ROLLS-ROYCE

SILVER SPIRIT & SILVER SPUR

BENTLEY

MULSANNE, EIGHT, CONTINENTAL, BROOKLANDS & AZURE

Other Veloce publications -

Colour Family Album Series
Alfa Romeo by Andrea & David Sparrow
Bubblecars & Microcars by Andrea & David Sparrow
Bubblecars & Microcars, More by Andrea & David Sparrow
Citroën 2CV by Andrea & David Sparrow
Citroën DS by Andrea & David Sparrow
Custom VWs by Andrea & David Sparrow
Fiat & Abarth 500 & 600 by Andrea & David Sparrow
Lambretta by Andrea & David Sparrow
Mini & Mini Cooper by Andrea & David Sparrow
Motor Scooters by Andrea & David Sparrow
Porsche by Andrea & David Sparrow
Triumph Sportscars by Andrea & David Sparrow
Vespa by Andrea & David Sparrow
VW Beetle by Andrea & David Sparrow
VW Bus, Camper, Van & Pick-up by Andrea & David Sparrow

SpeedPro Series
How to Blueprint & Build a 4-Cylinder Engine Short Block for High Performance by Des Hammill
How to Build a V8 Engine Short Block for High Performance by Des Hammill
How to Build a Fast Road Car by Daniel Stapleton
How to Build & Modify Sportscar/Kitcar Suspension & Brakes by Des Hammill
How to Build & Modify SU Carburettors for High Performance by Des Hammill
How to Build & Power Tune Weber DCOE & Dellorto DHLA Carburetors Second Edition by Des Hammill
How to Build & Power Tune Harley-Davidson Evolution Engines by Des Hammill
How to Build & Power Tune Distributor-type Ignition Systems by Des Hammill
How to Build, Modify & Power Tune Cylinder Heads Second Edition by Peter Burgess
How to Choose Camshafts & Time them for Maximum Power by Des Hammill
How to Give your MGB V8 Power Updated & Revised Edition by Roger Williams
How to Improve the MGB, MGC & MGB V8 by Roger Williams
How to Modify Volkswagen Beetle Chassis, Suspension & Brakes by James Hale
How to Power Tune the BMC 998cc A-Series Engine by Des Hammill
How to Power Tune BMC/Rover 1275cc A-Series Engines by Des Hammill
How to Power Tune the MGB 4-Cylinder Engine by Peter Burgess
How to Power Tune the MG Midget & Austin-Healey Sprite Updated Edition by Daniel Stapleton
How to Power Tune Alfa Romeo Twin Cam Engines by Jim Kartalamakis
How to Power Tune Ford SOHC 'Pinto' & Sierra Cosworth DOHC Engines by Des Hammill

General
Alfa Romeo Berlinas (saloons/sedans) by John Tipler
Alfa Romeo Giulia Coupé GT & GTA by John Tipler

Automotive Mascots by David Kay & Lynda Springate
British Cars, The Complete Catalogue of 1895-1975 by Culshaw & Horrobin
British Trailer Caravans 1919-1959 by Andrew Jenkinson
British Trailer Caravans from 1960 by Andrew Jenkinson
Bugatti Type 40 by Barrie Price
Bugatti 46/50 Updated Edition by Barrie Price
Bugatti 57 - by Barrie Price
Chrysler 300 - America's Most Powerful Car by Robert Ackerson
Cobra - The Real Thing! by Trevor Legate
Cortina - Ford's Bestseller by Graham Robson
Daimler SP250 'Dart' by Brian Long
Datsun/Nissan 280ZX & 300ZX by Brian Long
Datsun Z - From Fairlady to 280Z by Brian Long
Dune Buggy Handbook by James Hale
Fiat & Abarth 124 Spider & Coupé by John Tipler
Fiat & Abarth 500 & 600 by Malcolm Bobbit
Ford F100/F150 Pick-up by Robert Ackerson
Grey Guide, The by Dave Thornton
Jim Redman - Six Times World Motorcycle Champion by Jim Redman
Lea-Francis Story, The by Barrie Price
Lola - The Illustrated History (1957-1977) by John Starkey
Lola T70 - The Racing History & Individual Chassis Record New Edition by John Starkey
Lotus 49 by Michael Oliver
Mazda MX-5/Miata 1.6 Enthusiast's Workshop Manual by Rod Grainger & Pete Shoemark
Mazda MX-5/Miata 1.8 Enthusiast's Workshop Manual by Rod Grainger & Pete Shoemark
Mazda MX-5 Renaissance Sportscar by Brian Long
MGA by John Price Williams
Mini Cooper - The Real Thing! by John Tipler
Motor Museums of the British Isles & Republic of Ireland by David Burke & Tom Price
Porsche 356 by Brian Long
Porsche 911R, RS & RSR by John Starkey
Porsche 914 & 914-6 by Brian Long
Prince & I by Princess Ceril Birabongse
Rolls-Royce Silver Shadow/Bentley T Series Corniche & Camargue Updated Edition by Malcolm Bobbit
Rolls-Royce Silver Spirit, Silver Spur & Bentley Mulsanne by Malcolm Bobbit
Rolls-Royce Silver Wraith, Dawn & Cloud/Bentley MkVI, R & S Series by Martyn Nutland
Singer Story: Cars, Commercial Vehicles, Bicycles & Motorcycles by Kevin Atkinson
Taxi! The Story of the 'London' Taxicab by Malcolm Bobbit
Triumph Motorcycles & the Meriden Factory by Hughie Hancox
Triumph Tiger Cub Bible by Mike Estall
Triumph TR6 by William Kimberley
Veloce Guide to the Top 100 Used Touring Caravans by Andrew Jenkinson
Velocette Motorcycles - MSS to Thruxton by Rod Burris
Volkswagen Karmann Ghia by Malcolm Bobbit
Volkswagens of the World by Simon Glen
VW Bus, Camper, Van, Pickup by Malcolm Bobbit
Works Rally Mechanic by Brian Moylan

First published in 2000 by Veloce Publishing Plc., 33, Trinity Street, Dorchester DT1 1TT, England. Fax: 01305 268864/e-mail: veloce@veloce.co.uk/website: www.veloce.co.uk

ISBN: 1 901295 84 2/UPC: 36847-00184-1 Cloth hardback. 1 901295 68 0/UPC: 36847-00168-1 Leatherbound.

British Library Cataloguing in Publication Data -
A catalogue record for this book is available from the British Library.

Typesetting (Bookman), design and page make-up all by Veloce on AppleMac.
Printed and bound in the UK.

ROLLS-ROYCE
SILVER SPIRIT & SILVER SPUR
BENTLEY
MULSANNE, EIGHT, CONTINENTAL, BROOKLANDS & AZURE

MALCOLM BOBBITT

VELOCE PUBLISHING PLC
PUBLISHERS OF FINE AUTOMOTIVE BOOKS

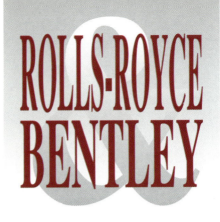

CONTENTS

ROLLS-ROYCE & BENTLEY

INTRODUCTION & ACKNOWLEDGMENTS

The Rolls-Royce Silver Spirit, its long wheelbase derivative the Silver Spur, and their Bentley counterpart, the Mulsanne, remained in production - albeit in a number of guises - for eighteen years. By modern standards, where manufacturers introduce new models at increasingly shorter intervals, this is a remarkable achievement, but then these are remarkable cars.

Codenamed SZ, the generation of cars from Crewe, launched in the autumn of 1980, were intended to withstand the test of time in respect of both styling and engineering. The architects were John Hollings, the company's engineering director, and Fritz Feller, a brilliant engineer turned stylist whose concern it was that the car should retain that particular presence so long associated with the marque. In short, it should be instantly recognisable as a Rolls-Royce. The fact that these cars successfully upheld Rolls-Royce tradition in every respect is evidence that the original recipe was entirely sound and Fritz Feller had achieved his ambition.

The Silver Spirit and its derivatives are also significant inasmuch as they are representative of a specific era in the history and fortunes of Rolls-Royce Motor Cars. Designed in the shadow of the early seventies collapse of the company's aero engine division, and subsequent separation of the motor car business, not to mention the burgeoning safety and emissions regulations emanating from America, SZ inherited, through economic dictate, many of its predecessor's attributes. In contrast to the Silver Shadow, which had been Rolls-Royce's most radical and innovative design for many years, Rolls-Royce directors demanded that that car's successor be conservatively cautious whilst building on its technology. Launched within days of the company being merged into the Vickers conglomeration, the Silver Spirit's demise coincided with the sale in 1998 of Rolls-Royce Motor Cars Limited to Volkswagen.

Much was achieved in the eighteen year period between 1980 and 1998. Several generations of cars ensued, each establishing new parameters of excellence and technical improvement to culminate in models which, whilst sharing the basic ingredients of the 1980 cars, were highly sophisticated and at the leading edge of automotive technology. Arrival of the Silver Spirit ll and Silver Spur ll for the 1990 model year brought adaptive ride and, with it, a degree of handling never previously experienced with a Rolls-Royce. Further development heralded a series lll nomenclature, progressing to turbocharging techniques which, at one time, would have been considered quite inappropriate on a car heralding the Spirit of Ecstasy.

It was also a period of resurgence for the Bentley marque. Having been allowed to fade into near oblivion like so many other famous names that are no more, the revival of Bentley sales proved just as dramatic as the arrival of the Mulsanne Turbo in 1982. From sales amounting to merely three per cent of total output in 1980, Bentley, at the turn of the millennium, was by

Rolls-Royce, established at Crewe since 1938, is as much part of the Cheshire town's heritage as the famous railway works. Here, the two industries have come together, the two generations of Crewe-built railway locomotives, the 1932 Pacific 'Princess Elizabeth' and the 1962 2700hp diesel hydraulic 'Western Prince', providing an emotive backdrop for the Silver Spirit which was introduced in the autumn of 1980, and was one of the most successful Rolls-Royce motor cars. The picture was taken at the grand opening of the Crewe Heritage Centre by HM The Queen and Prince Philip on 24th July 1987. (Courtesy Rolls-Royce Motor Cars Limited / Sir Henry Royce Memorial Foundation)

far the dominant product, outselling Rolls-Royce by three to one. In less than two decades some particularly potent motor cars bearing the Winged B emblem have emerged from Crewe: from the original Mulsanne Turbo, with its awesome performance that attracted a whole new type of customer, evolved the Turbo R which, in turn, was suc-ceeded by the mighty Turbo RT. At the opposite end of the scale the competi-tively priced Bentley Eight attracted to the marque many of those motorists for whom Rolls-Royce ownership might have previously seemed out of reach. In latter years the Mulsanne S and Bentley Brooklands have helped cre-ate a divergence from the Rolls-Royce marque, which undoubtedly will in-crease in the future.

In retrospect, that prudent and cautious design which emerged from Rolls-Royce's styling office under the direction of Fritz Feller, and latterly Graham Hull, has proved to be one of the most pioneering of Crewe's post-war cars. This is its story.

ACKNOWLEDGEMENTS
This book would not have been possible without the help and enthusiasm of many people. My thanks go to Richard Charlesworth, Head of Public Affairs at Rolls-Royce & Bentley Motors Cars Limited, for allowing me to search company records and photographic archives, and to his assistant Chris Ladley for painstakingly providing many of the illustrations which appear throughout. Graham Hull, Chief Stylist at Rolls-Royce, not only furnished me with much detailed information about the styling evolution of SZ, but also sought to provide a number of archive pictures which were taken during the car's formative years. Thanks also to Ian Rimmer, Senior Quality Engineer, who also contributed much information about the development of the Silver Spirit, Silver Spur and Bentley Mulsanne models.

I am grateful to Martin Bourne, retired Styling Engineer at Crewe, and Richard Mann, retired Senior Quality Engineer at Hythe Road, both of whom have spent untold hours talking to me and sharing their enthusiasm for the marque; to Jack Read, now of AVL(UK), for his assistance on preparing the Mulsanne Turbo story, and retired engineers Derek Coulson, John Astbury and Ron Maddocks.

Thanks also to Renée Feller, Roger Lister, John Bowling of Bowling-Ryan Limited, Michael Hibberd, and Paul Wood of P&A Wood. As always, Peter Baines, along with his team at the Rolls-Royce Enthusiasts' Club, has provided much assistance, as has Philip Hall, curator and archivist of the Sir Henry Royce Memorial Foundation. Annice Collett and her librarians at the National Motor Museum have, as usual, responded to my pleas for help with typical speed and efficiency.

Finally, my thanks to Rod Grainger at Veloce Publishing for suggesting I write this book, and my wife Jean for her usual patience, support and enthusiasm.

Malcolm Bobbitt
Cumbria, England

The Bentley Mulsanne was introduced at the same time as the Silver Spirit. Although it shared the Rolls-Royce car's fundamental technology, it was marketed to appeal to the Bentley enthusiast. Orders for Bentley badged cars were initially very limited, but with renewed interest in the marque created by the arrival of the Mulsanne Turbo in 1982, there began a divergence away from Rolls-Royce, resulting in these cars having a very definite sporting appeal that mirrored the company's impressive victories at Le Mans and elsewhere. Shown here is the Mulsanne's successor, the Bentley Brooklands, which remained in production until 1998. (Courtesy Rolls-Royce Motor Cars Limited/SHRMF)

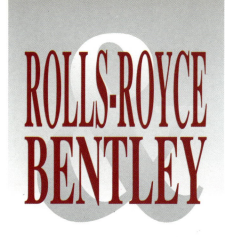

ROLLS-ROYCE & BENTLEY

1

ANCESTRY AND DEVELOPMENT

The introduction of a new model from Rolls-Royce is always an event, and, in the case of the Silver Spirit and its stablemate, the Bentley Mulsanne, the occasion in October 1980 was especially significant as the company had only a matter of days previously merged with the defence and engineering conglomerate, Vickers plc. Even more significantly, production of the Silver Spirit family of cars ended 18 years later, when Vickers relinquished its interests in Rolls-Royce and Bentley motors cars in an intensely hostile

The Silver Spirit and its Bentley stablemate, the Mulsanne, were introduced in October 1980. Two long wheelbase cars were included in the model range, the Rolls-Royce Silver Spur and its Bentley counterpart, which was known simply as the Mulsanne Long Wheelbase. Codenamed SZ, the cars replaced SY, the Silver Shadow and Bentley T models which had been introduced in 1965. Sales of the Bentley marque had fallen to around three per cent of total output and there was every reason to believe that the marque might have been allowed to drift into obscurity. This, of course, was not to be and the fortunes of the marque are chronicled, together with the Rolls-Royce models, in the following pages. (Courtesy Rolls-Royce Motor Cars Limited/ SHRMF)

At a casual glance early Silver Spirits appear virtually identical to later models. There were, however, many specification changes during the life of the car. This early production vehicle is pictured at the 1998 Rolls-Royce Annual Rally which was held at Cottesbrooke Hall, Northamptonshire, England. (Author's collection)

sell-off which attracted worldwide attention.

For Rolls-Royce the seventies had been a decade of disaster, frustration and change. The company went into receivership in early 1971 at the height of a bitter and harrowing crisis born out of technical and financial problems linked to the development of the RB211 aero engine project. Designed to power some of the world's new generation of wide-bodied jets, and the Lockheed Tristar in particular, the importance of the engine was such that it would enable Rolls-Royce to compete with American jet engine manufacturers on a previously impossible scale. Although the car manufacturing business was not directly affected by the problems at Derby, the effect at Crewe was nevertheless felt to no small degree, and the lead-up to the crisis was responsible for demoralising the entire factory personnel. Added to the corporate misery felt at Pym's Lane was the stringent motor vehicle safety and emissions legislation origi-

nating from America with which Rolls-Royce was obliged to comply. The demands imposed at all levels within the company were severe and particular strain was placed on design and engineering resources.

Under the guidance of Rupert Nicholson, the Official Receiver, the buoyant car division of Rolls-Royce was allowed to continue operating after a brief hiatus when all production was halted and the factory gates firmly shut, even to the most loyal and long-standing customers. Such was the spectacular collapse of Britain's most respected company that embarrassed and humiliated service personnel were forced to ask customers to pay their bills in cash before releasing vehicles from the factory. Ultimately, car manufacture was separated from the aero engine business and, as Rolls-Royce Motors, production of the most respected luxury cars in the world resumed.

The affairs of 1971 could easily have tarnished the shiny reputation of Rolls-Royce Motor Cars, and it would

not have been unreasonable to assume that sales might have suffered from the adverse publicity. In the event, the opposite happened and sales actually increased throughout and following this period. From those bleak days of February 1971, when it seemed that Rolls-Royce, a national institution and the epitome of Britishness, was threatened with extinction, life at Crewe gradually returned to some normality under the careful direction of David, later Sir David, Plastow, the new company's chief executive and managing director. Recognising that it would be difficult, indeed impossible, for Rolls-Royce to continue standing alone in industry, Plastow ultimately negotiated a merger with Vickers, an organisation he and his fellow directors considered best suited to maintaining the company's interests.

Possibly there were a number of companies or vehicle manufacturers with which Rolls-Royce could have formed a merger; indeed, during the sixties, serious consultation took place

SZ ancestry can be traced to the late fifties and the arrival of the V8 engine which was fitted to the Silver Cloud ll and lll and Bentley S2 and S3. Some of those Bentleys are represented in this photograph taken at Le Mans to welcome the Bentley SZ's successor, the Arnage. (Courtesy Rolls-Royce Motor Cars Limited)

with the British Motor Corporation, Associated Commercial Vehicles and Leyland. Plans for a full merger in this instance were abandoned and Rolls-Royce's suitors eventually, via a torturous route, emerged as the Rover Group, now under the BMW umbrella. Vickers, on the other hand, had a history of association with Rolls-Royce which extended as far back as Silver Ghost days when a number of these vehicles were equipped with Vickers guns. Not only had Rolls-Royce engines powered many of Vickers' aeroplanes - in post-war years the liaison between Vickers and Rolls-Royce to produce the Viscount turbo-prop airliner had been very successful - much co-operation had existed in various other fields, including tractor and tank development. Vickers was also closely involved in meeting the requirements of Britain's defence equipment, an area of business to which Rolls-Royce was equally committed.

At that time, the separation of Rolls-Royce Motors from Rolls-Royce

Aero Engines (later to become Rolls-Royce plc), seemed logical enough, but there was a sting in the tail which lay dormant for 27 years. Throughout the separation process and eventual merger with Vickers, the rights to use the Rolls-Royce name remained the property of Rolls-Royce Aero Engines, an all-important fact that was apparently overlooked by Volkswagen when it out-bid BMW to buy Rolls-Royce Motors for £470 million in 1998. A condition of the sale of Rolls-Royce Motors by the Official Receiver in 1971 permitted use of the Rolls-Royce name and trademarks only as long as the company remained in British hands. Under most bizarre circumstances, BMW, the loser in the battle, two months after its rival's victory and only weeks since the announcement that it

would be cancelling its engine contract with Rolls-Royce and subsequently Volkswagen, purchased the right to use the Rolls-Royce name and trademarks for £40 million, less than one-tenth of the price Volkswagen paid, for the manufacturing company. Nobody could have foreseen the injury that would be inflicted when that tail flicked and the sting was released: Volkswagen had no alternative but to surrender to the vanquished and retain only the Bentley marque. Thus, Rolls-Royce and Bentley will eventually separate after seventy years co-existence following a bid that was every bit as controversial as Rolls-Royce's acquisition of Bentley in 1931. The plan is that the Crewe site will continue to produce Rolls-Royce cars until 2002; at the start of 2003 BMW will build its own Rolls-Royce

SZ's direct antecedent was the Silver Shadow, SY being that car's codename. Both Rolls-Royce and Bentley versions are illustrated in this photograph taken within the confines of the Crewe factory. The occasion is unclear but all the cars, except for that on the far left, are either unregistered or carrying trade plates. (Courtesy Rolls-Royce Motor Cars Limited)

Soon after the Silver Shadow and Bentley T were launched in 1965, the international motor industry was rocked by a devastating report on vehicle safety. Penned by Ralph Nader, 'Unsafe At Any Speed' had far-reaching effects on car design. For Rolls-Royce this ultimately meant having to conform to the ensuing stringent American safety and emissions regulations to enable the company to continue selling cars to the USA. Much of this development, which was carried out during the seventies, was incorporated into the design of SZ. (Courtesy Rolls-Royce Motor Cars Limited)

During the seventies much experimental work at Crewe was done on conforming to America's Federal Safety Standards (FSS). This picture shows a two-door bodyshell being prepared for side impact tests. (Courtesy Rolls-Royce Motor Cars Limited)

models at a dedicated factory elsewhere, and Volkswagen will maintain Bentley manufacture at Pym's Lane in a considerably revamped plant, a £500 million investment in the premises having been announced in the autumn of 1998.

The full story of the 1998 debacle over Rolls-Royce and Bentley, Volkswagen and BMW has yet to be written. Anything more than the preceding paragraphs is not directly relevant to Silver Spirit history; it is sufficient to mention that BMW had had its sights on the Rolls-Royce marque for some considerable time, and had been deeply involved with the company in the design and building of engines to replace the aging V8. Ironically, the building of the Rolls-Royce V8 was contracted out to Cosworth Engineering in the closing months of Silver Spirit-based car production; Cosworth was acquired by Volkswagen a day ahead of it being announced that VW had won the battle for Rolls-Royce. In a completely separate venture which pre-dates any shared car engine development, BMW and Rolls-Royce plc worked together on developing aero-engines, a substantial factor in Rolls-Royce favouring BMW as owner of Rolls-Royce Motor Cars.

A further twist in the saga concerns Peter Ward who, during the early nineties, reigned as chief executive of

Rolls-Royce Motor Cars at Crewe. During that period some joint development was carried out with Mercedes, with Peter Ward in favour of the association. He considered Mercedes business acumen to be more akin to that of Rolls-Royce, a view not entirely shared by the Rolls-Royce Board of Directors. Despite Ward's entreaties to the Board, it opted for BMW and the relationship with Mercedes was abruptly abandoned. Peter Ward found himself in an untenable position and had no alternative but to resign. He took up another appointment in industry, while at Rolls-Royce car engine development

continued jointly with BMW.

In the lead-up to the sale of Rolls-Royce Motor Cars Limited, Volkswagen had made little pretence that its prime aim initially was anything other than to acquire the Bentley marque; not only for its obvious status and association with Rolls-Royce, but also its sporting distinction and sales achievements which, at the time of writing, accounted for 70 per cent of all production. The ratio of Bentley sales to Rolls-Royce illustrates the exceptional turnround in the marque's fortunes from a mere three per cent in 1980.

The Silver Spirit had been con-

The results of all safety testing at Crewe were closely monitored. Here, a hydraulic ram has simulated a side impact to gauge whether the vehicle's structure conforms to current or impending regulations and provides satisfactory passenger protection. (Courtesy Rolls-Royce Motor Cars Limited)

The effects of side intrusion can be clearly gauged from this picture. Door design incorporated maximum passenger protection. (Courtesy Rolls-Royce Motor Cars Limited)

ceived well before the RB211 debacle, and development, albeit considerably delayed, continued amidst political wranglings surrounding Rolls-Royce's future. Within a few days of the fusion with Vickers, the marriage between two of the most venerable names in British industry was consummated with the birth of spiritual twins, the Silver Spirit and Bentley Mulsanne.

From conception to birth, the Silver Spirit was 11 years in gestation, which was about the same time that it took to develop the Silver Shadow. New models do not materialise readily at Rolls-Royce and, since 1946, the year post-war car production was established at Crewe, this was only the fourth generation car to appear. The Silver Wraith, Bentley Mk VI, R-Type and Silver Dawn belonged to the first generation vehicles; Silver Clouds and S-Series Bentleys, recognised now as being possibly the finest of all post-war models and which formed the spiritual thinking behind the 1998 Silver Seraph and Bentley Arnage, were the second, and the Silver Shadow and Bentley T the third. Add to this are the Continental models, the two-door coachbuilt Silver Shadows, Camargue and Phantoms: the portfolio is impres-

Development work on the SY models had been extensive, calling for huge investment by Rolls-Royce. Together with work necessary for compliance with FSS, and the fact that the company was still in the shadow of the Aero Engine Division's 1971 collapse, it was decreed that the car to replace SY should be evolutionary rather than revolutionary. Although of completely new styling, SY's successor would utilise its predecessor's fundamental engineering. This publicity photograph depicts the Silver Shadow ll. (Courtesy Rolls-Royce Motor Cars Limited)

sive for what is essentially a low-volume manufacturer.

During the Silver Spirit's gestatory

period the mainstay of production was the Silver Shadow family of cars, which included the T-Series Bentley deriva-

Early thoughts about SY's replacement meant taking a close look at that car; in a quarter-scale wind tunnel test a coloured dye shows a rather unusual reverse airflow over the bonnet, due to the unique shape of the radiator shell. The tests were conducted at the MIRA research establishment. (Courtesy Rolls-Royce Motor Cars Limited)

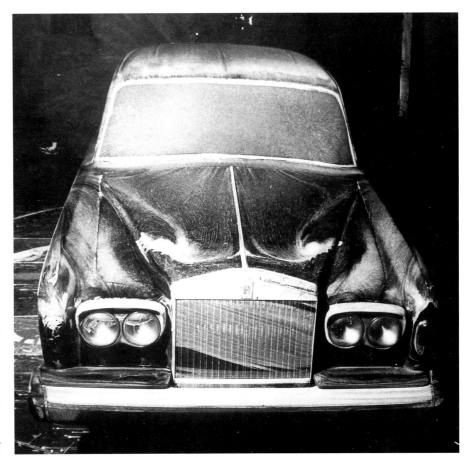

tive. The catalogue comprised both the Pressed Steel standard body and the long wheelbase saloons built in conjunction with Mulliner Park Ward. For the even more discerning customer the Mulliner Park Ward coachbuilt two-door models offered exclusivity and encompassed, after 1971, the Corniche and, in late 1984, a Bentley version named the Continental. Then there was the Camargue which Rolls-Royce considered its flagship; ultra-prestigious, it was never intended to be sold to any but the most discerning customer and, in fact, was planned primarily for America, from where the majority of orders were received. Despite its exclusiveness, the car was controversial, especially with styling penned by Pininfarina. Apart from the initial orders expected of any new model, the Camargue was not a good seller. It was very expensive and was like an exaggerated corporate Pininfarina style of that era. The Camargue had its enthusiasts, of course, but many believed its styling to be bland.

Hardly had production of the Silver Shadow begun in 1965 when Ralph Nader's far-reaching and contentious critique 'Unsafe At Any Speed' was published in America. Nader's views, which highlighted the American automobile's shortcomings and its apparent disregard for safety, triggered a massive and unprecedented consumer movement throughout the United States, the effects of which were felt worldwide, not as a ripple but a tidal wave. American motorists who, for years, had taken their cars for granted, were suddenly preoccupied with mak-

ing the motor car a haven of safety.

Safety consciousness reached levels of near-hysteria when Federal Safety Standards - FSS for short - legislation became a major issue in American politics. The requirements applied equally to imported vehicles and home produced cars, and any that failed to comply were ineligible for sale. To make matters especially difficult, California had its own dedicated emissions requirements: the nature of the west coast climate was such that in order to drastically reduce smog levels, acceptable exhaust emissions were far more stringent than elsewhere in the USA. The upheaval at Crewe to ensure that Rolls-Royce and Bentley cars satisfied both FSS and Californian legislation was enormous and contributed to the Silver Spirit's lengthy development programme. To digress; FSS regulations were born out of the American General Services Administration requirements (GSA for short) dating from August

1966, which were aimed at determining certain prerequisites for vehicles transporting government personnel. Crewe was first made aware of GSA in early 1967.

The Silver Spirit's ancestry lies deep within the Silver Shadow, although certain aspects extend even further into the annals of Rolls-Royce history. The nucleus of development can be traced back to the early fifties when Harry Grylls, then chief engineer at Rolls-Royce, together with managing director, Dr Llewellyn Smith, Ivan Evernden and John Blatchley, agreed that adoption of unitary construction techniques was inevitable if the company was to survive. The post-war demise of bespoke coachbuilding had, to a large extent, dictated future policies and if Rolls-Royce ignored the fact that the capacity to produce cars in volume using traditional methods simply would not exist, then the future looked bleak.

Most other builders of luxury cars

had already adopted chassisless construction techniques. Jaguar had adopted the monocoque body shell in 1955 for its compact 2.4 saloon, although it was not until 1961 that the first big saloons went unitary. Rover, too, forsook a separate chassis with the introduction of the 3 Litre in 1958, the car beloved by government officials. Mercedes-Benz had also taken the plunge by the end of the fifties.

The transition to unitary construction was, in fact, the logical step forward in a progression of events which originated in the immediate pre-war period. W.A.Robotham, the chassis division's chief engineer at Derby, had projected a series of measures which rationalised the use of common chassis components and engines in order to reduce costs and streamline production. His theories may have been considered far-reaching at the time, but history has shown that not only were they correct, but were responsible for maintaining the marque's existence in a period which might otherwise have witnessed its demise. When car production resumed after the war, not at Derby but Crewe, Rolls-Royce for the first time offered a complete vehicle and not just a chassis for which any number of coachbuilders could supply their own distinctive coachwork. The 'coachbuilder' in this instance was the Pressed Steel Company of Oxford, the result of a joint venture between the Nuffield organisation and the Budd Company of America. Hardly a coachbuilder in the specialist sense, Pressed Steel began building all-steel bodies in Britain in 1927 and for three

years supplied Nuffield exclusively. After 1930, when the Nuffield interest was sold, Pressed Steel began making bodies for the motor industry's major customers: Austin, Morris, Hillman, Humber, Standard, Rover and Vauxhall.

The policy of buying bodies from Pressed Steel was initiated by Robotham, who sought advice and experience from the Wilks brothers at Rover. Rolls-Royce's association with Pressed Steel continued with the introduction of the Silver Cloud models in 1955, although it remained possible for a customer to order custom-made coachwork instead of the standard product. Handsomely styled by John Blatchley, so good was the Silver Cloud and Bentley counterpart standard saloon coachwork, orders for coachbuilt cars generally declined. It was not all to do with styling and quality, of course, as price played an increasingly important part, especially when, in December 1955, a coachbuilt Silver Cloud by Park Ward cost £7078-17-0d, some £2000 more than the price of a Standard Saloon. Despite the bodyshells being made alongside those destined for many of Britain's popular makes of car, the quality which Rolls-Royce demanded was delivered by Pressed Steel. It should be remembered that, in many instances, the quality of products offered by specialist coachbuilders varied enormously, in some instances falling short of what was expected. It was indifferent quality that determined Rolls-Royce to adopt 'preferred' coachbuilders in an attempt to maintain quality levels; thus, the company

directed its customers to such firms as Park Ward, H.J. Mulliner, James Young, Hooper and Freestone & Webb, amongst others. Pressed Steel quality remained consistent and, despite the relatively poor quality steel available immediately after the war, the number of early Bentley Mk VIs that have survived demonstrates just how well their bodies were built.

The progression from rationalisation to standardisation was complete

What might have been ...
During 1977 Graham Hull produced this rendering of a Rolls-Royce concept car. Note the futuristic styling with semi-enclosed rear wheelarches, narrow pillars and large glass area, as well as some Camargue influence. A scale model built as a Bentley, and named Mulsanne after that section of the Le Mans circuit, was displayed in David Plastow's office at Pym's Lane for some time. (Courtesy Rolls-Royce Motor Cars Limited)

with the introduction of the Silver Shadow, with its modern monocoque bodyshell, again supplied by Pressed Steel. In fact, the Silver Shadow looked so modern many long-standing customers had difficulty recognising it as a Rolls-Royce. Certainly, the car had presence; the distinctive radiator shell adorned by the Flying Lady was the reason for that, and the quality finish expected of a Rolls-Royce and Bentley was fully evident. What was missing was the haughty stance of the separate-chassied car which one climbed aboard rather than lowered oneself into. Dave Tod, a sales manager with Rolls-Royce at the time of the Silver Shadow's launch, remembers several opposing facets of the car: existing customers

were slow in coming to terms with the car's smaller dimensions; it was designed with the owner-driver more in mind, and in appealing to a younger but still demanding clientele, who may not have previously considered Rolls-Royce or Bentley ownership, an insatiable demand was immediately created.

Rolls-Royce invested heavily in new technology and tooling to build the Silver Shadow which, bristling with innovation, was acknowledged as the most radical offering from the company in almost 60 years. The fact that it had been particularly expensive to design and build called for a major restructuring of the factory, necessitating not only an altogether higher

sales profile than any previous Rolls-Royce or Bentley, but also a long production career. In the event the Silver Shadow reigned for fifteen years during which time well over 32,000 standard saloons were built, making this by far the most prolific of all Rolls-Royce and Bentley models. By including the coachbuilt derivatives, the total build quantity of Silver Shadow cars is increased to 40,556, and it should be recognised that the Corniche and Bentley Continental were sold alongside the Silver Spirit until as late as 1996, over 30 years after the Silver Shadow's introduction. Such was the investment and engineering development within the company, the fundamental technology remained to form the basis of

The architect of the Silver Spirit was Fritz Feller. As chief stylist at Rolls-Royce Motor Cars from 1969 until 1983, he was backed by John Hollings who was technical director at the time. When he took over from John Blatchley, finding a replacement for the Silver Shadow was Feller's priority, and much work was necessary in keeping abreast of American safety and emissions regulations. Codenamed SZ, the Silver Spirit and its derivatives, the Silver Spur and Bentley Mulsanne, were introduced in October 1980, shortly after Rolls-Royce Motors merged with the defence conglomerate Vickers. (Courtesy Martin Bourne)

Before a car can be introduced a huge amount of development work is necessary. The Silver Spirit was no exception, and this picture shows Ron Maddocks, a member of Crewe's styling team in the seventies, preparing a one-eighth scale model of SZ (the car's codename) in readiness for wind tunnel tests at the MIRA experimental establishment. (Courtesy Ron Maddocks)

the successive generation motor cars.

The Silver Shadow and the Bentley T were completely different from any previous Rolls-Royce models. Gone was the peculiar satisfaction of the lofty driving position of the Mk VI Bentley, Silver Dawn and Silver Clouds, and the long, tapering bonnet stretching majestically into the distance, with the perfect form of the Spirit of Ecstasy or the Flying B presiding over all else on the road ahead. There were compensations, of course: the model was relatively compact, yet provided just as much, if not more, cabin space than its predecessors; the smooth V8 engine was almost inaudible, the GM 400 gearbox an absolute delight, and the power steering and disc braking made for effortless motoring. The car's ride quality, with its double wishbones and coil springs, together with hydraulic self-levelling, kept it at an even keel whatever the road condition. This was

particularly appreciated by the car's American customers who were more accustomed to the soft, wallowing comfort provided by most home-produced automobiles, and especially Cadillac. Not all owners favoured the ship at sea effect, however; some rear seat passengers complained of travel sickness in the Rolls-Royce. Radical and innovative the Silver Shadow certainly was, and justifiably acclaimed by the most discerning of motorist.

On a less positive note, the Silver Shadow era was a time when the Bentley marque, revered the world over, almost sank into oblivion. If any compensation was deemed appropriate for preferring the Winged B emblem to the Grecian Temple radiator with its R-R monogram and Spirit of Ecstasy, it amounted to the princely sum of £60 or thereabouts. With such a narrow price premium, is it any wonder that the vast majority of customers will-

ingly paid what was, after all, pocket money, even by 1960s standards, to acquire what many perceived as the most respected, if not the most famous, radiator shell in the world? After the austerity of the forties and early fifties, when Rolls-Royce and ration books hardly made good bedfellows, the late fifties and sixties were periods of growing prosperity. If the truth be known, Rolls-Royce directors all but forgot the very existence of the Bentley marque, even if it had once been the company's saviour. While orders for the Silver Shadow soared, those for the Bentley T dwindled during the seventies to a low point; just three per cent of all Rolls-Royce sales, giving rise to the theory that the marque might be dropped.

That the Bentley name was not allowed to fall into obscurity is a miracle, and today Rolls-Royce directors must be grateful for its reprieve. The

Design study. Early considerations about SY's replacement are evident in this photograph taken in 1971. The scale model in the centre represents the beginnings of SZ (model 'A') so that comparisons could be made with the Silver Shadow which, looking at the picture, is on the right, and Camargue, to the left. There are several points of interest: in the background can be seen a number of renderings depicting different styling ideas, a continuing facet of the styling department. More apparent are the modelling tables which give a clue to the proportions of the quarter-scale models. It is clear that Camargue had an affect on initial styling ideas; note the shape of the front wings and expanse of the bonnet. In the case of Camargue it can be seen that two styling arrangements concerning the headlamps have been evaluated. (Courtesy Rolls-Royce Motor Cars Limited)

This close-up view of SZ model A shows that by 1971 a clear styling theme was emerging. The model was carved by Ron Maddocks from solid pine. (Courtesy Rolls-Royce Motor Cars Limited)

From this rear three-quarter view, SZ's definitive styling is apparent, even at this early stage. (Courtesy Rolls-Royce Motor Cars Limited)

Bentley revival during the eighties and nineties will be discussed in greater detail elsewhere in this book, but it is pertinent to explain that the first glimmer of its renewed fortunes was seen a little before the Silver Spirit's introduction. George Fenn, then chief executive at Crewe, was entertaining a delegation from the Bentley Drivers Club at the factory when, rather surprisingly, he promised his audience that the Bentley name would return. One cannot help but speculate that there were many that day who remained cynical and unconvinced!

Essence of the Spirit

If previous experience is anything to go by, it can be presumed that the Silver Shadow's replacement was first thought about after the car's introduction in the autumn of 1965. After all, the design team had been made aware of the Silver Shadow project - or Tibet, to be precise - as early as 1955, immediately following the successful launch of the Silver Cloud and Bentley S. In fact, it was earlier than that the Tibet, and the almost parallel Burma project, were discussed behind closed doors along the top corridor at Pym's Lane. It is reasonable,

Styling is a very necessary and on-going function for all motor car manufacturers. In this photograph is illustrated the Rolls-Royce Silver Spur complete with American specification headlamps. Separate sealed beam lamps, which could be bought from any drug store and easily fitted, were a requirement for the US market for many years. There is much to interest the enthusiast in this picture: a number of styling ideas are hidden from view under those wraps, whilst on the wall in the background, wash renderings suggest some evocative designs, possibly on a 'Continental' theme. And what is concealed on the trestle? Standing alongside the Silver Spur is styling engineer Martin Bourne, and to the right stylists Ryan Lewis and Steve Everitt, an ex-TVR stylist. (Courtesy Rolls-Royce Motor Cars Limited)

Right: This close-up view of the stying mock up depicts the fine veneers and hide which are a feature of all Rolls-Royce motor cars. The air vent, known within the factory as 'bulls-eyes', are a traditional feature to be found on the facia. Different types of vents have at one time been considered but none are as efficient as this. (Courtesy Rolls-Royce Motor Cars Limited)

Right: Many hours can be spent in trying out and developing different styling ideas. Here much attention is being paid to the bumper and air dam arrangement. (Courtesy Rolls-Royce Motor Cars Limited)

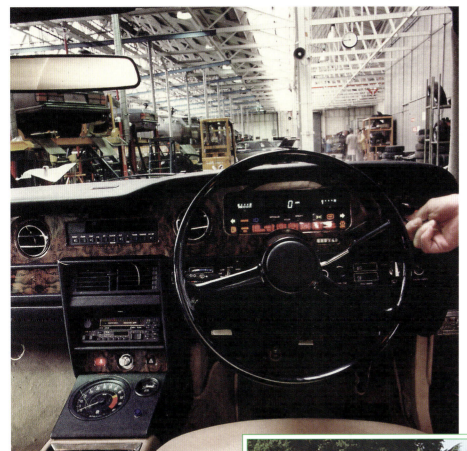

During the development of SZ many ideas were tried out, including a fully digitalised facia favoured by John Hollings. This is the result of the exercise, which no one appreciated except Hollings. Those who drove the maroon car with 'facia digitalis' were not impressed, and it appears a campaign was mounted to have the project abandoned, much to the chief engineer's regret but the relief of the stylists and engineers! (Courtesy Martin Bourne)

Work on SZ really got under way once preparations for Camargue had finished. To a large extent political issues within Rolls-Royce, combined with development work surrounding the Series ll Silver Shadows, affected the launch date of SZ. Had it not been for this, SZ might have been introduced as early as 1977. This is Camargue, an example of which was photographed at a Rolls-Royce Enthusiasts' Club event. Compare this with the scale model of the car shown, in 1971, with SY and SZ. (Author's collection)

therefore, to believe that a replacement 'Shadow' had been part of conversation at Crewe even before 1965.

All this is conjecture, of course, as, in the late sixties, there was a significant change of personnel at Crewe and, sadly, some of the key players in the story are no longer alive to relate the whole tale. Chief engineer Harry Grylls was not the sort of person to let such an important issue go undiscussed; John Hollings, taking over from Grylls, was abundantly aware of the urgent need to prepare a blueprint for the new car; Dr Llewellyn Smith, who had so prudently guided the car division through the fifties and sixties, would also have looked a decade or so ahead and seen beyond the Silver Shadow. The pragmatic John Blatchley, whose pen defined the Silver Shadow in the first instance, and later the Silver Shadow ll, obviously had thoughts upon the subject, al-

though he had elected to take early retirement in 1969.

More pressing at Crewe was the problem of what to do about the American FSS legislation. In this respect John Hollings, who was appointed chief

quality engineer at Crewe in 1965 and chief engineer in 1968, was thrown headlong into a difficult and deeply complicated issue which, had it not been properly addressed, could have threatened the valuable and irreplace-

able American market. Presenting a paper on the engineering of Rolls-Royce cars during the seventies, Hollings made the point that efforts were strongly influenced by the need to meet legal requirements concerning exhaust emissions and occupant safety. "As far as safety was concerned", he said, "we had to show that our cars would meet the safety requirements which were being developed by the authorities in America and Europe and elsewhere. Although certain countries such as Australia and Japan had their own specific requirements, the Federal Motor Vehicle Safety Standards in the USA were, generally speaking, the most stringent."

John Hollings was not involved with motor car design from an early age and joined Rolls-Royce from Cambridge University, having previously attended Stowe School. It was aero engine design with which Hollings was primarily involved before being appointed chief designer on nuclear reactors for submarines in 1957 and, from 1962, chief engineer Admiralty Reactor Test Establishment at Dounreay in northern Scotland. Joining the car division at Crewe, he admitted he knew less about motor car design than the

engineers under him, but his practical approach towards engineering nevertheless stood him in good stead to continue the outstanding work of Harry Grylls.

When full attention was turned to the Silver Shadow's replacement, much of the FSS work being concentrated upon at Crewe was, by necessity, incorporated in its design and, therefore, development work on the two projects was carried out in parallel. For this reason, and not forgetting any financial issues, what emerged as the Silver Spirit was to a large degree born out of the Silver Shadow. To be precise, all engineering developments were applied initially to Camargue, then Corniche and, eventually, the standard saloon. In some instances, developments were not initially incorporated on the standard saloon cars, a point in particular applying to the modified rear suspension, which was referred to as the 'Refinement Package'. While intended for the Silver Spirit, this was introduced on Corniche a short time prior to the new saloon's introduction.

Graham Hull, currently chief stylist at Crewe, recalls that serious work on developing the Silver Shadow replacement began in 1972. There were

several influencing factors concerning the date: by then the receivership issue was history and the Corniche, announced only weeks after Rolls-Royce's spectacular collapse, had survived a rather delicate launch and had done much to restore the company's good standing. In this respect it has to be said that David Plastow's marketing prowess in taking the rather obscurely-named Two-Door Silver Shadows and revitalising them with a revised and updated specification, along with a powerful and charismatic model nomenclature, was nothing less than inspirational. The launch of the Corniche, successful as it was, was nevertheless somewhat bizarre. Due to Rolls-Royce's difficult financial position, it was not possible to have invoices charged or to issue cheques in the usual manner; John Hollings once recalled that company executives were required to carry huge sums of cash in order to settle accounts. David Plastow, who only weeks before the 1971 collapse had been appointed managing director, had deftly guided Rolls-Royce Motor Cars back to the cutting-edge of respectability with every prospect of a long, profitable and exciting future.

There was further significance about the date of the Silver Spirit's introduction inasmuch that work was pressing ahead with the Series Two Silver Shadows which, had it not been

Bill Allen, a member of Fritz Feller's styling team, retired in July 1977. His fellow stylists, already hard at work on SZ, surround him on his final day at Pym's Lane. From left to right are: Norman Webster, Fritz Feller, Martin Bourne, Ron Maddocks, Bill Allen and Graham Hull. (Courtesy Rolls-Royce Motor Cars Limited)

Fritz Feller with his styling team. This picture was taken around 1980, after SZ's successful launch. With Fritz (on the far left) is Graham Hull (background left) who was appointed chief stylist following Feller's retirement. Standing alongside the chief stylist is Norman Webster, and looking on are Ryan Lewis (background centre), Ron Maddocks and, far right, Martin Bourne. Whatever the issue under discussion, it is obviously giving some food for thought! (Courtesy Rolls-Royce Motor Cars Limited)

for the Rolls-Royce collapse, would have been launched somewhat earlier than 1977. By 1972 most of Crewe's involvement in the design of Camargue was complete and, if one refers to the companion volume to this book on the Silver Shadow (Veloce), it will be understood that the workload at Crewe in the early seventies nearly reached breaking point. With a new managing director, new chief engineer and new chief stylist, the decision to commission Pininfarina with the styling of Camargue was met with universal relief from departmental heads. The styling team at Crewe was less impressed, however, and there was some resentment that Rolls-Royce's own styling engineers had been denied the opportunity to offer a design of their own. The ability of the Crewe team, having created design masterpieces in the form of the R-Type Continental and its successors, not to mention the Silver Cloud and Two-Door Silver Shadows, was

fully evident. Pininfarina, however, was well acquainted with both Rolls-Royce and Bentley models, and had produced a number of designs based on the company's post-war cars. In particular, it was the car designed around the Bentley T, displayed at the 1968 Earls Court Motor Show, which had most influenced the Rolls-Royce directors in their decision. What they saw was, in their opinion, an elegant motor car with a designer label which could be obtained without compromising other essential work.

Fritz Feller succeeded John Blatchley as chief stylist, the appointment being made by Geoffrey Fawn, who, only a short time before, had taken over from Dr Llewellyn Smith. An engineer - and a brilliant one at that - Feller's appointment created some controversy, although any dissent quickly melted away as soon as his commitment to Rolls-Royce was appreciated.

Austrian born, Fritz Feller escaped from his homeland in 1938 aged 12. His parents (FF's father was Jewish though not practising) had allowed the Quakers to take their son to England, whereupon the young Fritz wrote to the Prime Minister, Neville Chamberlain, to help get them out of Austria. The Feller's story is one of courage and they left Austria on the last train to leave for the west. On his arrival in England, Fritz was sent to King William School on the Isle of Man where he was so unhappy he ran away. Following arrival in Britain, Fritz's mother cooked for Doctor Dean at Newark, and his father helped look after the monks at Kelham in Nottinghamshire before he became an accountant with the LMS Railway at Derby. In 1941 Fritz successfully applied for a Rolls-Royce apprenticeship at Derby, one of the most respected and sought-after apprenticeships in British industry. In 1950 he had been promoted to a senior engi-

Surrounding a fibreglass shell of the final SZ body shape, Crewe's styling team discusses the project's progress. With Fritz Feller (foreground) are (left to right): Ryan Lewis, Martin Bourne, Graham Hull, Ron Maddocks and Norman Webster. (Courtesy Rolls-Royce Motor Cars Limited)

Building quarter scale models was customary for Crewe's styling department. As well as projecting specific ideas, such models were ideal for viewing purposes. In this picture, taken in late 1967, a proposal for a new Phantom model to succeed Phantom V can be seen. Although well before SZ's era, the scene gives a clear indication of styling trends of the period. The car on the right, incidentally, was known as Phantom Vl by styling engineers; Martin Bourne recalls that the model, built to the same scale as the Silver Shadow alongside, appeared gigantic. (Courtesy Rolls-Royce Motor Cars Limited)

neer and moved to Crewe and the car division of Rolls-Royce, where he was responsible for extensive development work on both the B (commercial) and K (military) ranges of engines, as well as much design work on the V8. Feller perfected the design of the diesel rotary engine for military purposes, which was funded by the British government, but despite its success was not adopted by the armed services. His work in this respect resulted in a close friendship with Dr Felix Wankel, and in 1970 Feller was awarded the Thomas Hawksley Gold Medal for a lecture paper on the exercise. It was the project's impending cancellation which acted as the springboard for Geoffrey Fawn's appointment of Fritz Feller as chief stylist.

The fact that he was neither a stylist nor a body engineer did present some initial difficulties during the early period of Feller's appointment as head of the department. It was almost unknown in the motor industry for an engineer to turn stylist and the appointment initially was made on a temporary basis. As an excellent manager with knowledge and expertise of engineering second to none, such adversity was swiftly overcome and he was able to guide his department through a particularly challenging and arduous period which, of course, included taking the fundamental steps in preparing for the new saloon car. Not surprisingly, Feller's 'temporary' appointment was very quickly confirmed as permanent.

One of Fritz Feller's prime concerns was the Camargue and he, for one, was extremely happy that Pininfarina had been commissioned to style the car. There was, nevertheless, considerable work to be done in conjunction with Pininfarina and the end result, whatever one's opinion of this very controversial motor car, displayed a number of Feller's ideas. As a 'front of house' man Fritz excelled: his delightful command of the English language, with a mere hint of an accent, was equal to his prowess in public relations and talent as a brilliant raconteur. His temperament was the complete opposite to his predecessor, the quiet, unassuming and self-effacing John Blatchley, who was never happier than when directing his department from the modelling table. For obvious reasons Feller preferred to leave scraper and wax to his stylists, but nonetheless led from the front, being assidu-

To some extent Silver Spirit, as SZ became known, was born out of Silver Shadow. Much existing technology was used and early design principles followed on from studies conducted around 1971. Model 'A' has already been illustrated; here is model 'B' shown during quarter-scale wind tunnel tests at MIRA. (Courtesy Rolls-Royce Motor Cars Limited)

Below, left: Model 'B', illustrated here at MIRA in 1971. The wind tunnel dye shows there is still a slight reverse flow over the bonnet.
Below, right: Model 'B's' rear styling has more SZ about it than SY. Wind tunnel tests give an idea of the car's profile.
(Both courtesy Rolls-Royce Motor Cars Limited)

ously interested in every stage of a project. Unlike Blatchley, who could grasp and complete a project with almost lightning speed, Feller insisted that no decisions be taken until at least several thoughts were fully considered at length. He was an ideas man who enjoyed the participation of those around him, and believed in management by confrontation: he revelled in political squabbles and was adept at fighting his corner whenever there was a policy disagreement, and expected the same from his staff.

Soon after his appointment, Fritz Feller expanded his design team, which comprised two highly experienced stylists, Bill Allen and Martin Bourne. Bill had been at Derby prior to the war and before that had served a premium apprenticeship with Arthur Mulliner, the reputable Northampton coachbuilder. After joining Rolls-Royce in 1935 to work on chassis design, during hostilities he moved to Clan Foundry, a disused iron works on the outskirts of Belper, along with other members of the car division who were not directly involved with aero engines. It was there that, at the end of the war, plans were made for a return to car production and Bill was instrumental, along with Ivan Evernden and John Blatchley, in designing the first cars built at Crewe under the direction of W.A. Robotham. Bill helped style all of the early postwar production cars and, as John Blatchley's deputy, worked on styling projects that resulted in the R-Type Bentley and the Silver Dawn and, later, the Silver Cloud and its Bentley equivalent, the S-Series. Having been associated with the styling of motor cars from the age of 16 in 1928, Bill retired in 1977, but not before he had contributed largely to the Silver Shadow cars: under John Blatchley's guidance, he is recognised as being largely responsible for styling the Silver Shadow's coachbuilt derivatives which eventually materialised as the Corniche.

It was with some amusement, and great pride, that Bill Allen came face-to-face with the last production Corniche in 1996. As the stylist looked along the car's aesthetic lines to the uplift above the rear axle, a feature which he termed coke-bottle shape, there was indeed pleasure on his face.

Martin Bourne joined Rolls-Royce in 1955 when he successfully applied for an engineering apprenticeship. In time he was appointed to the styling department under John Blatchley where he contributed to a wide range of projects, not least being the Silver Shadow. for which he was responsible for much of the interior design. Some of his most challenging work centred around the FSS requirements, which led to the Silver Shadow's facia being extensively modified to comply with the then current regulations. In addition to applying his skills to designing the Silver Shadow ll's facia (which formed the basis of that designed for the Silver Spirit), Martin was at a much earlier stage involved in countless projects the outside world never saw, including Tibet, Tonga, Borneo, Bengal, Rangoon and Alpha. Before taking early retirement and establishing his own styling studio - where he still undertakes projects for Rolls-Royce and Bentley - his final project was, fittingly perhaps, an SZ hearse!

This quarter-scale model of SZ, model 'B', set against a most realistic background, illustrates how the car's styling arrangement had progressed from the ideas suggested in model A. Frontal styling, headlamps excepted, is more in keeping with later trends. (Courtesy Rolls-Royce Motor Cars Limited)

Model B as viewed from a three-quarter rear position. The styling is much more progressive than that of the first model. These photographs were taken on the steering pad in a corner of the company sports field. (Courtesy Rolls-Royce Motor Cars Limited)

Newcomers to the styling department were Ron Maddocks and Norman Webster, along with two graduates from the Royal College of Art, Chris Johnson and, later, Graham Hull. Ron was appointed as a full-time modeller and Norman as a project designer. Chris left after a year but Graham remained, taking charge of the department on Fritz Feller's departure in 1983. In 1998 he unveiled the Silver Seraph and Bentley Arnage only weeks before Vickers' sale of Rolls-Royce Motor Cars to Volkswagen in early June and, ultimately, the acquisition of the Rolls-Royce name by BMW at the end of July.

In recalling those now distant and halcyon days at Crewe, Graham remembers that his first project was not styling motor cars as he had imagined, but the much more mundane task of designing a knee pad for Alex Moulton's car. The engineer famous for designing the innovative bicycle was a long-standing Rolls-Royce customer, whose unique position at the wheel of his vehicle meant that, to be comfortable, he required a specially designed knee pad to be fitted to the driver's door ...

Styling techniques began to change to an extent during the late seventies and early eighties, and there came an end to building quarter scale models for viewing purposes, although these were still used during the early stages of a project. The reason for this was the introduction of styling committees, unknown during John Blatchley's days, who were largely unable to look at a scale model and see it as a finished car. Only a few engineers were adept at this, such as Dr Llewellyn Smith, Harry Grylls and the stylists

Model B on the styling table. Here, the size of the model is highlighted by the positioning of the one foot ruler. This picture was taken around 1971/72. (Courtesy Rolls-Royce Motor Cars Limited)

Further development shows model B with paired headlamps with quartic bezels set within single surrounds, giving a more positive appearance. Note also that frontal styling is cleaner, the result of redesigned sidelamps and turn indicators. (Courtesy Rolls-Royce Motor Cars Limited)

By the time this model was constructed the car's body shape was almost in its final form. There was, however, much to do regarding the form of the tail. Styling engineers had been contemplating a low tail section, hence the need for wing markers. (Courtesy Rolls-Royce Motor Cars Limited)

themselves. Instead, full-size models were constructed, complete with paint and imitation glass and brightwork which, as far as the styling committee was concerned, was the next best thing to an actual car.

Small scale models had always been built within the styling department, and this policy continued. Instead of total use of wax it became practice to prepare certain examples in solid wood, which produced a most attractive finish. With the advent of full-size modelling, however, responsibility for their construction was transferred to the experimental department, a directive which resulted in the stylists being prevented from actually working on the models themselves. Not surprisingly, some antagonism resulted, but eventually what might have become an unpleasant situation was avoided and the two departments agreed on a working practice which, although not perfect, was at least harmonious (up to a point).

Elsewhere at Crewe, personnel that had been responsible for the engineering of the Silver Shadow turned their attention to the new model. Under John Hollings was J. Macraith Fisher, the chief engineer's assistant; with him was Derek Coulson and Jock Knight, who, between them, formed a formidable and highly experienced team of engineers.

Emerging from the Shadow

It would be easy to say that the Silver Spirit was designed on a clean sheet of paper; although this is true to a certain extent, the origins of the car suggest otherwise. The board of Rolls-Royce directors, when meeting to discuss proposals for the Silver Shadow's replacement, took a very guarded view which, considering the company's fragile and battle-scarred position, was hardly unexpected. The ink in the accounts ledger was barely dry concerning the investment poured into

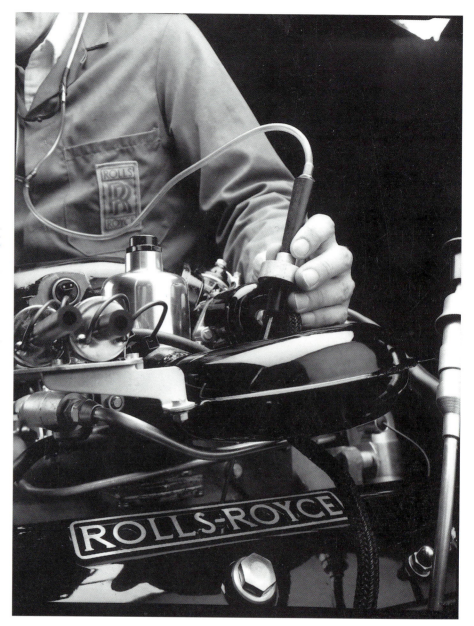

the Silver Shadow programme, and Rolls-Royce's future - following reconstruction of the company - was still uncertain. It was fully recognised that a new model was needed, but the message from the boardroom was loud and clear: proceed with extreme caution.

The criteria in developing the new car was to keep costs to a minimum and use as much existing technology as possible. This precluded designing a new engine, but the car had to be visually different with modern and distinctive lines. By designing a new bodyshell for use with a similar platform to that specified for SY, the drive train would, in essence, represent that already proposed as a progression of ideas being planned for future generation Silver Shadows and, in particular, the Corniche and Camargue. The same applied to the suspension, although in the case of the SY replacement, this was heavily modified to include what was known as the 'refinement package'. The Silver Shadow's handling had come in for some criticism and the revised suspension was intended to redress this. So we have it, a blueprint for the future which incorporated all that was good about the Silver Shadow and its derivatives: underframe, engine, transmission and basic suspension layout, all of which was contained within a new suit of clothes. Rather than being revolutionary, as in the case of its predecessor, the Silver Spirit would be evolutionary.

As far as the coachwork was concerned, Pressed Steel readily agreed to continue supplying complete bodyshells, even if the short production runs, when compared to those for other makes of car, did impose some limitations. In the early days of the Silver Spirit development programme, Pressed Steel had been engulfed within the massive empire that was British Leyland and, despite the company's commitment to BL and other manufacturers for volume bodyshell production, the Rolls-Royce contract was considered particularly prestigious. It wasn't as if Pressed Steel was the only source of manufacture: within the Vickers group of companies there existed the facility at Vickers Pressings in Newcastle-Upon-Tyne to supply bodyshells. Other sources also existed from which pressed steel panels could be obtained; Motor Panels at Coventry being one.

There were other implications, even if somewhat diverse, for maintaining the Pressed Steel contract, including the fact that the company was the UK's largest producer of motor bodies. One such was an agreement signed in the sixties between the then

British Motor Corporation and Rolls-Royce in respect of joint liaison. That project ultimately failed, but, had it not, Rolls-Royce may have acquired a 'small Bentley' for a much wider market, and BMC a prestigious motor car. (BMC eventually got its prestige marque when it acquired Jaguar.)

The sole outcome of the Rolls-Royce-BMC affair was as ill-fated as the partnership itself: the Rolls-Royce engined Vanden Plas 4-Litre Princess R, the bodyshell of which was built by Pressed Steel. The appointment of the car was too much akin to the standard Vanden Plas product, with its Austin roots, and, despite the Rolls-Royce association, few buyers were found. The cruel hand of fate has a habit of striking a second time for, in 1998, following the debacle over the sale of Rolls-Royce Motors Limited, Volkswagen promised an all-new small Bentley with an annual production of around 10,000 units, in addition to a traditional model. BMW once proposed moving production of Rolls-Royce cars to Birmingham to combine it with Rover - the successor to BMC and British Leyland - which it owns. The possibility of a prestige Rover adorned by the Flying Lady and dubbed as 'the poor man's Rolls-Royce' may yet be a possibility ...

The familiar V8 that was to power the Silver Spirit can trace its ancestry to long before the Silver Shadow, and dates, in effect, from the immediate post-war era, although it did not appear until 1959 in the Series II Silver Cloud and Bentley S2. The engine it replaced, the faithful inlet-over-exhaust straight six, had reached the limit of its development and any further enlargement would have resulted in serious cooling problems. The Rationalised Car Engine - be careful not to confuse this with the B engines, with their all-iron construction, which were designed for commercial and military use and therefore provided torque rather than performance - had served well, having powered all the post-war cars up to the end of the fifties, apart from the handful of Phantom IVs which relied upon the enormous 5675cc straight-eight.

Another straight-six could have been developed but the vogue, especially in America, was towards the compact V8. Was Rolls-Royce's V8, the first the company had produced apart from an engine designed to power the Legalimit in 1905, inspired by Detroit? Possibly; Ivan Evernden had purposely visited Detroit in the fifties to study the American motor industry, and it was his report that had sealed the decision to proceed with a monocoque bodied car. He would have had a first-hand opportunity to study the American V8s which were filling the bonnet space of America's cars from the turn of the decade. Rolls-Royce's V8 featured hydraulic tappets sourced from Chrysler although, in time, these were produced in-house at Crewe. Harry Grylls had also given food for thought when, explaining the engine, he compared it directly with the General Motors product. It was a matter of trend which dictated the design and sale of motor cars, and neither Rolls-Royce nor its engineers were bashful about admitting looking around at the rest of the motor industry to gauge fashion and development. Why build a straight-six when the motorist clamoured for a V8?

For the design and engineering of the Rolls-Royce V8 we have the late Jack Phillips in particular to thank, for it was he who masterminded the engine's development. A masterpiece in engineering, the 6230cc, light-alloy engine weighed much the same as the straight-six, but was considerably more powerful, by around 25 per cent.

The 6.230 litre V8 reigned for several years and was installed in the Silver Cloud II and III, as well as the early series Silver Shadows. When fitted to the latter it underwent design changes which modified the combustion chambers, a development which did away with having to remove the front wheels and panels in the wheelarches to access the sparkplugs. In 1970 the engine was enlarged to 6.750 litres, the extra capacity intended to compensate for power loss caused by all the emission gear, not necessarily to make it go faster. Emissions control and concern about fuel conservancy ultimately scuppered any idea of an even larger engine, despite a $7^1/_4$ litre unit having been developed and tested in a number of experimental cars.

The gearbox, too, owed its origins to the sixties when the GM400 was specified for export: Silver Shadows from the outset of production and home market cars from the end of 1968. A General Motors four-speed gearbox, the Hydramatic, had already been in use in Rolls-Royce and Bentley cars and, when the time arrived for a new

Changing styles. The comparisons between these two models are interesting. The model on the right is fitted with a headlamp styling arrangement which is pretty near its definitive form; side lamps and indicators have been moved from the horizontal to the vertical, and a close look at the bumper will reveal a design modification.
(Courtesy Rolls-Royce Motor Cars Limited)

Viewed in conjunction with the previous photograph, the two models, now nose-to-nose, illustrate the styling changes implemented in accordance with pending USA FSS regulations. The comparison shows what was required 'on nose' to 'survive' a 50mph impact. (Courtesy Rolls-Royce Motor Cars Limited)

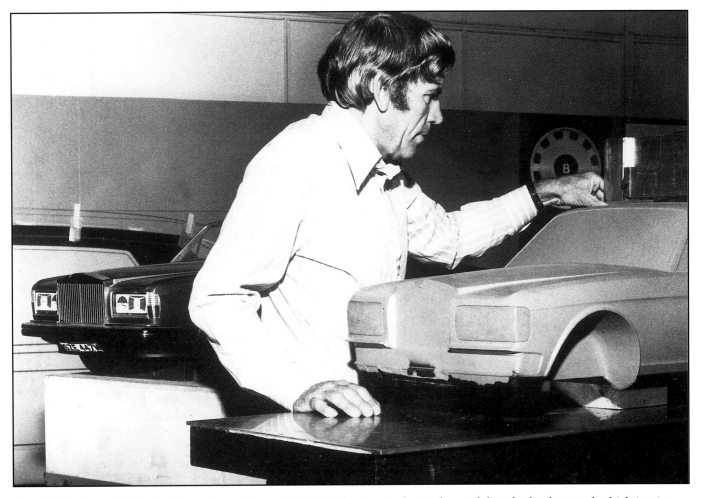

Ron Maddocks with the final quarter scale model of SZ. Of interest also is the model in the background which is at a more advanced stage. (Courtesy Rolls-Royce Motor Cars Limited)

automatic box, it was pointless looking any further than Detroit for a replacement. As a matter of interest, the 6.230 litre engine and four-speed transmission continued to be used in the Phantom Vl until 1978. The GM400 was specified for inclusion in the best of America's cars, but even when installed in the Cadillac it did not have the benefit or luxury of electric actuation enjoyed by Rolls-Royce and Bentley owners. Unlike the earlier four-speed unit, many of which were built under licence by Rolls-Royce at Crewe, the GM 400 remained a proprietary unit and was delivered to Rolls-Royce as a complete item ready for installation.

For the new management team at Crewe, the prudent decision to remain faithful to existing technology was seen as satisfactory, even without allowance for the already burgeoning workload. There were no more fanciful project names either: the Far-Eastern connection so dearly loved by Harry Grylls was consigned to posterity, and SZ, progressing from SY and evolving into Silver Shadow, was the adopted nomenclature for the new car. Eventually, of course, SZ became Silver Spirit after exhaustive checks that the name did not have any unfortunate connotations when translated. An embarrassing situation was only narrowly avoided at the last minute when it was realised that the preferred name for SY - Silver Mist - was highly unsuitable in German as it meant 'rubbish' or words to that effect, and Silver Shadow was hurriedly adopted instead! The 'Silver'

appellation, of course, is steeped in tradition and follows a pattern set by Claude Johnson in 1907 when he named the 12th 40/50 model, chassis 60551, with its handsome Barker touring coachwork finished in aluminium paintwork, and silver-plated fittings and headlamps 'The Silver Ghost'. The Silver Spirit's ancestral names, Silver Dawn, Silver Cloud and Silver Shadow, were all patented in 1938, although remained unused until the post-war years.

One assumption that can be made is that SZ was originally to be known as Silver Shadow lll, and the long wheelbase derivative, Silver Wraith lll. Badges had already been prepared but were eventually scrapped, although one or two escaped this fate.

As for the Bentley derivative, use

Following on from quarter scale models, full-size models were built. These were not constructed within the styling department but in the experimental workshops. Whereas the small scale models were normally created from clay, those full-size were made from epowood, a plastic wood-type material. This is FS-1 in its preparatory stage, photographed on 23rd May 1973; it is slightly larger than the final offering. (Courtesy Rolls-Royce Motor Cars Limited)

of chassis nomenclature R, S, and T, was abandoned in favour of a dedicated model name. Rolls-Royce did not have to search too far as the Bentley marque immediately rekindled thoughts of Le Mans and the era of the Bentley Boys. For Graham Hull, the vision of pre-war Bentleys roaring down the Mulsanne Straight perfectly evoked the marque's sporting image. The directors, approving Graham's suggestion, thought so too, and Mulsanne it was. To be accurate, the name Mulsanne first appeared on a little freelance $\frac{1}{16}$ scale model Graham and Ron concocted for Fritz Feller's desk - one wonders what became of it ...

The styling of SZ was all-important if the car was to have a major impact. Just as John Blatchley before him, Fritz Feller had to ensure that the car still looked modern at least a decade ahead, possibly nearer two, and the chosen shape would therefore be required to stand the test of time and trend. What was fashionable at the time of the car's introduction would have to be completely acceptable years later, which gave little scope for anything controversial or flamboyant. When talking to Graham Hull about the styling process of SZ, he recalled that the most important objective was to make the car appear considerably bigger than it was, and proportionally larger than the Silver Shadow. Despite it having become virtually a legend in its own lifetime, especially in Britain and Europe, in America, the Silver Shadow was considered somewhat delicate when compared to such cars as the Cadillac Lincoln and Buick. The

FS-1 completed and ready for viewing. Even at this stage the definitive shape is apparent, although further work was carried out on the design's frontal area. (Courtesy Rolls-Royce Motor Cars Limited)

classic shape, so typically British, was, quite simply, considered too small by the average American motorist.

By retaining the basic underframe design as the Silver Shadow, modified

to support the revised suspension and rear axle layout, building the SZ appreciably bigger than the Silver Shadow would have been simply impossible. The prime requirement to keeping the

FS-1 being compared with a Mercedes 350SE. This picture was taken in 1977. It was customary for Rolls-Royce to compare designs in this manner, if only to ensure that when viewed against different motor cars they retained that particular presence so evocative of the marque. (Courtesy Rolls-Royce Motor Cars Limited)

FS-1 with a Jaguar XJ6 for comparison purposes. Rolls-Royce had a policy of acquiring different cars for evaluation and using them as company vehicles. (Courtesy Rolls-Royce Motor Cars Limited)

Comparing a Rolls-Royce with a Ford Granada, however unlikely in some people's opinion, was nevertheless all part of the evaluation process. (Courtesy Rolls-Royce Motor Cars Limited)

FS-2 followed FS-1; this again was constructed from epowood and is pictured within the experimental workshop. The difference in styling between this and FS-1 is most obvious with the kick-up on the rear doors. (Courtesy Rolls-Royce Motor Cars Limited)

Photographed on 7th October 1974, FS-2 has been completed. Of particular interest are the wheelarches, which appear almost out of proportion to the rest of the car, and which were designed around Dunlop's Denovo Run-Flat tyres which are fitted. (Courtesy Rolls-Royce Motor Cars Limited)

important and lucrative US market, which comprised around 35 per cent of total sales, was the need to devise a car which was attractive to American motorists without in any way compromising the vehicle's character. The interests of the home market had also to be protected, and so a careful styling approach was essential. An influencing factor in the overall dimensions of the SZ actually lay in the FSS requirements, inasmuch that, whilst the Silver Shadow had been designed to withstand a 30mph barrier impact, the Silver Spirit was engineered to 40mph-plus limits. Building in the required strengthening to the platform therefore added a couple of inches or so to the overall length, although initially this was going to be much greater. In order to absorb much of an impact without deforming the passenger cabin, early proposals had suggested ten inches be added between the front wheel centres and the leading edge of the bumper.

So stringent were the safety re-

Even at this relatively early stage in SZ's development, there were definite plans to produce a Bentley version. Unlike SY, which employed separate bonnet pressings, Rolls-Royce and Bentley versions of SZ were to utilise identical pressings, so therefore the Bentley radiator grille had to be remodelled. This full-size model of a Bentley SZ was fitted with a clay radiator shell crafted by Ron Maddocks. (Courtesy Rolls-Royce Motor Cars Limited)

This close-up of Bentley styling not only illustrates Ron Maddocks' careful remodelling of the radiator shell to fit the Rolls-Royce bonnet, but also the first (failed) attempt to make the US Federal headlamps (sealed beam units that could be bought at any drug store and easily fitted) appear right. (Courtesy Rolls-Royce Motor Cars Limited)

Due to the curvaceous design of the Bentley radiator shell it was necessary, in order to give adequate protection, to pull out the bumper. This is the reason why, on production Bentley SZs, the bumper is curved and adds an inch or so to the car's overall length. (Courtesy Rolls-Royce Motor Cars Limited)

33

This early prototype car, Z-3, pictured on 30th November 1977, wears a dummy Bentley radiator grille. It was also the first road-going pre-production car and carried the registration BCA 831S. Note the slave Silver Shadow bumpers and Corniche wheel trims. The car was designed to be fitted with Dunlop Denovo tyres, so did not carry a spare wheel which accounted for the boot having a lower floor. (Courtesy Rolls-Royce Motor Cars Limited)

Dunlop's run-flat Denovo tyres were abandoned and Z-3 ultimately had a secondary role as far as road testing was concerned. Nevertheless, the car was put through its paces first by test driver Derek Mason, and later by Derek Rowlands. Taken out of service in April 1979, Z-3 served as a test rig for noise and vibration evaluation; the car was later rebuilt and underwent further testing before being scrapped in early in 1985.
(Courtesy Rolls-Royce Motor Cars Limited)

External viewings were, and still are, a feature of any model development. Here, the SZ full size model makes an interesting comparison with a Series l Silver Shadow and Camargue. (Courtesy Rolls-Royce Motor Cars Limited)

Pictured on the Rolls-Royce sports field, SZ, along with Silver Shadow and Camargue, seen from the rear. (Courtesy Rolls-Royce Motor Cars Limited)

In preparation for an external viewing, this full size model of SZ is transported to the Rolls-Royce sports field by lorry. On the left of the picture is (left to right): Ron Maddocks, John Fox, head of the experimental department, and Norman Webster. (Courtesy Rolls-Royce Motor Cars Limited)

Dated 18th December 1974, this photo records the occasion when the final mock-up of SZ was presented to David Plastow, managing director, and John Hollings, technical director, at Rolls-Royce's sports field. Following the viewing, it was decided to change the body coloured front air dam to black. Also, the flush door handles weren't liked ... (Courtesy Rolls-Royce Motor Cars Limited)

... and were subsequently changed, as depicted in this photograph. (Courtesy Rolls-Royce Motor Cars Limited)

quirements that not even the Flying Lady herself was allowed to remain untouched. It was decided that the majestic Spirit of Ecstasy was too prominent, and so she was made to instantly disappear within the radiator shell on impact. Needless to say, this was not easy to do, and many

hours were spent ensuring that the Lady Vanished!

Getting the shape of SZ right took a considerable time; about three years, in fact. Making the car look considerably larger than the model it replaced required some careful razor-edged styling techniques in conjunction with

greatly increased glass areas. There was the danger of the shape becoming wholly angular and, if any of the early styling projects are anything to go by, this nearly happened. The first sketches were undertaken by Chris Johnson in 1970-71, and Martin Bourne recalls the artist using large, spirit-based felt

Attention to detail is one of the many aspects of car manufacture for which Rolls-Royce is rightly acclaimed. This is a styling mock-up of the Silver Spirit / Silver Spur showing burr walnut detail, box wood inlay and cross banding of the veneers. Note also the exquisite hide and carpeting. (Courtesy Rolls-Royce Motor Cars Limited)

External show-ings are all part of the styling process and here we have a prototype SZ along-side a Silver Shadow (first series) and Camargue. As can be seen, styling con-trasts between the models are much in evidence. (Courtesy Rolls-Royce Motor Cars Limited)

Prototype cars are subjected to gruelling testing. Occasionally accidents happen and, in this instance, ACH01009 received extensive frontal damage. The car was ultimately written off as to repair the damage would have cost in excess of £12,000. (Courtesy Rolls-Royce Motor Cars Limited / SHRMF)

maker pens - a technique new to the Crewe styling office - which, when being drawn across paper, were both smelly and irritatingly noisy. When it came to producing scale wax models, preliminary ideas show a car with a very wide windscreen and massive bonnet, which was almost entirely flat apart from the slightly raised crown line that conformed to the radiator shape. With its slab-sides and boot that sloped downwards not very gently, the car did initially appear enormous. The boot eventually became more horizontal, in order to get the trailing edge high enough to be seen when reversing the car. The ideal shape was still some time away but the de-

finitive outline was apparent. Possibly the most disconcerting aspect of the styling was the headlamp treatment: four round lenses that somehow were lost in the abyss that was the frontal area.

This was design 'A' from the styling studio; design 'B' was considerably more aesthetic, the angular shape giving way to some extent to a more flowing pattern. Headlamps were more in proportion if only because the lenses were encompassed into almost square bezels, a feature that was revived on some future models. Indicators and sidelamps were positioned above the bumper instead of being beneath it, and a swage line provided the side

profile with greater definition. Style 'C' was even more improved but it was not until the fourth model, 'D', that the frontal shape of the car appeared proportionally correct, with a headlamp arrangement more definitive of the production car.

The Camargue had some influence on SZ's styling because, at one time, the two-door Coupé's headlamps and door handles were used. Several other ideas were considered, even a radiator with horizontal vanes, which was intended to disguise prototype cars when used for roadtesting purposes.

Other quarter scale models followed before the first full-size model was built, representative of design 'F'

Severe accident damage befell pre-production car ACH011010. The extent of the damage does indicate the car's 'crumple zone' which allowed the passenger compartment to remain generally unaffected. Note how the bonnet has folded, thus preventing it intruding into the windscreen. (Courtesy Rolls-Royce Motor Cars Limited/SHRMF)

and referred to as FS1. At first glance the model had all the hallmarks of the definitive car, but closer examination showed differences to the shape of the front wings and design and positioning of the indicators and side lamps. The bumpers were similar to those fitted to the Silver Shadow ll, and the shape of the rear wings and boot was not fully developed. The first prototype car, Z-1, had also been built and was based on scale model design 'C', and it was the arrival of this which catapulted the project into reality. That first prototype, like so many Rolls-Royce experimental cars, has long since been scrapped, but if it were possible to stand it side-by-side with an early pro-

duction vehicle, several notable design differences would be seen.

The roof was wider than on production vehicles, which illustrates just how much work had been undertaken in revising the 'tumblehome', a situation calling for a major reappraisal as it alters the very element you start with when designing a new car; the side-glass planes. The headlamps appeared out of place and really did not blend in with the overall styling. In order to get the car on the road, the car was, similarly to FS-1, equipped with a host of Silver Shadow ll trim components, and also the bumpers front and rear. One of the more radical aspects of the car was that plastic fillers were used as an

alternative to lead, which was accepted as being environmentally hazardous. A principal measure of the design was that it was built with fewer panel joints than would have been usual and immense care was taken to perfect, as far as possible, the seal facings. Plastic fillers nevertheless failed to produce the same degree of quality as lead and its use was ultimately abandoned. Lead, despite its dangers, was retained for use on production cars but in much reduced quantities.

Z-1 entered service in April 1975 and, once initial tests had been carried out at the MIRA proving ground, the vehicle was entrusted to Derek Coulson and Peter Brocklehurst for road test-

ing in Italy. Part of the car's evaluation consisted of wind tunnel tests, and on the high speed test track it was subjected to some pretty gruelling trials which measured the degree of body lift. Twenty-three years after the event, Derek still has strong memories of that car, and the test programme. As far as the car's engineering was concerned, this was fairly well proven, having been developed for the Camargue and Corniche, but it was the bodyshell which posed the majority of problems. Not only were the doors and seals a dreadful fit, but the car suffered from extensive vibration and, it has to be said, fell somewhat short of what was expected of a production vehicle. Such an evaluation is hardly unusual for an initial prototype, and in the case of the early experimental Silver Shadows the findings were not dissimilar. One of the more niggling problems concerned keeping the side windows clear of rainwater, and this was resolved by fitting a defector each side of the windshield, the modification being incorporated into the car's final design.

The demise of Z-1 occurred in 1979 when the car was used for crash testing purposes with only 12,000 miles recorded. Demolishing a car in this manner is truly expensive and in Rolls-Royce fashion the most economical method of disposing of a car was used. By adopting both left and right hand steering simultaneously, which meant fitting a steering rack with two pinions, and, therefore, dual steering columns and wheels, along with a specially adapted instrument board, a single crash barrier test produced two inde-

pendent results, which satisfied both left and right had steering criteria. To check what was happening inside the car, a hole was cut in the roof and a perspex panel inserted for photographic purposes. After the crash the remains of Z-1 were unceremoniously scrapped.

Z-2, the second of the prototype cars, built to Swiss specification, had an even shorter stay of execution and was scrapped after only 8000 miles. There were all sorts of problems with this car, particularly the bodywork, which showed large gaps and rattled and vibrated excessively. The purpose of the car was not so much endurance testing but evaluation of the key components, such as suspension and transmission. It was not until Z-4 arrived on the scene in October 1977 that the definitive shape of the car was seen. Z-4 pre-dated Z-3 by several weeks and was fitted with left hand steering, which made it compatible for long-term endurance testing throughout mainland Europe.

Z-3 was lighter than Z-4, which was used for type-approval purposes, and was notably different by the fact that it was designed with a lowered boot floor, made possible by the absence of a spare wheel, and which conveniently offered greatly enhanced luggage space. The intention was to equip SZ with Dunlop Denovo tyres which were theoretically capable of running flat, even after a puncture, thus obviating the need to carry a spare wheel. Richard Mann, former Senior Quality Engineer at Mulliner Park Ward, recalls that the Denovo tyres, on their special wheels, were incredibly heavy. "We had a Corniche fitted with Denovos, it came with a spare wheel, the idea being that you could run on a flat tyre for up to 50 miles at reduced speed until a service station or similar could be found. Certainly on a Corniche, with its high boot panel, one had to be very strong to lift a wheel in or out."

Despite advances in tyre technology, the potential risk of supplying a car without a spare tyre or wheel, not to mention customer criticism, was too great to consider, even if the Denovo tyres operated as they were supposed to. Z-3 was ultimately seconded to subordinate duties, which included road testing mainly in the vicinity of Cheshire and Derbyshire. The design was similar to the second full-size model, FS-2, and incorporated the increased tumblehome and used by Pressed Steel for tooling purposes to produce bodyshells. Styles D and E had also emerged from the styling studio and served as productive steps towards design improvement.

Z-4 was still in use with the Experimental Garage when the Silver Spirit went into production in 1980. At around the date of the car's launch it was used for engine development purposes, with particular attention being paid to American emissions requirements. It was for such a role that Z-5 was purposely designed and, fitted with left hand steering, together with cloth seats and headlamps that complied with US regulations, the car was dispatched to Rolls-Royce Motors Inc. New Jersey, in August 1979. Between April 1978 and its departure to the USA, the car underwent several modifications, including fitment of a $7^1/_4$ litre engine, although this was exchanged for a $6^3/_4$ litre petrol injection unit before departure.

Z-5's visit to America was a gruelling experience, with 8000 miles being covered over a period of six weeks. John Gaskell was initially in charge of the test programme; based in Denver, he took the car on a proving run northwest across the USA to Canada and the Rockies before heading south to Phoenix, Arizona. The heat of the desert was ideal to test the car under extreme conditions and proved invaluable when evaluating the car's air-conditioning and cooling systems.

Z-6 represented the definitive production model and was finished with all the correct SZ fittings, to include a Rolls-Royce radiator shell. For a time the car was displayed in the styling studio at Crewe with selected personnel being invited to view it before it was dispatched for endurance testing, which included skid-pan trials. Before leaving the factory the Rolls-Royce radiator grille was removed and, in accordance with usual road test practice, a dummy Bentley grille was fitted.

Up to this point all experimental work had centred around the standard wheelbase cars. From the outset of planning the model range the intention had been to include a long wheelbase car to supersede the Silver Wraith ll and LWB T2, and both Z-7 and Z-8 were representative of the SZ derivation. Unlike the long wheelbase Silver Shadows which were jointly prepared at Hythe Road, Willesden and Crewe, arrangements were made for the forthcoming Silver Spur, the long wheelbase version of Silver Spirit, to be constructed entirely at Cowley with Pressed Steel adding the four inch extension to the platform and bodyshell. Only Z-8 was used for road work as Z-7 had been specially built for crash test purposes, which included the mandatory side impact and rollover tests, before being subjected to final destruction on the barrier test. Before its demise, Z-8 was flown to New York for publicity purposes, leaving the Weston Road (Crewe) car bond on 25th July 1980.

Z-9 and Z-10 were the final experimental cars, Z-9 being a standard 120 inch vehicle registered ULG 948V which was severely damaged in an accident, resulting in the car being written off as the repair charges amounted to over £12,000 including labour costs. Z-9 should have been painted Ice Green but, due to an error, was actually finished in Georgian Silver. John Gaskell recalls this car as amassing over 100,000 miles in 8 months, most of which were acquired in France. It accompanied Z-6 to Italy for high speed trials and tyre testing and, for a period, carried the publicity registration RRM1 when being filmed in readiness for the Silver Spirit's launch. Z-10 was widely used at Crewe by Production as a test-bed in advance of general production; as many as 40 times the car was stripped down and rebuilt, providing production personnel with much valuable experience. The car spent a month in America, from late December 1985 until the end of January 1986, and at

Car Test at Crewe. The car in the foreground is a Mulsanne Turbo. (Courtesy Rolls-Royce Motor Cars Limited)

one time suffered severe accident damage which proved expensive to repair. In all, some 25 pre-production cars were built, some of which were used for publicity and launch purposes.

Recalling the development programme, John Gaskell likens the early cars to mobile test-beds. These were by their very nature somewhat crude and had little in the way of the sophistication expected of production vehicles. As each prototype was evaluated so its

shortcomings were reduced; hence the later experimental cars were capable of extreme mileages over a short period. John remembers that one of the most difficult problems to rectify was the rear axle noise. When fitted in a Silver Shadow, the axle was no problem whatsoever, but as soon as it was installed on SZ an intrusive whine was apparent. Many hours were devoted to trying to correct this, which involved prolonged testing following redesign-

ing and experimenting with sound deadening materials. Although the floorpan was called over from the Silver Shadow, the 'noise paths' would have been quite different. At Mulliner Park Ward at Hythe Road, many of the axles rejected as being too noisy for a Corniche were fitted, untouched, to four-door cars without problem. Corniche cars destined for North America were fitted with only Grade 1 axles, Grade 2 being acceptable for all

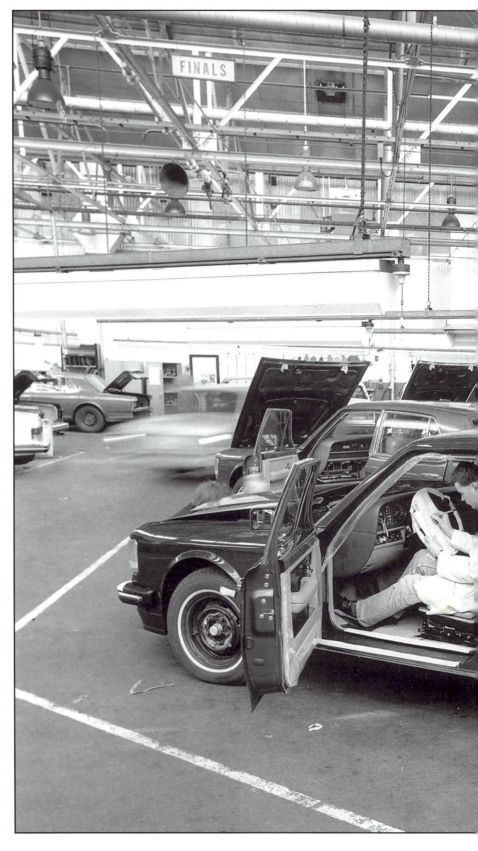

other than American cars.

Preparation for production

The Silver Spirit was launched to the
media in Nice a couple of weeks before
being officially announced only a few
days before the opening of the 1980
Birmingham Motor Show. The car's
impending debut had not been a secret
- Rolls-Royce had advertised the car's
existence in the company's annual
report published in May 1980 - and for
several months before launch the
motoring press had followed
development. When the model was
unveiled, some commentators were
surprised to see a car of such
proportions, especially as the double
oil crisis of the seventies had made
manufacturers and the general
motorist acutely aware of the need for
fuel conservancy. It had been suggested
that a smaller engine might have been
developed, but, of course, there had
been no time for this. Neither was the
car any smaller than the one it
succeeded and was, in fact, fractionally
larger. Although it used what was
essentially the Corniche floorpan and
running gear, the Silver Spirit was
three inches longer than the Silver
Shadow ll and a fraction under three
inches wider. In the case of the Silver
Spur, this was proportionally larger
than the Silver Wraith ll. The stylists
had been successful in their objectives
and the car appeared very much bolder
than its predecessor. Straight lines
and flat surfaces had produced the
right illusion, complemented by a 30
per cent increase in glass area.

To put the 'chassis' design in its

SZ was introduced to the media in Nice ahead of it's official Geneva Motor Show debut. Journalists with Rolls-Royce test drivers and personnel are pictured here before experiencing the Silver Spirit and Bentley Mulsanne for themselves. (Courtesy Rolls-Royce Motor Cars Limited)

proper perspective, the Silver Shadow floorpan, was, essentially, the same for Corniche, Silver Spirit and Continental R, Azure and Continental T, although modified for the latter. From chassis 5000, Corniche and Camargue underframes were modified at the rear end to accommodate the forthcoming Silver Spirit's rear suspension. A ma-

jor change was the adoption of mineral systems fluid, these cars being CYZ and DYZ respectively. When the modified front of the Silver Spirit underframe was incorporated on the Corniche, it became CZ; there were no production DZ cars.

For all its evolutionary nature, getting the car ready for production had nevertheless been an awesome task and Derek Coulson, who was closely associated with the car's development, remembers a protracted period when, it seemed, there were no

solutions to many of the problems that continually arose. Getting the refinement package right proved such a headache that it held up development considerably, even to the point where it prevented work elsewhere on the project. One of the most challenging

49

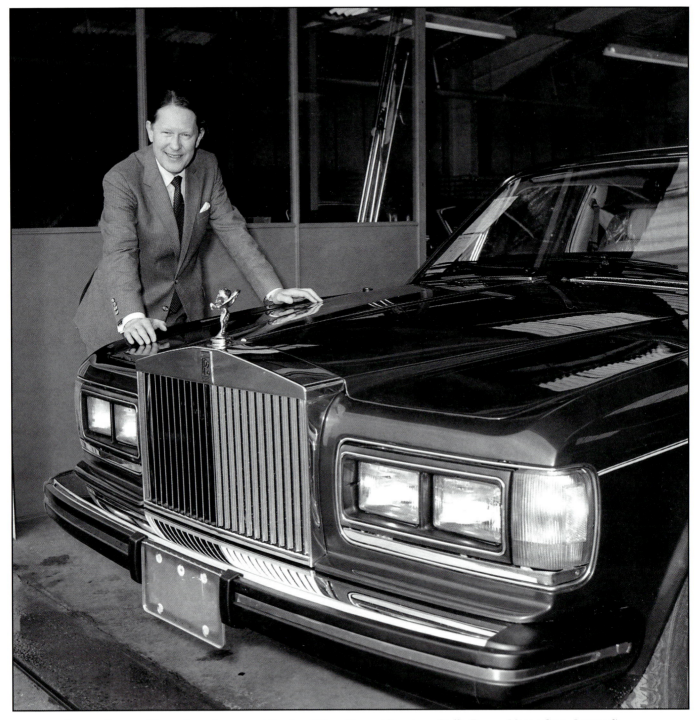

George Fenn with an American specification Silver Spur. (Courtesy Rolls-Royce Motor Cars Limited)

modifications was to the design of the suspension, which was changed to run on mineral oil instead of the usual vegetable RR363 brake fluid. Brake fluid is highly corrosive and lacks the lubricating properties of a mineral oil, and is unable to withstand the 2000 lbs per sq.in. pressure the hydraulic system required. Girling also advocated the use of mineral oil for its shock absorber height control units, and developed suitable components in parallel with Rolls-Royce for use in the new model.

The 'refinement package' which was designed to transform the car's handling was developed with the help of computer-aided engineering, the first time such a technique was used at Rolls-Royce. Derek Coulson instigated the use of computers in this respect and brought in a specialist company, SDRC of Hitchin, Hertfordshire, to prepare the programmes. The task, in the event, was enormous and it transpired that not a single computer existed in Britain which had the capacity to undertake the many complex calculations that were required. Instead, a computer system in Brussels was used and the bottom line of the experiment was that development was concluded in a matter of months rather than years of trial and error which otherwise would have been the case.

Getting the refinement package to the point where it was ready for production came perilously close to disaster. Rear axle noise had bedevilled development to the point that getting the car on the production line in time for the 1980 launch very nearly did not happen. Even when the rear axle assemblies were fitted to production cars there were problems and, ultimately, the best installations were reserved for export cars and those destined for the USA. For home sales vehicles the problem was not considered as acute because rectification could be managed under warranty through the main agent.

Prior to the Silver Spirit's media and dealer launch in Nice, ten cars were made available for publicity purposes, and each was scrutinised to the extreme to eliminate even the most minor problem. Behind the scenes the exercise took countless hours with Derek Coulson in charge of affairs and John Gaskell looking after the cars and acting as 'site manager'. Such attention to detail was worthwhile for the Silver Spirit, and its stablemate, the Mulsanne, were generally well received by the inquisitive, if not critical, media and motoring journalists.

ROLLS-ROYCE & BENTLEY

2

THE SPIRIT EXPOSED

"We will have succeeded in our task of maintaining the Rolls-Royce tradition if, late on a winter's evening, in a dimly lit street, someone looks out of a window and catches a glimpse of a dark and travel-stained Silver Spirit and says 'a Rolls-Royce has just gone by'."

These were the words of chief stylist Fritz Feller, describing the presence he intended the car to convey. The occasion was the unveiling of the Silver Spirit and Bentley Mulsanne at their launch in 1980.

The aim of stylists and design

Silver Spur

The new Rolls-Royce Silver Spur is different and distinctive, the supreme embodiment of the Rolls-Royce motor car, and a milestone in the history of the marque. From the delicate modification of the celebrated radiator, complementing the new styling, to the reshaped rear body, this new design is smooth, clean, more integrated.

Providing its owner with the ultimate in luxury and elegance, yet harnessing the world's most advanced automotive technology, the Silver Spur ensures exceptional comfort for driver and passengers alike.

When styling SZ, it was Fritz Feller's intention that the Silver Spirit and, for that matter, of course, a Silver Spur or Bentley, should retain a presence that made it instantly identifiable as a Rolls-Royce. Nothing has changed since Feller voiced this wish at SZ's introduction in 1980, for his successor, Graham Hull, twenty years on, clearly believes in that philosophy. Today, the Silver Spirit and Silver Spur have a charisma which is internationally recognised and respected. (Courtesy Rolls-Royce Motor Cars Limited)

Silver Spirit at the 1980 Geneva Motor Show. The car made its debut within weeks of Vickers' acquisition of Rolls-Royce Motors. (Courtesy Rolls-Royce Motor Cars Limited)

engineers alike was not merely to ensure that the Silver Spirit *looked* like a Rolls-Royce - or that the Mulsanne should have the appearance of a Bentley - but that, as far as the customer was concerned, both should *perform* in the manner expected of those marques, and therefore offer the ultimate in quality and driver satisfaction.

Two decades on, the observer will have been able to decide whether Fritz Feller succeeded in maintaining Rolls-Royce tradition. As far as owners and enthusiasts are concerned, there is little doubt that the Silver Spirit and its Mulsanne stablemate lived up to the promise that a Rolls-Royce or Bentley offered: certainly, the charisma is there, as is the luxurious appointment and excellence of engineering, not to mention the peace of mind that a car of its ilk gives driver and occupants. These cars, along with every example of the marques which preceded them, are instantly recognisable; there aren't

many who do not feel some measure of pride and pleasure at seeing something so distinctively British.

If, to the untrained eye, the Silver Spirit appeared both wider and lower than its predecessor, then the car's stylists were wholly successful in their objective: to provide the vehicle with a contemporary form. It will be appreciated from the preceding chapter that, by utilising the basic floorpan of the Silver Shadow ll, there was, in fact, little room for manoeuvre. Nevertheless, by lowering the body waistline, disrobing it of trim, and accentuating the horizontal (which became known as Fritz Feller's 'dustsheet look'), it was possible to create an illusion of width and length. It was not totally illusional, of course: the Silver Spirit is actually longer and wider than the Silver Shadow, but only marginally. The effect of width, however, was achieved by careful attention to styling detail, such as headlamp design and rear lamp

arrangement, and by increasing the glazed area by 30 per cent so that the upper mass of the car was reduced, in turn, emphasizing the horizontal.

Wheelarch size, larger than on the Silver Shadow, is responsible for visibly decreasing body mass: the wing panel area is reduced and, when viewing the car in profile, the eye is directed downwards from the car's upper structure.

The familiar shape of the Grecian Temple radiator, an inch lower and 3.5 inches wider than that fitted to the Silver Shadow, also adds to the desired effect. Close scrutiny of the radiator shell reveals it has slightly rounded edges, this design conforming to certain regulations in some countries where, for safety reasons, a sharp edge is illegal. This detail, in fact, is very similar to that for German market Silver Shadow lls, where rounded, softer-styled edges were required. The prominent rectangular headlamps are sig-

This publicity picture taken for the launch and brochure presentation shows the Silver Spirit in its definitive form. Although modern in appearance, the SZ range of cars relied on the technical prowess of its predecessor, the Silver Shadow, but nevertheless proved to be the right car at the right time. (Courtesy Rolls-Royce Motor Cars Limited)

nificant as they are shaped to incorporate dominant direction indicators and side lamps. Being neatly sculptured around the leading edges of the front wings, the lamp units help give a softened appearance in an otherwise angular style. This was the first time Rolls-Royce had used this design of headlamp which, on close examination, is seen to incorporate twin lamp units. The reason for agreeing upon a rectangular shape was not simply one of aesthetics: advances in lighting technology meant it was possible to maximise efficiency as well as utilise the horizontal aspect to balance the car's frontal styling.

American market cars were equipped with separate twin rectangular sealed beam headlamps without covers, imported from the USA to comply with that country's lighting regulations. The headlamps - fitted to home and other market cars - were not legal in the USA as they had to be readily available from drug stores or parts outlets, and capable of being fitted with nothing more complicated than a screwdriver. It also meant that the wash and wipe facility fitted to other market cars, and which was easy to install, had to be omitted as it would have been very difficult to design a suitable system. This situation, which, it has to be said, did little for the car's looks, continued until almost the end of production, when it became possible to fully standardize headlamp design.

The styling effect on the Mulsanne, with its more curvaceous Bentley radiator grille, was an even softer ap-

American market cars were fitted with paired rectangular headlamps to conform to that country's Federal Safety Standards (FSS). The sealed beam lamps could be purchased at a drug store and fitted to the car with no more mechanical expertise than knowing how to use a screwdriver! (Courtesy Rolls-Royce Motor Cars Limited)

pearance, enhanced by a curved and deeper bumper which added an extra 1.6 inches to the car's length. For the first time both Rolls-Royce and Bentley motor cars received exactly the same bonnet pressings, a feature which added to production cost effectiveness and made the badge-engineering aspect of the cars all the more evident. From a design point of view common bonnet pressings may have saved on production expenses, but in terms of styling this was not wholly acceptable. The Bentley's bonnet shell overlapped the shoulders of the Rolls-Royce bonnet by quarter of an inch, a situation not resolved until a new shell with sharper corners was designed by Martin Bourne in 1986.

Despite the use of flat surfaces and a 30 per cent increase in the glazed

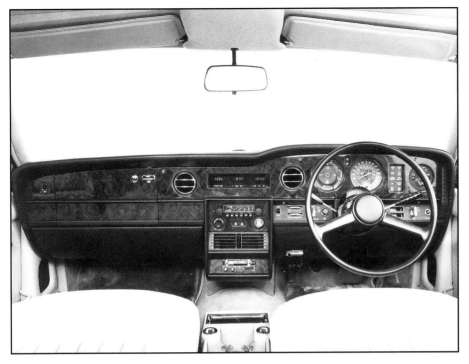

SZ had an all-new exterior but the facia was largely that from Silver Shadow ll. There were modifications, of course, as the car was slightly wider, but in essence Fritz Feller decided that change for change's sake was unnecessary. In fact, this was not quite the case: there had been too little time in which to devise a new style of facia and, ultimately, Martin Bourne's design was extended by $1^1/_4$ inches at each end. (Courtesy Rolls/Royce Motor Cars Limited/SHRMF)

area, the car's dynamic efficiency was not compromised. The increased rake of the windscreen and adoption of a downward slope of the front wings were an aid to visibility. Stability at high speeds was provided by maintaining a high body line at the rear with a relatively sharp cut-off, together with an air dam below the front bumper, which kept the front of the car down and moved the centre of pressure rearward, thus lessening the effects of drag and side winds. Nor was passenger privacy compromised; regardless of the larger windows, rear seat occupants could recline in seclusion within the confines of the substantial rear quarters. A feature of all post-war Rolls-Royce and Bentley cars is the fitting of the familiar 'companions' - illuminated mirrors in the rear quarter panels - an elegant touch continued with the Silver Spirit and Mulsanne.

The efficient exterior of the Silver Spirit belies the fact that the car's interior styling, and that of the facia in particular, remained largely unchanged from that of the Silver Shadow ll. The reason for carrying over the facia styling from the previous model was, as stated by Fritz Feller, simply because it

was considered unnecessary to change it. In Feller's view, the 1977 facia provided all the information and controls a driver needed and, whilst it would have been possible to modernise, this would not have made it any more efficient. Change for change's sake should be avoided at all costs, was the official line. In fact, the true reason for carrying over the facia, the first time this had occurred on a Rolls-Royce, was because there had been insufficient time to design a suitable replacement.

In the event Martin Bourne's facia styling proved completely acceptable for the Silver Spirit, but it did mean adding $1^1/_4$ inches at each end in order for it to fill the Silver Spirit's slightly wider body. For the Silver Spirit and Mulsanne owner there was the opulence of the finest walnut veneers, the familiar switchbox and easy to read instrumentation. The circular shaped switchbox with its Yale lock is as much part of a Rolls-Royce as the car's R-R monogram or, in the case of the Bentley, its delightful Winged B emblem, for contained within the roundel is the key to the car's power system. And we must not forget the chromium plated 'bulls-eye' air outlet ventilators, a

throwback to the early Silver Shadow and something which really could not be bettered.

As far as seating was concerned there were some initial problems. Seat design was modified from that of the Silver Shadow. Instead of the conventional springcases for cushion and squab, the seats had moulded foam cushioning fixed to a 'flexolator', a wire mesh base joined to a frame by small coil springs. The shape of the seats differed from those on the Silver Shadow, giving greater comfort by improved lateral and lumbar support. Instead of a rear bench seat there were two individual seats, styled to resemble armchairs and providing armchair comfort. With the central armrest raiised, it was possible to seat a third passenger in the rear compartment, and a lap-type seatbelt was provided for this purpose. Prototype cars were trimmed in the experimental garage and the trimmers tensioned the hides exactly to provide the optimum shape. With the establishment of a mean driving position it had been possible to gauge the most comfortable height at which to locate the arm rests. On production, cars were trimmed by the works' upholsterers, who considered the hides should be somewhat tauter, so that one sat *on* the seat rather than *in* it. The arm rests were kept at the same height as on pre-production cars, which resulted in a number of complaints from owners who found the seating position uncomfortable. The situation was quickly addressed and the armrests raised, especially after

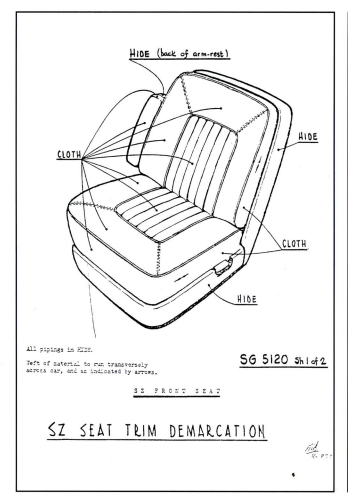

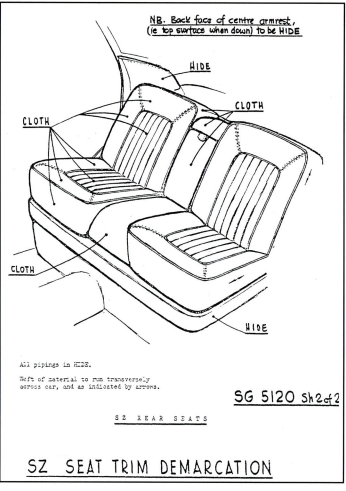

HIDE (back of arm-rest)

CLOTH

HIDE

CLOTH

HIDE

All pipings in HIDE.

Weft of material to run transversely across car, and as indicated by arrows.

SG 5120 Sh1 of 2

S Z F R O N T S E A T

SZ SEAT TRIM DEMARCATION

NB. Back face of centre armrest, (ie top surface when down) to be HIDE

HIDE

CLOTH

CLOTH

CLOTH

HIDE

All pipings in HIDE.

Weft of material to run transversely across car, and as indicated by arrows.

SG 5120 Sh2 of 2

S Z R E A R S E A T S

SZ SEAT TRIM DEMARCATION

Not all cars were specified with full hide seating as these seat trim demarcations show. Customers were offered a combination of hide and cloth as well as the traditional full hide. Some early Silver Spirits suffered from teething troubles in respect of armrests but, ultimately, this was rectified. (Courtesy SHRMF).

Sir Joe Nickerson, who acquired one of the first production Silver Spirits, was moved to write to Rolls-Royce to complain that "the only arm rest that's any good on this car is that between the front seats - when I'm in the back I can rest my feet on it!"

Selling the Spirit

Traditionally, Rolls-Royce and Bentley enjoyed a select and discerning clientele, many of whom regularly traded with either the London Showrooms at Conduit Street, or from the relatively few designated agents, which included a number of Rolls-Royce and Bentley appointed coachbuilders such as Hoopers, Freestone & Webb and James Young. Some customers dealt directly with David Tod or David Buckle, Rolls-Royce's sales managers. David Tod was responsible for Scotland, Northern Ireland and the north of England, while David Buckle took responsibility for the remainder of the British Isles. Upon introduction of the Silver Shadow, Rolls-Royce, in effect, widened the marque's appeal and attracted a new, and often much younger, customer. Shortly after introduction of the Silver Shadow, all the independent coachbuilders had disappeared, leaving only H.J. Mulliner and Park Ward, the latter having been an intrinsic part of Rolls-Royce since before the Second World War, to offer specialist-built, two-door versions of the Standard Saloons. The Silver Spirit was built on a new direction and a more aggressive marketing policy was adopted in keeping with the vagaries of market forces. However, the gentlemanly approach to selling Rolls-Royces continued, especially where long-established dealerships were concerned.

Company policy was about selling more cars so much as reminding potential customers that exclusive Rolls-Royce or Bentley ownership could be more widely enjoyed. A new generation of motorists, some of whom were owner/driver company executives, found themselves being courted by rival manufacturers such as Jaguar and Daimler, Mercedes and, to a degree, Rover. All had designs on the market

Rolls-Royce does not approve of trendy and pretentious publicity material, the like of which is published by some motor car manufacturers. Instead, the company's brochures were, and are, factual, combining essential information with superb photography. (Courtesy Rolls-Royce Motor Cars Limited)

that Rolls-Royce had dominated for many years, and, after all, was not Her Majesty the Queen the owner of a Rover 3 litre? To an extent Bentley was especially suited to changing markets: the marque, arguably slightly less pres-tigious, especially in respect of the Bentley Eight, was introduced in 1984 and brought Rolls-Royce ownership

Considering Rolls-Royce's close association with aviation and the aero industry, it's hardly surprising that aircraft, especially those powered by Rolls-Royce engines, often featured in Rolls-Royce Motors' publicity brochures. This particular photograph is a good example; it also features the Bentley Mulsanne which, despite being stationary, nevertheless gives an impression of speed and performance, thanks to the Cranfield Aerodrome surroundings with RR Continental-powered Formula I aircraft hurtling by. The brochure itself refers to the 'Return of The Silent Sports Car'; although it was unknown by enthusiasts generally, Rolls-Royce had definite plans which would revive Bentley sales in no small way. (Courtesy Rolls-Royce Motor Cars Limited)

within reach of many more people.

As far as Rolls-Royce was concerned, nothing had ever existed to rival its cars; the company had traded on the accolade given to the Silver Ghost, and most people believed it was The Best Car In The World. Jaguar, however, with its 1972 V12-engined version of the XJ12, marketed under the Daimler marque as the Double Six, found an ally in *Motor* magazine which declared the vehicle to have better handling and high speed cruising ability than the Silver Shadow, and at half the price. The Double Six did enjoy a certain exclusivity, and did have a luxurious specification courtesy of Vanden Plas, but it lacked that certain element of sophistication a Rolls-Royce or Bentley has. Mercedes, too, challenged Rolls-Royce for the upper-crust customer with its massive 600 series - almost too ostentatious to be true. Two versions - one with a 126 inch wheelbase, and the other 153 inches - boasted air suspension, air-conditioning and power for everything, including seats and windows. Only slightly less flamboyant was the 450 S-Class Mercedes with its 5-litre V8 engine: a number of commentators saw this as the great challenger to Rolls-Royce from Europe. Cadillac also challenged the Flying Lady in the form of the Seville, which was retro-styled in the fashion of the R-Type Bentleys. Whilst America's most formal motor car might have aped Rolls-Royce, it was always the Crewe product that American motorists chose when only the best was good enough.

Rolls-Royce had always been noted for discreet, high quality publicity material, a far cry from some manufacturers' glossy brochures and sensational approach when it came to sales technique. The publicity material generated by Rolls-Royce was factual and unpretentious, providing exactly the information a client familiar with the company's products would wish to know. Rolls-Royce and Bentley cars hardly needed trendy sales aids; the best adverts for Rolls-Royce and Bentley were, and still are, their names and trademarks. With the introduction of the Silver Spirit, sales brochures still featured stately mansions as discreet backdrops to many of the photographs, whilst the sales message reminded potential customers that the new car was every inch a Rolls-Royce. Bentley photographs depicting the Mulsanne relied heavily upon a familiar background of aircraft wearing the R-R monogram on engine cowlings; the Bentley revival, still in its infancy, had yet to make its mark.

Body beautiful

Preparation for the Silver Spirit's

production was co-ordinated by John Astbury, project engineer at Rolls-Royce in charge of the programme. John had formerly been involved with engine design and had largely been responsible for fitting the V8 engine into the Burma bodyshell during development of the Silver Shadow. Overall responsibility for building the car fell to Ian Nelson, director of production resources and special products and, between the two engineers, they established new plant and tooling facilities, as well as modernising the Crewe factory.

The re-tooling programme, which took several months to complete, called for a £22 million investment by Rolls-Royce. Liaison with the company's suppliers in respect of necessary components was similarly protracted and Pressed Steel (now Pressed Steel Fisher), Rolls-Royce's principal subcontractor, invested £12 million installing new presses and tooling at its Cowley factory. To facilitate produc-

tion of Silver Spirit bodyshells, Pressed Steel invested an additional £4 million in refurbishing a redundant building which had once supplied body panels for the Hillman Hunter.

Following close monitoring of Silver Shadow production, several improvements were incorporated in the manufacturing process of Silver Spirit bodyshells. Instead of the panels being clipped by hand to clean edges and flanges, the operation became automated with die-trimming, which reduced the possibility of distortion and promised greater accuracy in both manufacturing and assembly stages of production. The manner in which bodyshells were handled was changed so that body sections were moved on tracks instead of being lifted by cranes at various production stations. Not only did this relieve stresses but ensured a better fit of doors and windows when cars were assembled.

As had been the case with the Silver Shadow, bodyshells for the Sil-

ver Spirit were delivered to Crewe by road transport. Along with the usual checking process, where the 'Bodies In White' were carefully examined for accuracy and blemishes rectified, it was mandatory to select two bodyshells each week, one having been immediately received, the other having been in storage for a longer period, to be measured using a Portage three-dimensional manual measuring machine. The data obtained from these randomly selected bodyshells was checked against datum measurements to highlight any variations from specification.

Reg Spencer, an engineer who had joined Rolls-Royce when the Crewe factory was being converted to produce motor cars after the Second World War, was manager of quality control and inspection, and responsible for liaising with Pressed Steel's engineers to make necessary tooling modifications. This system of checking bodyshell accuracy was designed not only to keep costs to a minimum by reducing the amount of rectification work at Crewe, but also to ensure consistent high quality.

Throughout production, bodyshell quality came under permanent scrutiny. As director of associate and dealer programmes before taking retirement in 1998, this was one of Bernard Preston's main areas of criticism: no doubt the question of quality was partly responsible for Rolls-Royce choosing to produce its own bodyshells for the Silver Seraph and Bentley Arnage models.

The task of preparing bodyshells for production began as soon as the

The finishing process allowed for at least ten coats of paint, sometimes more according to colour, manually applied and hand rubbed. These built up to a protective layer at least twice as thick as that on most other cars. The underbonnet colour of black was achieved by applying black stove enamelling or air-dried black enamel, depending upon specification or supplies.

The finishing touch was the coachline applied to the body sides: this was once carried out with great care by a craftsman using a small camel-hair brush. Eventually, this tradition of coach finishing, maintained for many years by Jack Hassle, ceased, and in the Silver Spirit's era was achieved by a jig assembly which located under the wheelarches, giving a profile from which an operator with a wheeled lining tool applied the coachline. It took about 10 seconds to complete each side of the car depending upon whether single, double or different colour coachlining was specified.

Some decorative exterior and interior metallic components were formed from stainless steel, other items being chromium plated. Much plating was bought out but, where a special finish or specific extra thickness was required, this was undertaken at the Crewe factory. Steel components, and the Bentley radiator shell in particular, required very high standards of perfection, and were given an acid copper treatment in the plating process to produce the desired finish. Aluminium alloy components were mostly anodized for protec-

shells arrived from Pressed Steel. The oil-based rust inhibitor applied at the factory was removed by steam cleaning, after which the bodies were subjected to a rigorous soak cleansing process. Formed from two special aluminium alloys and welded with anti-corrosive fluxes, the doors were fitted to outriggers so as to allow access to all concealed surfaces, while the boot and bonnet, built of the same materials, were left open. Following two cold rinses and the application of a phosphate wash, there were three more cold rinses, the last being in demineralized water to ensure removal of any residual salts which, if allowed to remain, would attract moisture. Drying the bodyshell was carried out in an oven at a temperature of 115 degrees centigrade.

Following immersion in an anti-corrosion dip to fully protect both external and internal surfaces, vulnerable areas on the underside of the bodyshell were given a protective coat of zinc. Corrosion-resistant oil, a petroleum wax, was then sprayed onto sub frames, and some 70lbs of anti-drumming compound applied to the whole underside of the vehicle, in addition to sealing compound being injected into all underfloor joints. Furthermore, external body surfaces were given a spray coating of acid etch primer which, as well as neutralizing residual phosphates, provided a key for subsequent painting, as well as adding a thin layer of chromate paint on the phosphatized steel surfaces. Before painting, a plastic compound was applied to interior joints and crevices, a process designed to prevent the ingress of moisture.

Two coats of epoxy primer, each a different colour to obviate excessive paint removal during the rubbing down process, were applied to all external areas and interior surfaces of the engine and boot compartments. These were then treated to a black guide coat.

Crewe's production techniques made the building of components more cost-effective. Doors were built as separate units and then fitted to the bodyshell. It will be noticed that curved side glass is being used; this was new to Rolls-Royce, and construction of accurate frames were conducted in-house. (Courtesy Rolls-Royce Motor Cars Limited)

tion; stainless steel was, and is, used for the Spirit of Ecstasy, together with Rolls-Royce radiator shells, wheel discs, window frames, some door handles and boot badge mouldings. Where the likelihood of condensation has been eliminated or reduced, such as in some exhaust applications, a ferritic grade of stainless steel was sometimes used. The Silver Spirit era also saw the use of plastics, albeit limited initially, especially where weight saving was essential; as plastics technology developed, its use became ever more widespread.

The changeover to Silver Spirit production was achieved without loss of production to the then current models, the Silver Spirit ll, Silver Wraith ll, Bentley T2, Corniche and Camargue. A separate production line had been installed in the car assembly area and, initially, 12 pre-production cars were constructed to evaluate the best build methods. Two particular sub-assemblies had proved very difficult to put together on Silver Shadow cars: doors and instrument boards. With improved quality control on behalf of Pressed Steel and greater accuracy, it became possible to pre-assemble both items on specially designed jigs. This meant that ready-assembled instrument boards were fitted to cars on the production line, and doors were made as complete units, and hung in their apertures rather than being built up piece-by-piece within them.

By building up doors as separate units, the task of fitting them into position was made all the easier and reduced production time. The door assembly jig was designed so that part of the frame supporting it connected directly with the lifting machine, itself counterbalanced so that the door was, in fact, weightless as it was manoeuvred into position. The whole assembly was designed to be adjusted with the touch of a finger and remained in place whilst the hinges were tightened by a fitter. Considered a big step forward, curved side glass was something new to Rolls-Royce and constructing the accurately curved frames was carried out in a separate workshop within the factory. This was the first time the company had produced the glass frames in-house, except, of course, for the hand coachbuilt cars.

The fitting *in situ* of instrument boards had always been a difficult and time-consuming operation, carried out in confined conditions and hampered by continual modifications, new equipment and diverse and complicated actuation motors, sensors, switchgear and wiring. By enabling instrument board assemblies to be built up as complete units outside the bodyshell, Rolls-Royce engineers were able to undertake a complete functional check to ensure correct operation before each unit was installed. In similar fashion to the door jigs, a lifting device provided a single-handed operation to transfer the instrument board, or 'unit dash' as it came to be known, into the car.

Much of the drive train was developed from the Silver Shadow ll and was actually installed in the Camargue and Corniche ahead of the Silver Spirit. The engine had already received a rise in compression ratio in March 1980, from 8:1 to 9:1, some six to seven months before the Silver Spirit was announced, although North American cars continued to have the lower ratio. Changes to the car's carburation and ignition timing, intended to improve fuel economy, were carried out with the Silver Spirit in mind; modifications were made to the size of the crankshaft bearings and new types of seals were designed to prevent oil leaks in the event of the sump being overfilled with oil.

The cooling system on the Silver Spirit was pressurised to 15psi and a plastic expansion tank was fitted to the left hand side of the underbonnet. A new device, using a small vacuum motor, successfully mixed the intake of cold air, sourced from the right hand

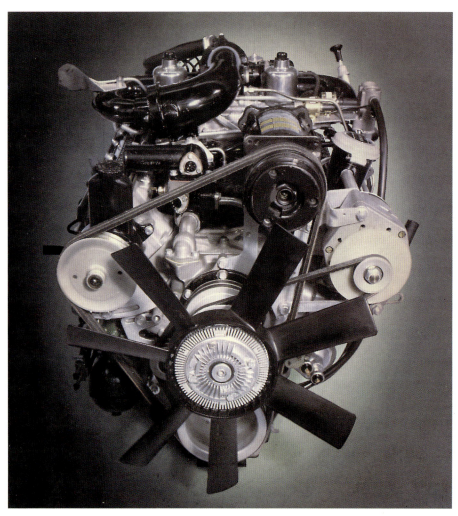

Modifications to the Silver Shadow ll's drive train (it was not fitted to SY four-door cars) were applied to Corniche and Camargue before introduction of SZ. The engine, too, underwent some revision before announcement of the new car. In essence, the format was the same as that designed by Jack Phillips in the 1950s, and originally fitted to the Silver Cloud ll models in 1959. Forty years on, the same engine, albeit heavily modified, is still being fitted to the Continental models as well as the Bentley Arnage Red Label. (Courtesy Rolls-Royce Motor Cars Limited)

side of the front bumper, and warm air collected from near the exhaust to the right of the engine.

Anyone expecting to see marked changes under the bonnet was disappointed, for here the trusty 6.75 litre V8, carried over from the Silver Shadow ll, remained a snug fit surrounded by the usual profusion of pipes and ancillaries. The Silver Spirit's wider bonnet, however, gave better access to the engine compartment. The gearbox, too, was carried over from the Silver

Shadow, the faithful GM400 providing superlative transmission.

The real differences were contained in the suspension system which completely transformed the car's ride. The suspension of the Silver Shadow had gradually been improved: compliancy had been introduced for the front in 1972 and had aided handling considerably with the help of radial ply tyres. Specification of larger tyres in 1974 and introduction of rack and pinion steering had shown the rear suspen-

sion to be in need of urgent modification if it was to match performance of the front. Priority development was ordered in 1974 with three objectives: improved ride, better handling and reduced road noise. The result was first seen on the Camargue in 1978, then on the Corniche but never, as has already been discussed, on the Silver Shadow four-door saloons.

Swing axle effect

In redesigning the rear suspension system, the semi-trailing arms, which had been an intrinsic feature of the original design of the Silver Shadow and Bentley T, were retained but with greater inclination of the arm pivots. The result was a change of camber; more pronounced than before as the wheels rode uneven surfaces to provide a greater swing axle effect. Attention was paid to the roll centre height of the car; by raising it, the wheels not only remained more upright, but the car rolled less and gave a flatter ride. A contributing factor to ride quality was that the rear track was 3 inches wider than on early Silver Shadow cars. The benefits were immediately noticeable: surer handling, reduced tyre wear and greater cornering power, all of which enhanced road holding and driving pleasure, not to mention improved passenger comfort. When comparing ride quality of the Silver Shadow to the Silver Spirit, one is often reminded of its shortcomings. In fairness to both the car and its designers, it should be appreciated that throughout the Silver Shadow's production, much was established in the way of new

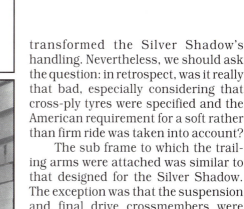

A feature of SZ was its redesigned rear suspension. The new geometry improved both cornering and comfort and, in conjunction with gas springs and rubber mounts, ride adjusted to load conditions. (Courtesy Rolls-Royce Motor Cars Limited)

A Silver Spirit experimental car (GCH14351) on the computerised bump rig at Crewe, which was designed to simulate any road surface at any speed. (Courtesy Rolls-Royce Motor Cars Limited)

transformed the Silver Shadow's handling. Nevertheless, we should ask the question: in retrospect, was it really that bad, especially considering that cross-ply tyres were specified and the American requirement for a soft rather than firm ride was taken into account?

The sub frame to which the trailing arms were attached was similar to that designed for the Silver Shadow. The exception was that the suspension and final drive crossmembers were formed as a single rear axle unit, secured by tie bars and attached to the car's platform at each corner by cylindrical rubber mounts having a horizontal fore and aft axis. The rubber mounts which replaced the Vibrashock stainless steel mountings, otherwise known as 'pan-scrubbers', performed well and were able to smooth out many of the higher frequency bumps, such as 'cat's eyes' and rough surfaces, in a manner much improved, compared to the previous design. They also helped reduce road noise, a factor long campaigned for by some critics within the motor industry who drew parallels with the less expensive Jaguar saloons. The redesign as a whole was responsible for enhancing ride and handling, both of which were made possible by efficient lateral suspension control.

An inherent part of the Silver Spirit's suspension was the self-levelling and gas springs, the latter intended to reduce the degree of body roll. The system was never meant to replace the car's coil springs, which provided the essential means of suspension, but to supplement and provide a constant ride height, irrespective of loads car-

technology. When introduced, the vehicle's suspension and handling were considered innovative and technically advanced when compared to many other British cars. By the end of the seventies successive improvements had

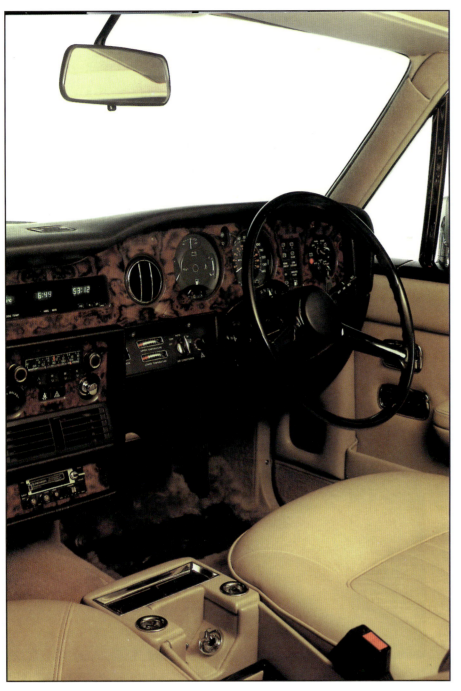

Quality and comfort, hallmarks of any Rolls-Royce or Bentley, were to be found on SZ. The facia styling was essentially carried over from the Silver Shadow, and in this photograph can be seen the digital display showing outside temperature, clock and journey time indicator. Between the seats, the eight-position spring-loaded joystick had the power to move the sublimely comfortable front seats to the desired position. Also visible are the air conditioning controls. (Courtesy Rolls-Royce Motor Cars Limited)

those taking up less space and which did not intrude as much into the boot area. The Girling self-levelling system used each of the rear dampers as struts which maintained a pre-determined height via the mineral oil pressure system and, being connected to gas springs, made it unnecessary for levelling rams to be fitted. Regardless of a vehicle's load or its distribution, the levelling valves in the dampers kept the car's attitude constant at all times.

The change to a hydraulic system mineral oil - HSMO for short - in preference to the previously used RR363 brake fluid has already been discussed. The advantages of HSMO are many, but in particular it gives improved lubrication, reducing friction between moving parts in the braking and levelling systems. It also has better damping properties than brake fluid and absorbs shocks and vibration far more ably. Being non-hygroscopic, HSMO does not absorb water, thus preventing the risk of water-induced corrosion. Neither does its performance fall off: in severe cases, water being absorbed into brake fluid could result in the liquid boiling and brake failure. Another benefit is that it is not chemically corrosive like brake fluid and increases the longevity of hydraulic components, with the further advantage that should any fluid be accidentally spilt on paintwork there's less likelihood of damage.

An element of danger does exist with HSMO inasmuch that if it is introduced to a system intended for RR363, or vice versa, much damage can result. Mixing fluids can cause severe con-

ried and weight distribution. It did mean, however, that the larger and heavier springs employed in the original suspension were superseded by

During the seventies some facia styling exercises were conducted. Ultimately, the facia from the Silver Shadow II was favoured for SZ with only minor modification. (Courtesy Martin Bourne)

tamination of the hydraulic system, which could lead to complete failure. It's not surprising, then, that Rolls-Royce, recognising the danger of mixing HSMO and brake fluid, paid strict attention to advising its dealer network and, accordingly, training was provided so that anyone in any way connected with the servicing and maintenance of Rolls-Royce and Bentley motor cars was made fully aware of the correct use of fluids. The Crewe factory and dealerships operated a colour-coded safety system so that all labels and stickers pertaining to HSMO cars were green, and RR363 cars were amber. Owners soon realised that yellow and green did not mix, particularly if, as a result, it was necessary to replace all seals and hoses which, at that time, cost around £2000! A particular problem Rolls-Royce encountered was that one brake fluid manufacturer coloured its brake fluid green, with potentially disastrous results ...

Spiritual comfort

When introduced, the Silver Spirit and Mulsanne displayed a level of comfort and quality which fully lived up to the expectations of Rolls-Royce and Bentley owners. There existed the traditional attention to detail, the aroma of fine hides, expertly designed fittings and a level of craftsmanship to satisfy the most discerning motorist. By means of an eight-position, spring-loaded

Several designs of steering wheel were considered: the centre one was eventually adopted and replaced the Silver Shadow type that was initially fitted to SZ. Two of Rolls-Royce's styling engineers, Ryan Lewis (left) and Martin Bourne, conducted the exercise. (Courtesy Rolls-Royce Motor Cars Limited)

joystick switch, it was possible to move the front seats to exactly the desired position, adjusting fore and aft as well as for height and tilt, although manual adjustment was required for rake. Mirrors and windows, too, were adjustable with equal precision. Leaving nothing to chance, the speedometer was both silent and totally accurate, the trip indicator being correct to within nine yards in every mile. The facia display included a quartz crystal digital clock, together with journey time and external temperature indicators.

Additional comfort was made possible by 3 inches being added to the car's interior width, although the lower

door switches within a padded area, and a central locking system that allowed individual control of a single door if required.

The split-level air-conditioning, each level being separately adjustable between 17 degrees and 33 degrees centigrade, needed no further adjustment once set to the required temperature. Three temperature sensors regulated the system, which was claimed to be accurate to within one degree centigrade. Both front and rear windscreens had automatic demisting and de-icing facilities and, for the ultimate in luxury, the electrically-operated aerial was automatically raised when the radio was switched on.

Exporting the Spirit

Fuel injected engines became available in January 1980 when the Silver Shadow ll was prepared for California. That state's extremely severe emissions legislation had encouraged Rolls-Royce to devise an engine that was as clean running as possible; ultimately all Silver Spirit cars destined for America were equipped with the Bosch K-Jetronic fuel injection system, together with exhaust gas recirculation, a three-way catalytic converter and injection of air to the exhaust manifolds during cold starting. Types of fuel injection equipment other than the K-Jetronic received consideration but all were

roof line did mean sacrificing half an inch of rear seat head room which, to a certain extent, was recouped by increased rear squab rake. Instead of the veneered door cappings found on the Silver Shadow, those on the Silver Spirit

were crafted from solid walnut and, instead of being fixed, movable carpet-trimmed footrests were provided for rear seat passengers. Safety features included head restraints for both front and rear seat passengers, recessed

It will be noticed that the front wheels appear out of centre to the wheelarches on this full-size model of SZ. The reason is that the wheelarches were designed around Dunlop's 'Runflat' Denovo tyre, which was abandoned immediately prior to the car entering production, leaving it too late for any restyling and retooling. Fritz Feller fought ardently to have the design modified but was overruled by circumstance as well as company directors. (Courtesy Rolls-Royce Motor Cars Limited)

rejected for various reasons, including that of inadequate testing. The choice of system was made on the grounds of reliability, particularly as Mercedes had already been fitting it to its eight-cylinder cars destined for California, and its application to the Rolls-Royce V8 engine meant that there were minimal tooling and development costs.

There was a penalty to pay for developing such a clean emissions system: development work with the Silver Shadow cars had been carried out using an engine compression ratio of 7.3:1, which meant a power loss of around 15 per cent. This was compensated for on the Silver Spirit by raising the compression ratio to 8.0:1 but, nevertheless, performance and fuel economy suffered severely. The top speed of American specification cars was no higher than 105mph, a figure achievable two decades earlier by the straight-six engined Silver Cloud and S-Type Bentley. On the positive side, however, such a performance sacrifice in theory should have gone unnoticed

with the blanket 55mph national speed limit. For a period of time American cars were fitted with speedometers graded to a maximum of 80mph. Neither was fuel consumption satisfactory: at somewhere around 12mpg even American motorists used to relatively inexpensive petrol found the car thirsty, and may have baulked at it being subjected to an additional tax due to this excessive fuel consumption. Rolls-Royce at least did not pass the $650 penalty on to its customers, but absorbed it from the profit margin.

Different markets had their own particular requirements; Japan, for example, did not require air-injection for cold starting, while Australia continued to allow cars to be fitted with carburettors rather than fuel-injection. All this meant careful planning at Crewe in order to prepare individual cars for specific markets.

Silver Spirits exported to America were, similarly to Silver Shadows, not fitted with air dams. There was no technical reason for this other than the

steep ramps associated with American car parks, which were likely to cause damage to any under-bumper protrusions; in any case, the overall national speed limit of 55mph hardly warranted the stabilising affect of the air dam at much higher speeds. Air dams were not the only styling casualty and it was not legal to fit fog lamps, which were normally specified on British and European specification cars. Unlike the bumpers fitted to home market cars, those specified for American vehicles were designed to be energy absorbing with Menasco struts incorporated within them, and capable of withstanding 5mph impacts without damage. The design was particularly clever and allowed the bumpers to retract into a recess within the body; at the rear, the long flexible wrap-around extensions were provided with spring-loaded toggle attachments at their ends which lifted themselves away from the paintwork if strongly pushed forward. Depending also on the market, particular types of tyres were specified: cars exported to North America, South Africa and some Middle-East countries were fitted with the Michelin XVS, while European cars were fitted with either Michelin, Avon or Dunlop tyres, the latter being the D7 design which Dunlop had developed specifically for large luxury saloons and which Rolls-Royce was the first to specify the use of.

A careful look at a Silver Spirit in side profile will reveal that the front wheels are out of centre to the wheelarches. The reason for this is that the wheelarches were designed

specifically around Dunlop's 'Runflat' tyre, the idea of which was scrapped before the car went into production but too late for the wheelarch styling to be modified. The tooling had already been finalised and, to complicate the matter still further, last minute design changes to the front suspension meant that not only did the wheelarches look too big for the car's wheels, the wheels themselves appeared out of alignment. Needless to say, the styling engineers at Crewe were far from happy with the situation: Fritz Feller went to great lengths to have the design modified but this was one argument the chief stylist did not win!

At the time of the Silver Spirit's introduction, export vehicles accounted for 60 per cent of the total output of all Rolls-Royce and Bentley cars, with 35-40 per cent being American sales. 1980 was a difficult year for Rolls-Royce, for not only was the company recovering from a damaging engineering dispute the year previously, but a recession in the American economy meant that fewer orders were being placed for luxury goods, motor cars being a particular casualty. The amount of work needed to certify a new car for the American market was simply not warranted and the consequence was that export of the Silver Spirit to the USA was delayed until 1981. That decision was taken by John Carpenter, then Rolls-Royce marketing director, who considered the American economy would, by 1981, be in a substantially stronger position. This meant there were more cars for sale in the UK and, unusually, home market sales topped

Designed in conjunction with the Silver Spirit was a long wheelbase derivative, the Silver Spur. Technically, the two cars were virtually identical, although the Silver Spur afforded greater space and comfort for rear seat passengers. When specified with a division, which was seldom, there was increased privacy for the rear compartment, but to the detriment of leg room. As can be seen from this publicity photograph, Silver Spurs were mostly equipped with Everflex roofs. (Courtesy Rolls-Royce Motor Cars Limited)

50 per cent of total vehicle output.

American customers were far less used to waiting for a car than their British counterparts, who were accustomed to delivery dates extending to several months or more. American enthusiasts expected to take delivery of a new car immediately and delays were unacceptable. American car-buying habits meant that Rolls-Royce Motors Inc. of Lyndhurst, New Jersey, which handled all Rolls-Royce and Bentley (and Lotus) imports, were usually committed to keeping a substantial number of cars in stock, a situation rarely experienced in Britain. However, the fact that the Silver Spirit was not available in America until 1981 did not overly affect Rolls-Royce sales. Demand for the Silver Shadow and Silver Wraith ll continued in the USA, even though the car was officially out of production, and ultimately the total number of vehicles sold in 1980 was only six per cent down on that of the previous year. Demand for the Silver Shadow remained buoyant because production had ceased and enthusiasts were eager to obtain one of the last models. The fact that the purchase price was as much as $25,000 to $30,000 less than the cost of a Silver Spirit possibly did much to encourage orders.

ROLLS-ROYCE & BENTLEY

3

EVOLUTION OF THE SPIRIT

No sooner was the marriage between Rolls-Royce Motor Cars and Vickers consummated with the successful introduction of the Silver Spirit and Bentley Mulsanne, than a downturn in business seriously affected production. Demand for cars which, in the wake of SZ's birth had been buoyant, suddenly dwindled, leaving Rolls-Royce with unsold vehicles well above usual stock levels. As far as the coachbuilt cars were concerned, this amounted to as many as 200 Corniche models. Of the cars sold in America, relatively few were to individual customers; dealers ordered cars which, in their estimation, would sell, hence the majority of vehicles were supplied with a fairly standard specification. Colours, too, were fairly uniform: white and magnolia were popular, as was black when matched with tan hood and trim.

Rolls-Royce was not the only motor manufacturer to suffer diminishing sales: the teeth of recession, having

In this picture the Silver Spirit makes an interesting comparison with the Camargue. Despite the latter being the flagship of the range, it sold in relatively few numbers, which adds to its exclusivity, and was, by many marque enthusiasts, not generally revered. Many were exported to America, expected to have been the car's prime market, where it was particularly appreciated. The Camargue does, of course, have its devotees, but when the Silver Spirit was announced in the autumn of 1980, its looks and more balanced styling were welcomed. Ironically, the introduction of SZ coincided with an international downturn in business, the effects of which were experienced in the USA before the UK and Europe. (Courtesy Rolls-Royce Motor Cars Limited/SHRMF)

J. A. Duckworth arriving at a Rolls-Royce Enthusiasts' Club rally with his early production Silver Spirit. Identifying features of series l cars include the wash/wipe headlamp cleaning system, which was superseded by pressure jet washers for 1985 model year cars. Soon after SZ was announced, car production at Crewe fell dramatically due to recession. Luxury items, including bespoke motor cars, were hardest hit and lay-offs at Crewe resulted. (Courtesy Colin Hughes & SHRMF)

already been felt in the USA, were beginning to bite hard into British and European economies, and it was the makers of luxury and specialist cars, relying to some extent on export sales, which felt the first chill of economical blight.

Rolls-Royce, possibly, had been too engrossed in matters at home to take heed of the warnings that the export sales bubble was about to burst. For several years demand from overseas had steadily climbed until, quite abruptly, the boom plunged into decline. Instead of introducing the Silver Spirit in the USA at the same time as in Britain and Europe, the decision was taken to delay the American launch by a year, by which time, it was confidently assumed, the 'blip in the economy' would be safely over.

As it happened, the economy took rather longer to recover: British Leyland, having already forecast a drop in export orders, had rapidly pulled out from North America. Not so Rolls-Royce, for whom the American market had traditionally been so lucrative. Due to

the need to maintain stocks of readily available cars to satisfy the American habit of impulse buying, the company was burdened with increasing numbers of vehicles it could not sell, a weak dollar against a strong pound not in the least helping the situation. It's an ill wind that blows nobody any good, and Rolls-Royce and Bentley motor cars, perceived as the ultimate luxury goods, were amongst the first casualties when the recession fully impacted on the British economy.

The situation at Crewe was critical: vehicle production, having reached nearly 3000 cars annually, was drastically cut by around a third, to approximately 2000 per annum. Wholesale redundancies were announced in 1982, and it wasn't only shop floor personnel who went: large numbers of managerial posts were also axed. In a desperate move to reduce overhead costs, it was not necessarily a case of last-in, first-out; in many instances long-standing employees with years' of experience were informed, sometimes with instant effect, that they no longer had

jobs. In cases where sensitive information or technology might have been at risk from potentially aggrieved ex-employees, it was not unknown for personnel to be escorted away from their workplace by security without notice. Queues at employment offices in Crewe and nearby towns were filled with ex-Rolls-Royce staff:

Morale at Crewe was gloomy: all sense of security and job satisfaction evaporated and those fortunate enough to remain, though in fear of losing their jobs, witnessed the loss of countless highly qualified crafts-people. Sir David Plastow, at the time chief executive of Rolls-Royce Motor Cars, admits there were many personal tragedies: experienced men and women who had been loyal to the company all their working lives were suddenly and cruelly dispensed with. It was the manner in which the culling of jobs was carried out that gave rise to a crippling strike, the most serious in the company's history of otherwise excellent working relations, which closed the factory for several weeks.

When the strike action ended, working practices at Crewe and Hythe Road Willesden returned to some normality. Production of the Silver Spirit resumed, as did that of the Bentley Mulsanne and the long wheelbase cars,

When the Silver Spirit was introduced a number of other luxury car makers were keen to penetrate the market Rolls-Royce and Bentley had long enjoyed. Not all cars had a presence that is so unique. (Courtesy Rolls-Royce Motor Cars Limited/ SHRMF)

Introduced at the same time as the Silver Spirit, the Silver Spur, with its extended wheelbase, offered even greater comfort. (Courtesy Rolls-Royce Motor Cars Limited/SHRMF)

but at a vastly reduced rate. From a figure of 2500 Silver Spirit based cars built in 1982, production dipped dramatically in 1983 to fulfil only 1551 orders. From this low point, annual production gradually increased, so that, by the early nineties, it was again in excess of 3000. Thereafter, another decline in sales had a catastrophic effect, more about which is explained later in the chapter.

The early eighties were, therefore, difficult times for Rolls-Royce. Added to the misery the business downturn caused, the company was having to fight off some strong competition from other makers of luxury cars. Only a few models, such as the Aston Martin Lagonda, were more expensive than the Crewe products and, not surprisingly, these vehicles commanded a strictly limited, albeit loyal, following. The real challenge was by cars such as the Daimler Double-Six HE and Mercedes-Benz 500SEL, which could offer, at around half the cost of the Silver Spirit, all that a Rolls-Royce could in terms of performance and running costs. What these cars could not match, of course, was the prestige and elegance, not to mention distinctive quality, that only a Rolls-Royce or Bentley had. Despite the fact that Rolls-Royce did obviously lose a number of

orders to rival manufacturers, to many customers nothing else could equal the thrill of looking along the bonnet to either the Spirit of Ecstasy or, when fitted, the Flying B on the radiator shell. (As a matter of interest, the Bentley mascot was illegal for a number of markets, including latterly the UK, as it was fixed. Where appropriate, Rolls-Royce supplied a bonnet moulding extension, known as a motif, together with a separate mascot; the motif could be released and the mascot secured using the $5/32$ inch Allen key included with the small tool kit.)

A derivation of the Silver Spirit was the Silver Spur, the long wheelbase successor to the Silver Wraith ll, which was announced at the same time as the standard four-door saloon. The Silver Spur, the name evoking a theme once more closely associated with the Bentley Continental, enhanced passenger comfort by having a wheelbase measuring 124 inches, an inch longer than its predecessor's.

Long wheelbase (LWB) versions of the Silver Shadow had proved very popular, and from the outset the Silver Spirit was designed to be built as body in white in two wheelbase lengths. The base platform for the LWB Silver Spur utilised the Silver Shadow floor panels

and double skinned transmission tunnel, the latter serving as a heater duct for the rear compartment, the extension being created forward of the rear seat heelboard by incorporating new pressings. LWB Silver Shadows were modified in London by Rolls-Royce's coachbuilding division, Mulliner Park Ward, where the bodies were extended by being cut in two aft of the centre pillar (BC post) and four inches added. However, in the case of the Silver Spur, the structural modifications were undertaken at Cowley by Pressed Steel. The conversion included fitting lengthened rear doors and a completely new roof, which was initially made from two standard roof panels, welded together across the joint at mid-length. So discreet was the conversion that, at first glance, the Silver Spur appeared almost identical to its sister car.

A standard feature of the long wheelbase cars was an Everflex vinyl roof, which successfully concealed any signs of the conversion process. An optional feature was a division between the front and rear compartments which, it was hoped, would be appreciated by owners accustomed to using their cars for business purposes who were often chauffeur-driven. For more leisurely pursuits, when the owner

This picture of a Silver Spur shows the car off most elegantly. Note the special wheel trims which helped identify this from the standard wheelbase Silver Spirit. (Courtesy SHRMF)

Distinguishing features of the Silver Spur included dedicated wheel trims and an everflex roof, both of which are clearly visible in this photograph. The car's registration, incidentally, is one that is used by Rolls-Royce on company vehicles for publicity and road test purposes.
(Courtesy Rolls-Royce Motor Cars Limited / SHRMF)

might be driving, the division glass could be lowered, but it did mean that rear seat passengers were at a considerable disadvantage in respect of leg room. Whereas the Silver Wraith ll had air conditioning units positioned in the boot, those on the Silver Spur were housed in the division which, despite the lengthened platform, severely encroached into the rear compartment. For these reasons the option was not popular and no more than seven or eight such cars were produced. Those owners who chose not to have a division were rewarded with a rear compartment that was particularly spacious and which afforded near-limousine comfort. The Silver Spur's identification features included dedicated badging on the boot lid and rear quarter panels, and adoption of Corniche-style wheel trims.

Apart from the Silver Spur's overall length and greater amount of inte-

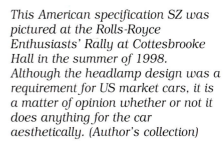

This American specification SZ was pictured at the Rolls-Royce Enthusiasts' Rally at Cottesbrooke Hall in the summer of 1998. Although the headlamp design was a requirement for US market cars, it is a matter of opinion whether or not it does anything for the car aesthetically. (Author's collection)

rior space, fundamental differences between it and the Silver Spirit were few. One could even be forgiven for thinking that the driver's handbooks were identical, until one or two seemingly insignificant variations became evident, such as wheel trim removal. More obvious were those differences concerning technical specifications, such as vehicle weight and dimensions. Due to the longer wheelbase, Silver Spur cars were some 60lbs heavier than the standard four-door saloons, and there were also differences in weight depending on which market specific models were intended for. The kerb weight of British and European market cars was 5010lbs (4950lbs, Silver Spirit); Australian and US market vehicles were 10lbs and 30lbs heavier respectively, whilst Japanese cars were 35lbs lighter than the British and European models. The equivalent model to the Silver Spur in the Bentley range, the Mulsanne L, was made available at the same time, but only 49 - compared to 6238 Rolls-Royce badged cars - were produced. These numbers are, however, in contrast to those later built cars which are discussed in the next chapter.

This Silver Spur has an American specification, identified, apart from the Massachusetts registration, by the twin rectangular headlamps. The longer wheelbase of the Silver Spur was especially appreciated in the USA where customers were used to cars being generally larger than those produced in Europe. (Courtesy SHRMH)

With four inches added to the wheelbase, SZ as the Silver Spur, afforded extreme comfort for rear seat passengers. Note the folding picnic tables built into the backs of the front seats. (Courtesy Rolls-Royce Motor Cars Limited / SHRMF)

Other derivatives of the Silver Spirit were the Hooper conversions. Designed around the Silver Spur platform, these cars were evocative of the grand coachbuilding era and were intended as a strictly limited venture. The demise of separately-chassied Rolls-Royce and Bentley models had determined an end to this great name, which was often closely associated with royal cars, and for a time the revered name of Hooper fell into decline. The fortunes of the company were revived when Colin Hyams, a young Australian businessman, rescued it from near extinction in 1981 when coachbuilding, or body engineering to be precise, was given a re-birth in respect of a number of cars which were based on the Silver Spirit and Bentley Mulsanne but did not carry Rolls-Royce approval. Hooper conversions were carried out on customers' own cars, or if new cars were required, they had to be purchased through a dealership.

The first of the Hooper conversions, Silver Spurs with completely remodelled and luxuriously equipped interiors, was named the Hooper St. James, and was displayed at the 1982 Birmingham Motor Show. The conversions were largely carried out to specific requirements, with some being fitted with a sliding glass roof panel over the rear compartment, and a smaller rear window. All cars were built to comply with American specifications. Some later work undertaken by the coachbuilder concerned converting a standard saloon to a two-door model, which Hooper displayed at the 1985 Geneva Motor Show. In a

number of respects the conversion rekindled that which James Young undertook on early Silver Shadow and Bentley T cars, and which pre-dated the Mulliner Park Ward Two-Door models. By lengthening the front doors and repositioning the BC pillars, the coachbuilder produced an eye-catching alternative to the four-door saloon. Hooper was the builder of a State Limousine variant of the Silver Spirit which

had the standard wheelbase lengthened by nearly two feet. Not only were the body sides entirely restyled, but also the roof was raised, which added to the car's fine proportions.

Robert Jankel Design (RJD) of Weybridge, Surrey, also produced a number of stretched Silver Spurs, which had either two or three feet added to the wheelbase. Prototype Robert Jankel cars were built as six-door saloons,

The Silver Spur was not the only model to have an extended wheelbase. Both Hooper and Robert Jankel Design (RJD) offered 'stretched' versions of SZ; the vehicle illustrated here is a Hooper conversion. Note the four rear seats which face each other. (Courtesy SHRMF)

and all conversions were Rolls-Royce approved which meant the vehicles carried the usual 50,000 miles or 36 months warranty. The cars were, in fact, commissioned by Rolls-Royce in an attempt to prevent unauthorised 'stretching' of the Silver Spirit and Silver Spur models, especially in America where such conversions, applied to various motor cars, were popular. The interior of these vehicles was lavishly appointed with a cocktail cabinet, television, and full in-car entertainment, as well as the usual Rolls-Royce refinements. Ultimately, the centre doors were omitted from production Robert Jankel cars as they served no practical purpose.

Other RJD Silver Spirit/Silver Spur conversions included the Val d'Isere, a four-wheel drive estate car with front wheels driven hydraulically via motors built into modified front hub assemblies. Selecting either low or reverse gear ratios engaged drive to all four wheels, but once vehicle speed

exceeded 30mph, drive to the front wheels automatically disengaged. Special commissions were undertaken, one for a car with a 71 inch stretch, possibly making it the longest Silver Spur ever built.

Crewe-built Silver Spurs were never offered as anything other than four-door saloons, apart from approved limousine variants. There was, however, a shortlived proposal for a convertible model which was reminiscent of the Corniche styled by John Blatchley in the heady days of Silver Shadow development. Sketches were completed by Peter Wharton, Mulliner Park Ward's chief stylist, and the project had progressed to the building of a full-size model before the project was abandoned. Retention of existing Corniche models was favoured, including renaming the Bentley model to revive the Continental nomenclature for the 1985 model year. As it happened, Corniche and Continental Convertibles remained available until the mid-nineties, after

A close-up view of the Hooper interior. Every luxury is provided, including cocktail cabinets and a fold-away audio unit. (Courtesy SHRMF)

Hooper, one of the great names in coachbuilding, was responsible for this 'stretched Spur'. Hooper fell into decline once coachbuilding finished but was resurrected in the early eighties by Colin Hyams, a young Australian businessman. (Courtesy R-REC/SHRMF)

This Hooper conversion created much interest at the R-REC's 1998 Harewood House meet in Yorkshire; note the convertible styling and enclosed rear wheelarches. (Author's collection)

Side-by-side, the post-1989 model year Rolls-Royce Silver Spur and Bentley Turbo R.
(Courtesy Rolls-Royce Motor Cars Limited)

which orders were accepted on a commission-only basis.

During May 1984 it was announced that Fritz Feller was to retire early, due to ill health. For 42 years the chief stylist had contributed to the prosperity of Rolls-Royce, and the Silver Spirit is a lasting tribute to his talents. Graham Hull, who had played a significant part in the development of the Silver Spirit and Bentley Mulsanne, and had been responsible for styling in Feller's absence, continued as acting chief stylist until permanently and officially appointed to the position.

Also during 1984 there was a move to change the facia styling of the Silver Spirit and Bentley Mulsanne in an attempt to do away with the, by now familiar, 'bulls-eyes' ventilation and air conditioning outlets. These were considered heavy and expensive to produce and in their place it was proposed to fit the 'cheese grater' type found on contemporary Jaguars. Several styling proposals were drawn up but, to everyone's relief (within the styling department at any rate), the idea was abandoned and the bulls-eyes remained.

Celebrating the 100,000th motor car built by Rolls-Royce, the company made available in August 1985 a spe-cial edition Silver Spur, which was limited to twenty five vehicles. Rolls-Royce considered it appropriate to combine the occasion with the 100th anniversary of the British motor industry, and the final car of the series to be built, the 100,000th car, was retained by the company for posterity. The car, its keys and documentation, were officially handed over to Richard Perry, chief executive of Rolls-Royce Motor Cars Limited, by the company's two longest-serving employees, Margaret Green and Jack Goodwin, at a special ceremony held at the factory. The limited-edition 'Centenary Spurs' were,

Graham Hull was appointed chief stylist at Crewe upon Fritz Feller's retirement in May 1984. Graham had much to do with SZ's styling and in 1998 unveiled his creations, the Silver Seraph and Bentley Arnage, which replaced the Silver Spirit range of motor cars. (Courtesy Rolls-Royce Motor Cars Limited)

Both Hooper and RJD offered a complete design service for their customers. This Hooper conversion is fitted with a television monitor as well as an audio console. (Courtesy SHRMF)

therefore, 'replicas' of the definitive car; all were finished in Royal Blue, had matching blue carpets and champagne-coloured hide. The attention to detail was meticulous and included specially engraved door sill plates and monogrammed waist-rails; even the picnic tables in the rear compartment were inlaid, and a commemorative plaque was fitted to the inside of each glovebox door. For those customers fortunate enough to acquire one of these very prestigious motor cars the price was £77,740, which was £9995 above the price of a production Silver Spur. These cars are undoubtedly cherished and should appreciate in value.

The ceremony to record the build-

Plans once existed for SZ to be built as a convertible in similar fashion to Corniche. The proposal was ultimately abandoned, but not before sketches had been completed. (Courtesy Rolls-Royce Motor Cars Limited)

Styling proposals in 1984 included changing the facia of SZ, with particular emphasis on replacing the familiar 'bulls eyes' ventilation and air conditioning outlets, which were considered rather heavy and expensive to produce. The 'cheese grater' or 'potato chipper' variety as found on a number of cars was favoured as a replacement by some personnel, but ultimately, and to the relief of the styling engineers, they were not adopted. This mock-up of a facia, photographed within the styling studio, illustrates how the proposed facia might have looked.
(Courtesy Rolls-Royce Motor Cars Limited)

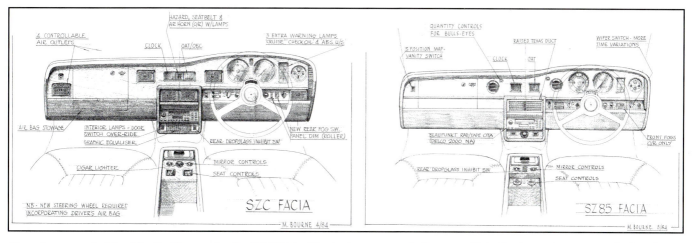

Drawings created by Martin Bourne in April 1984 to illustrate proposed changes. Note that one drawing includes the 'cheese grater' vents, the other the more familiar 'bulls eyes'. (Courtesy Martin Bourne)

ing of the 100,000th car by Rolls-Royce proved to be a grand occasion. The factory was opened to invited guests and the car park on the opposite side of Pym's Lane cleared to make way for an arena. Where the first car parking avenue had been, a stage was built to accommodate a procession of Rolls-Royces and Bentleys of each type from the earliest examples to the then present models. Possibly the most dramatic event, and one which caused intense excitement, was a demonstra-

tion of the Bentley Mulsanne's power and acceleration. Jim Armstrong, one the company's most celebrated test drivers, was invited to put the car through its paces along the staging: after carefully manoeuvring the car into position at one end, he unleashed almost all the car's full power so that it leapt along the short distance, reaching over 60mph before pulling up under a controlled emergency stop within an inch or so of the edge of the staged roadway. Had Armstrong miscalculated

his timing, the outcome could have been disastrous ...

As for the 1985 model year standard saloons, there were some minor revisions which mainly concerned the facia and interior trim, although, externally, the headlamp wash/wipe system gave way to high-pressure spray jets mounted on the bumper, which eliminated the need for separate wipers. In addition to some subtle restyling, the cars received burr walnut veneers that were of even greater el-

Unlike the Silver Shadow, which was built as a two-door Convertible and Coupé, the Silver Spirit and Silver Spur were built as saloons only. Plans at one time did exist for a Silver Spirit Coupé but these were abandoned. That did not stop at least one American customer from having his Silver Spur specially converted, however ... (Courtesy SHRMF)

egance than before, and their use was extended to the door cappings, which, on the early Silver Spirit cars, were limited to finishers formed from walnut. Operation of the cruise control was simplified; the air-conditioning outlets were slightly repositioned within the central console, and the digital display modified to be all the more informative.

From a styling engineer's point of view, this was a particularly busy period which involved preparing a host of new ideas, some of which did not come to fruition. Before ill health had prevented him from working, Fritz Feller had chosen not to present styling committees with a single theme, but instead allowed selection from a multiple choice. This meant much detailed work, and once his engineers had produced their drawings, the experimental wood shop was able to prepare full-size mockups. One such styling arrangement which never materialised was the adoption of a fully digitalised instrument board, which was especially favoured by John Hollings. This particular

project kept members of the styling team busy for months, but it has to be said that there was considerable opposition to the idea throughout the design departments. Eventually, a fully digital facia was produced and fitted to John Hollings' maroon Silver Spirit: although Hollings adapted to it very easily, those who drove the car did not in the least share his enthusiasm for it. The main difficulty experienced with a digital read-out was, apart from instrument board aesthetics, comprehending all the information given in the little time available to look from the road. John Hollings ultimately lost his argument for this type of facia when, it is said, a drawing was given to him of Big Ben with a digital face ...

Nor was Fritz Feller averse to adopting somewhat novel ideas whenever the need arose to resolve certain styling issues. On one occasion, when he wanted to study seat adjustment design, the chief stylist arranged to borrow a pilot's seat from a British Aerospace HS125 aircraft, which was being constructed at the De Havilland

works near Chester. Aeroplane crew seats are renowned for having excellent adjustment, with those fitted to the HS125 being particularly remarkable, and some of the features were incorporated in SZ's seat technology. On another occasion, Feller acquired a skeleton from a doctor friend, which was used to good purpose to study seat ergonomics. By careful examination of the manner in which the bones were positioned, styling engineers could decide which part of the seat should be soft. As to be expected, the skeleton provided much in the way of amusement, but it was a positive and invaluable design aid.

Changes to specification

The Rolls-Royce policy of continuous development and improvement included modifications to the cars' cooling systems, and the engine compartment itself benefited from improved airflow. Close scrutiny of the car's frontal design reveals that cooling was enhanced by the repositioning of the registration plate from beneath the

The achievement of building 100,000 motor cars called for a celebration and one of the attractions was the gathering at Crewe of many of the company's historic motor cars. Pictured here is the Centenary Spur with its famous forebear, the 40/50hp (chassis 60551) Silver Ghost, which has the registration number AX 201. (Courtesy Rolls-Royce Motor Cars Limited)

The registration of this car shows it to be one of H.A. Fox's (R-R agent) demonstrators. Amongst some of the 1985 model year revisions was the adoption of spray jet washers in place of the headlamp wash/wipe system. Other model year modifications included some facia restyling and changes to trim specification. (Courtesy Rolls-Royce Motor Cars Limited/SHRMF)

bumper, to being mounted upon it. The suspension was also modified so that smoother cornering was afforded with greater resistance to the car's tendency to roll. New and distinctive stainless steel wheel trims identified the 1986 Silver Spur cars, which were also equipped as standard with a cellular car-telephone housed within the front central armrest.

Although fuel-injected engines had been fitted to cars destined for the USA and Japan from the beginning of production, and Australia from 1986, it was not until the 1987 model year that this feature became standard for all markets.

Fuel injection helped achieve a 20 per cent gross power boost as well as enhancing economy. Rolls-Royce figures claimed a 16 per cent improvement in petrol consumption - at a constant 56 mph - but, ultimately, such results depended on speed and driving conditions. It was not entirely fuel injection which improved petrol consumption: redesigned pistons reduced the amount of friction in the engine, and new cylinder heads were fitted to enhance both performance and fuel efficiency.

In order to comply with the strict emissions regulations, Rolls-Royce, like any other manufacturer, had to prove their engines could actually achieve, and surpass, the mandatory requirements. To do this, a production-standard motor car was subjected to a gruelling 50,000 mile test which, even allowing for 24-hour evaluation by a team of selected test drivers, took a minimum of 16 weeks to complete. The schedule, which was planned with precision and conducted with the efficiency of a military exercise, included all the necessary service intervals and statutory emissions tests. Unlike some manufacturers, Rolls-Royce undertake

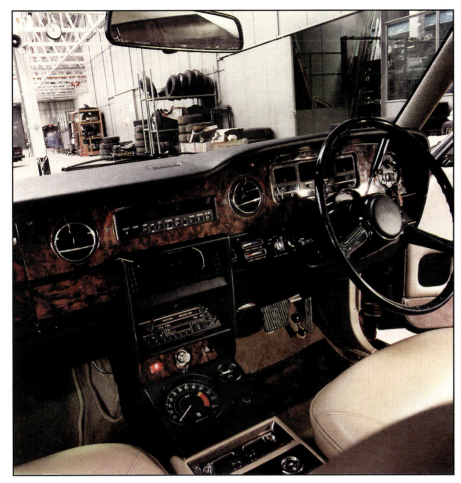

The mid-eighties were a busy period for company styling engineers. As well as working on future models, they also had to contend with designing a digitalised facia, which is shown here fitted to chief engineer John Hollings' maroon car. Everyone except Hollings disliked the digital facia, and those who drove his car found the system most difficult to read. Nevertheless, Hollings persisted with his campaign until one day when he was given a picture of Big Ben with a digital face superimposed ... Shortly afterwards work on 'facia digitalis', as the project was known, was abandoned. (Courtesy Rolls-Royce Motor Cars Limited)

such extensive testing on public roads which is completed in two stages. In the case of the Silver Spirit, an experimental car initially undertook the 50,000 mile test in order that results could be compared against the required specifications; from those figures, Rolls-Royce engineers were able to adjust or change components as necessary on production cars. The test proper followed, carried out by three test drivers, each working a daily shift of eight hours during which time they drove a total of 558 miles. Drivers were re-quired to follow a predetermined route of 46.5 miles incorporating various road and traffic conditions designed to fulfil the test schedule. Each course took $1^1/_2$ hours to complete, during which time certain parameters had to be met, such as obligatory stops and periods of driving at 70mph. American emissions testing is so stringent that two per cent of production vehicles have to be evaluated: Rolls-Royce, anticipating nothing less than total satisfaction, went as far as testing ten per cent of its production, a figure which is maintained to this day. During these 50,000 mile tests the opportunity was taken to evaluate production components for the suspension and transmission, whilst also observing how well the driver's seat, carpet and trim fared.

A number of other specification changes were implemented for the 1987 model year cars. Anti-locking (ABS) brakes were introduced, except for the North American market; the ABS system electronically measures wheel speed and adjusts braking pressure to avoid 'locking-up' in icy, wet, or heavy braking conditions. A new starter motor of Japanese origin was fitted, more powerful and quieter than that previously used. Within the passenger compartment, restyled seats offered even greater comfort with increased lateral support, and fully-adjustable head restraints were provided; for the first time on Rolls-Royce cars, electrical operation of the seat squab was added. An addition to comfort and convenience was electric front seat adjustment, linked to an electronic memory device to provide any one of four preferred positions for both driver and passenger. Door mirror positions could also be logged in the memory system.

One significant change that is often overlooked concerns the company name which, from 14th October 1986, became Rolls-Royce Motor Cars Limited. The new name was considered a better statement of the nature of business, particularly as the company no longer had the same commercial interests as it once did when diesel engines were produced at Shrewsbury. Coinciding with the opening of the British

For the 1987 model year, fuel injection was standardised on SZ throughout the entire market range. It had been fitted to American and Japanese specification cars from the outset in 1980, and for Australian cars since 1986. Rolls-Royce is renowned for its engineering standards and continual quality control is a way of life at the Crewe factory. (Courtesy Rolls-Royce Motor Cars Limited)

sophisticated in-car entertainment system was provided, together with restyled cantrail finishers. Technically, the major change concerned the engine and gearbox, the former having a strengthened and cross-bolted crankcase, and the latter giving even smoother operation.

A new generation

Almost exactly nine years after introduction of the Silver Spirit and Silver Spur cars, a Series ll designated model was unveiled at the Frankfurt Motor Show in October 1989 for the 1990 model year. The complexity of model improvements was enough to warrant a second series nomenclature, but the model range, halfway through its production expectancy, was felt to be in need of a fillip.

For Rolls-Royce Motor Cars Limited, 1989 was certainly looking to be a 'vintage' year. Car production increased by over 15 per cent from 2801 vehicles in 1988, to 3243, which represented a increase in sales turnover of over 23 per cent to £253.2 million. Profits before interest also increased by 6.5 per cent to £24.7 million, despite a £22.5 million investment in equipment and tooling, the largest single project being a new paint shop at the Crewe factory at a cost of some £10 million.

The new models were unveiled to the United Kingdom dealership in September at Turnberry, on the Ayrshire coast of Scotland. The official dealer launch was the first of a number of promotions around the country which culminated in two important events, the London Motorfair and the Scottish

International Motor Show at Birmingham, the name change was intended to be part of a plan to strengthen the company's identity, especially in view of the planned privatisation of Rolls-Royce PLC, the gas turbine engine company, in the first half of 1987. Some confusion existed about a supposed connection between the two companies, and every effort was made to establish strongly and clearly the substantial differences between the motor

car company, then part of the Vickers Group, and the aero engine company at the time owned by the British Government.

Minor improvements to the Silver Spirit and Silver Spur cars were made for 1989, although these were largely overshadowed by changes to Bentley cars, details of which appear in the next chapter. Externally, Rolls-Royce badged cars were graced with new front air dams whilst, internally, a more

In 1986 Graham Hull prepared a series of styling proposals for a face-lift for both Rolls-Royce and Bentley versions of SZ. Note the integral air dam incorporating fog lamps and, in the case of the Bentley, the round paired headlamps. (Courtesy Graham Hull and Rolls-Royce Motor Cars Limited)

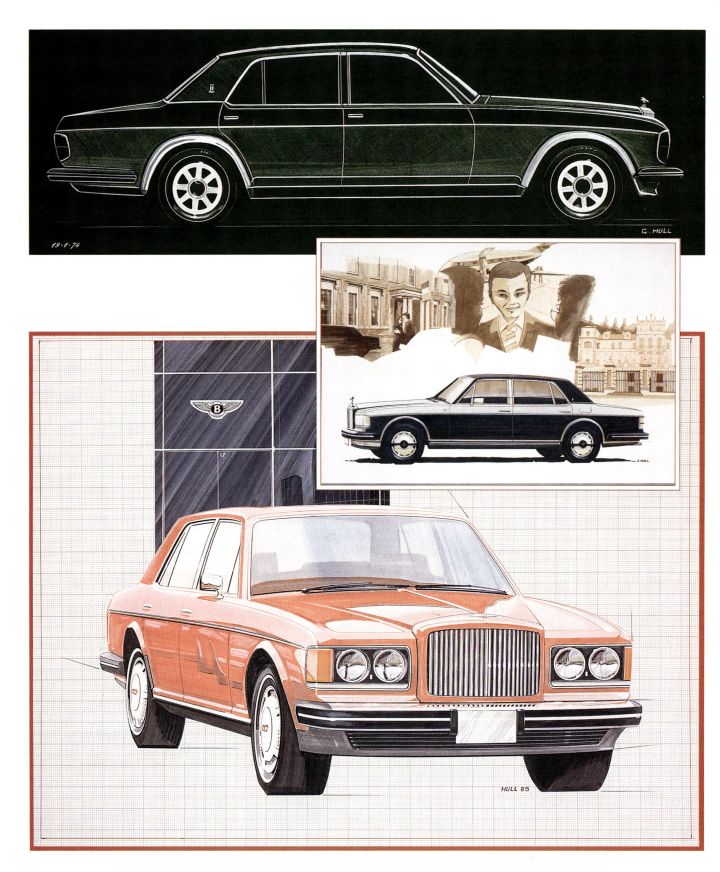

G. HULL

19·1·74

HULL 85

The Silver Spirit ll and Silver Spur ll were introduced at the Frankfurt Motor Show in October 1989 for the 1990 model year. External features of series ll cars were their alloy wheels and stainless steel trims, the long wheelbase models having wheel trims with a painted ring. Apart from some interior restyling, the major modifications affected the car's mechanicals and included the fuel injection management system adopted from the Bentley Turbo R which helped increase maximum speed to 126mph. It was the car's adaptive ride and much improved handling which customer's most appreciated. Automatic Ride Control (ARC) transformed SZ and had required a huge amount of development on behalf of Rolls-Royce engineers, much of it under the direction of Mike Dunn, who replaced John Hollings as chief engineer. (Courtesy Rolls-Royce Motor Cars Limited/SHRMF)

Motor Show. The Rolls-Royce sales force was given the prime objective of demonstrating the new range of cars to 1000 potential customers by November that year, a target which was exceeded by over 50 per cent. Contributing to this achievement were various 'ride and drive' events around the British Isles, which gave potential customers an opportunity to experience the new cars. Elsewhere around the world the cars went on show in Tokyo, Sydney, Washington, Beverley Hills and throughout Europe.

The launch of the Series ll models at Turnberry was a most spectacular event which involved, to everyone's surprise and delight, a flypast from a visiting Spitfire. The Rolls-Royce Griffon-engined fighter was carefully timed to arrive at Loch Doon at precisely the moment Bernard Preston was introducing the cars to his audience, and it goes without saying that only a considerable amount of preparation made the spectacle possible. The Spitfire arrived in the vicinity of Loch Doon shortly before the scheduled time and was circling around an adjacent valley waiting for a signal from a member of the Rolls-Royce team; flying time to the rendezvous was no more than a couple of minutes, but even so, timing was crucial. As a particular reference was made to the cars' engines, so the aircraft roared across Loch Doon.

Was this 'new' Rolls-Royce still worthy of the grand accolade of "The Best Car In The World"? According to its critics you might not have thought so, but delve into the pages of *Autocar* and *Motor*, and the verdict is some-

what different. Certainly, the Silver Spirit ll wasn't the fastest of motor cars, and neither did it score on economy. However, almost without doubt it was the most expensive and finely-built of the world's luxury saloons. Rolls-Royce, of course, did not intend the car to be an out-and-out sports saloon; it was far too sophisticated for that. In reality, no other manufacturer could achieve such a level of finesse, acquired from generations of dedicated craftsmanship.

Externally there is little to distinguish a Series l Silver Spirit from a Series ll, apart from the wheels, that is, which on the Series ll cars are of alloy construction with stainless steel trims. The $6^{1}/_{2}$ inch alloy wheels were designed to assist ride comfort by reducing the unsprung weight, as well as

improve overall performance. Apart from a limited edition of the Camargue, alloy wheels had not previously been fitted to a Rolls-Royce; they were, however, also fitted to the Silver Spur ll, but the wheel trims fitted to these cars differed slightly from those on the standard saloon by having a painted trim ring. From the rear, a Series ll car could be identified by its dedicated badging on the bootlid.

Internally, both the Silver Spirit ll and Silver Spur ll were furnished with a restyled facia, which incorporated additional 'bulls-eye' air-conditioning outlets, one at each end. Inlaid and crossbanded burr walnut was featured, and instrumentation layout was revised to include a new ignition and lighting switchbox, and a modified warning light panel. The steering wheel

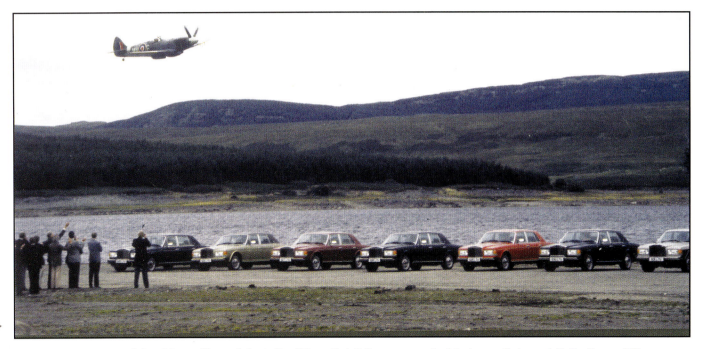

Prior to its Frankfurt Motor Show debut, the Silver Spirit ll was unveiled to journalists and Rolls-Royce UK dealerships. The venue was Loch Doon in Ayrshire and the highlight of the event was the timed-to-the-second flypast by the company's Griffon-powered Mk 14 Spitfire, flown by Rolls-Royce test pilot, Andy Sephton. (Courtesy Rolls-Royce Motor Cars Limited)

was trimmed in leather, and vanity mirrors, which were built into the sun visors, had sliding burr walnut covers. Both front seats were electrically heated and, additionally, had power-operated pneumatic lumbar supports, with switches located within the central console. The Silver Spur ll's rear seats were electrically adjustable, the cushion moving fore or aft to increase or decrease the rake of the seat squab, and a separate telephone jack socket installed in the rear compartment enabled the car's cellular telephone to be used by either front or rear seat occupants. The in-car entertainment system fitted to the Series ll cars was the best available, and the system incorporated no less than ten speakers which had a richness of sound and power that was virtually unequalled.

A remotely controlled, ultrasonic anti-theft alarm, a device which at that time was relatively innovative, added to the car's security. A decade later, of course, the most popular models of many a lesser car have this as standard equipment. Electric front window

lifts featured a single-action, 'one-shot open and close' operation for the driver's door, but it was the parking brake, with its automatic release linked to the gear selector, which provided the ultimate in driver convenience.

Other than the specification changes mentioned, the most important developments concerned engine, suspension and handling characteristics. The Silver Spirit ll could boast of a modest increase in power, attributable mainly to the Bosch K Motronic fuel injection management system adopted from the Bentley Turbo R. This took the car's top speed up to 126mph with a gain of two per cent peak power which was acknowledged as being 226bhp at 4300rpm. These were the days when Rolls-Royce was still coy about publishing the power output of its cars, preferring merely to call it 'adequate'.

All 1990 model Rolls-Royces and Bentleys were designed to use unleaded or super unleaded petrol. Owners of cars which used leaded fuel were encouraged to switch to lead-free petrol,

and Rolls-Royce sent out over 6000 invitations to UK customers, inviting them to take their vehicles to a franchised dealer where the conversion would be undertaken free of charge. One particularly significant customer to have her fleet of Rolls-

Series ll SZs were fitted with alloy wheels and stainless steel trims. The painted ring distinguishes this as belonging to a Silver Spur ll. (Courtesy Rolls-Royce Motor Cars Limited / SHRMF)

The front compartment of a series II car showing the restyled facia. Front seats were heated and had power operated pneumatic lumbar support. (Courtesy Rolls-Royce Motor Cars Limited)

Royce Phantoms converted to unleaded petrol was Her Majesty the Queen. Two employees from the Rolls-Royce London Service Centre were sent to the Royal Mews to convert the cars, an undertaking which, at the time, received widespread media coverage and did much to promote the use of unleaded fuel.

When Mike Dunn took over as chief engineer from John Hollings at the end of 1982, he was adamant that changes to the way Rolls-Royce cars handled were necessary. On his appointment, the new chief engineer's

views about matters relating to a car's suspension and handling left some Rolls-Royce engineers reeling. Dunn had little experience of Rolls-Royce motor cars other than when, as chief engineer at Alvis, he was instrumental in having bodies for the TD and TE21 models built by Park Ward at Willesden. There is some indication that the relationship between Alvis and Park Ward, in the latter years of Alvis' car manufacturing history, was at times less than agreeable. Alvis had complained about poor workmanship in respect of Park Ward's work, and the coachbuilder

went some way towards addressing the major grievances, which mainly concerned water leaks and dropping doors. In the event, Park Ward could do little about the doors, which were ash-framed and panelled in steel and which, it had been claimed, were too heavy for the car's wooden A-posts. Park Ward also advised Alvis that the chassis was of insufficient strength, an opinion that Alvis strongly disputed. The major issue, as far as Mike Dunn was concerned, was that Park Ward had built down to a price, and did not produce for Alvis the same quality as it

94

The rear compartment of the Silver Spur ll had electrically adjustable rear seats.
(Courtesy Rolls-Royce Motor Cars Limited)

did for Rolls-Royce and Bentley, its parent-company cars. In defence, Park Ward presumably would have preferred to have built Alvis bodies using alloy doors but was reliant upon Alvis' specifications, which were controlled to a certain degree by cost constraints. Alloy doors would certainly have been more expensive to produce than steel, and the fact that wood framing was used serves to illustrate Alvis' approach to traditionalism.

Following his tenure with Alvis, Mike Dunn had taken up an appointment with Ford, before accepting the

position at Rolls-Royce. Some Rolls-Royce engineers, it has to be said, were sceptical about their new chief's intentions. Dunn, however, completely overhauled some of the company's working practices and, in hindsight, many personnel now agree he was the right person at the right time for the job. Those who worked closely with the chief engineer recall his great sense of humour and appreciated his professional approach to engineering matters.

Under Mike Dunn's guidance, continued efforts were made to improve

the handling of Rolls-Royce and Bentley cars, and the culmination of several years' research and development was the introduction of the Silver Spirit ll and Silver Spur ll. Rolls-Royce was not alone in revising its suspension systems, as both BMW and Mercedes had concentrated their efforts in that area. Rolls-Royce engineers developed the Silver Spirit ll's suspension in-house at Crewe over a period of four years. Automatic Ride Control (ARC) was the panacea which transformed the cars, a computer-aided system which successfully adapted to both

Above: The extended wheelbase of the Silver Spur ll is more evident in this illustration than others, and gives an indication of the car's interior space and comfort. (Courtesy Rolls-Royce Motor Cars Limited / SHRMF)

The technology for the Automatic Ride Control as fitted to series ll SZ cars took four years to develop; it enabled the suspension to adapt to both road and driving conditions so unobtrusively that passengers remained quite unaware of its existence, other than to enjoy a most comfortable ride. (Courtesy Rolls-Royce Motor Cars Limited / SHRMF)

driving and road conditions and provided the ultimate in comfort and safety.

Adaptive ride, in reality, was hardly novel, as over forty years previously the first post-war cars produced by Rolls-Royce and Bentley featured a type of ride control. On the Bentley Mk VI and R-Type, and Rolls-Royce Silver Wraith and Silver Dawn, this amounted to a small lever attached to the hub of the steering wheel which allowed a driver to select, whenever the need arose, stiffer suspension control on the rear shock absorbers. The system devised for the Silver Spirit ll was all the more sophisticated as it eliminated driver input and gave what, at that time, was considered a ride control without equal. Until adoption of Automatic Ride Control there existed a compromise in a conventional suspension system to achieve good ride comfort and handling. With ARC such compromise was unnecessary as technology made it possible to select between 'comfort', 'normal' and 'firm' suspension modes quite imperceptibly.

The suspension layout was in itself familiar: coil springs, lower wishbones, anti-roll bar and telescopic dampers at the front, and coil springs with semi-trailing arms and anti-roll bar at the rear. The differences were that the front upper levers were compliant controlled and the dampers, front and rear, were electronically control-

led. With automatic ride control monitoring both front and rear axles, self-levelling was retained at the rear. At the heart of the computer-aided system, a micro-processor altered damper settings to within 1 / 100th of a second in response to several factors, i.e. acceleration or deceleration, steering and road surface conditions.

The system was designed to be totally automatic and so completely unobtrusive in operation that it was impossible for the driver or passengers to detect any changes in the car's stance, whatever suspension settings the micro-processor had selected. Occupants would notice only that the vehicle gave the finest possible ride.

First considerations for an adaptive ride system included a prototype design produced for Rolls-Royce, which automatically compensated for roll tendency. The system was oil-based, and as roll sensors fed information to a computer, so the system spontane-

ously pumped oil to the relative suspension units to maintain a prerequisite level whatever the angle of roll. Derek Coulson remembers that, in principle, the system worked well enough, although there were a number of disconcerting tendencies, not least that gallons of oil were being pumped around the car at almost alarming pressure and speed.

Development of ARC was intensive and evolved as a state-of-the-art electronics package which, with the aid of vertical and longitudinal accelerometers, continually monitored every part of a car's progress. Each of the three suspension mode settings were determined during the system's development, and the micro-processor, at the heart of ARC, was programmed from data collected during the extensive evaluation period. Continual information, passed to the micro-processor from the accelerometers and predictive sensors while the car was on

the move, was recorded by an 'electronic brain', so that if any of the threshold values were exceeded the damper settings would be altered in milliseconds. Such was the versatility of the system that, depending upon road and driving conditions, a 'firm' mode selected on entry to a corner could be superseded by either a 'normal' or 'comfort' mode for the manoeuvre depending on car speed.

Typically of Rolls-Royce, the ARC system was designed to be fail-safe even though rigorous testing and development had proved it completely reliable. To avoid any handling problems, the Crewe engineers, with their usual meticulousness, arranged for all dampers to automatically switch to 'firm' in the event of a fault. Firm mode was always employed when the car was stationary, ready for a rapid start or instantaneous selection of another mode for more gradual acceleration.

The newly-designed handling packages for the Silver Spirit and Silver Spur (and Bentley) begged close scrutiny from motoring journalists inquisitive about how they compared to those of other vehicles contending for a share of the luxury market. During 1993 in Britain alone, some 10,000 customers shopped for a luxury car, and that output of Rolls-Royces and Bentleys was around 1500 vehicles says much. Worldwide sales in the luxury sector accounted for approximately 200,000 vehicles, which made the Crewe products extremely exclusive. So, just how did the rest of the

pack compare?

In relation to BMW's 7-Series and the V12 Daimler Double-Six, *Autocar & Motor* kindly described the Silver Spur's cornering as 'stately'. This is not as patronising as it sounds when considering the car's overall size and weight; it did, in fact, prove far easier to handle than might have been imagined. On a six-car test, the Rolls-Royce did not come top-of-the-class in terms of outright speed, nor did it return the most miles per gallon. It did, however, win in a lot of respects; quality, comfort and ride were beyond criticism, and who would buy a Rolls-Royce just for performance, anyway?

Variations on a theme

Although the revisions applied to the standard wheelbase cars were similarly employed on the long wheelbase Silver Spur, a particular derivation was a strictly limited edition, the Silver Spur ll Mulliner Park Ward, 71 of which were built. Known in-house as 'Mulliner Spurs', it was the original intention to build just 25 of these cars, but they proved so popular that production was extended. These cars, all painted in a

Despite the car's advanced technology, the basis of the Silver Spirit ll's suspension remained as before: coil springing , lower wishbones, anti-roll bar and telescopic dampers at the front. At the rear, coil springs with semi-trailing arms and an anti-roll bar was combined with self-levelling. A computer-aided system, ARC altered damper settings in accordance with road and driving conditions within 1/100th of a second. (Courtesy Rolls-Royce Motor Cars Limited/SHRMF)

During the Silver Spur's reign there were a number of 'special editions', including the Silver Spur Mulliner Park Ward. Shown here, the car is fitted with American specification headlamps for that particular market. (Courtesy Rolls-Royce Motor Cars Limited & Queste magazine)

distinctive shade of red known as Bordeaux, were built in co-operation with the Mulliner Park Ward factory at Willesden, and incorporated many special features which were that coachbuilder's hallmarks. To contrast with the paintwork, which extended to the roof, thus eliminating the more usual Everflex roof covering, bumpers and headlamp surrounds were colour-coded; stainless steel body trim, running the entire length of the body sills and continuing around both front and rear wheelarches and along the lower portions of the rear wings, added to the car's striking appearance. This roof embellishment made from 18-gauge stainless steel, was crafted by hand in true coachbuilding tradition. Other specific external features included discreet twin magnolia coachlines along the sides of the car, polished stainless steel bumper inserts and a chromium-plated badge bar mounted on the front bumper. A unique

badge on the boot lid proclaimed the car's coachbuilding pedigree.

Designed essentially for export, the cars were built at Crewe but finished at MPW, and completed to exceptionally high standards of excellence which included interiors styled and furnished in the most exquisite manner. MPW started the theme for the limited edition Silver Spur ll where Crewe had left off with the Silver Spur Centenary five years previously.

The limited edition Mulliner Park Ward cars therefore had a specification to meet the requirements of only the most discerning owner. Waist-rails crafted from specially selected veneers, and complemented by silver inlays and R-R monograms, graced each car; the four door panels were veneered in American burr walnut, the same being used for the picnic tables fitted to the backs of the front seats and to the companion surrounds in the rear quarter panels. The facia, naturally, re-

ceived the special veneer treatment, extended to include the inner surface of the rear seat armrest that also served as an outer panel for the built-in refrigerator housed between the rear seat squabs.

Such was the careful attention to detail that the refrigerated compartment was both illuminated and temperature controlled, and could hold two one-litre bottles of wine. Discreetly concealed within the luggage compartment, the refrigerator compressor was designed to operate only when the ignition was switched on; a voltage-drop cut-out ensured the car battery was not drained in the event of the refrigerator being left on for too long without the engine being run. Everything had been painstakingly considered: below each picnic table in a compartment of its own was a cocktail cabinet made from American black walnut. The cabinets contained two crystal tumblers and a pair of crystal decanters, each

Known in-house as 'Mulliner Spurs', 71 examples of these custom-built Silver Spurs were sold. All were painted a distinctive red Bordeaux, and incorporated many features that were the coachbuilder's hallmark. The cars were devoid of the usual Everflex roof, and bumpers and headlamp surrounds were colour-coded. The stainless steel waist trim gave the car a most unique appearance. (Courtesy Rolls-Royce Motor Cars Limited & Queste magazine)

with distinctive silver screw tops and monogrammed MPW. The driver's central armrest contained a coin rack and trinket box, whilst the passenger armrest housed a Motorola cellular telephone. The rear lower armrest opened to reveal not only space for a separate telephone and its connection, but also a silver pencil and a R-R monogrammed leather-covered notebook.

There was more: the left-hand picnic table housed writing materials, whilst that on the right contained a smoker's companion comprising humidor, cedar-lined cigar compartment and Dunhill silver-plated cigar cutter. In addition to the roof-mounted lamps, chromium-plated swivelling reading lamps enabled rear seat passengers to read the *Financial Times*, *Country Life*, or whatever. Within the glovebox, the driver's handbook was contained in a magnolia hide wallet that matched the car's interior furnishings and, on the inside of the glovebox lid, a silver com-

memorative plaque recorded the car's serial number. Special attention paid to the interior finish of each car was such that the air conditioning sensors and speakers for the optimum in-car entertainment system were all colour-coded. The car's sound entertainment was truly impressive: powered by two 100-watt amplifiers positioned in the boot, the ten-speaker system featured a compact disc player with a six-disc stacking facility, as well as stereo cassette unit and radio. Remotely controlled from within the cabin, the CD player was installed in the boot, for reasons of security and conservation of interior space.

In a combined operation involving Crewe and Willesden, the Silver Spur ll Mulliner Park Ward cars were extensively tested at both locations. In contrast to the production Silver Spirit ll and Silver Spur ll, the 'Mulliner Spur' models took rather longer to build with delivery extending to several months

instead of the more usual average twelve weeks.

These were among the last of the Rolls-Royce models to be built at Willesden. A serious decline in orders in 1991 led to a decision to close the London factory which, during the previous decade, had undergone immense restructuring. In May 1991, Rolls-Royce announced the relocation to Crewe of its coachbuilding interests, and there followed a running down period at Willesden. Although Hythe Road effectively closed at the end of 1991, the finishing of Corniche and Continental models continued until around April 1992. During 1992, the first and second floors were cleared, and the Touring Limousine body build was relocated on the ground floor, near the Convertible build line. Hythe Road continued to produce bodies for the Convertible and Touring Limousine until 1996-7, after which production of the 'Mulliner Spur' continued at the

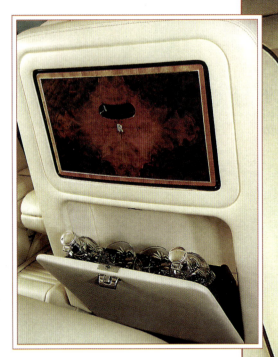

Attention to detail: Mulliner Spurs were fitted with a refrigerated compartment as well as an inlaid cocktail cabinet, which was concealed within the back of the front seat. (Courtesy Rolls-Royce Motor Cars Limited & Queste magazine)

dedicated MPW department at Crewe.

Out of the brief of this book, the Phantom Vl, the final link between Rolls-Royce and traditional coachbuilding methods, had also been the product of Mulliner Park Ward at Willesden. The demise of that car occurred in the early part of 1992 when the last examples left the factory. Its replacement was designed around a limousine version of the Silver Spur ll, known officially as the Mulliner Park Ward Silver Spur ll Limousine but referred to in-house as the Touring Limousine.

The Touring Limousine was unveiled at the Frankfurt Motor Show in September 1991, and made its first appearance at the British International Motor Show at Birmingham in the autumn of 1992. This impressive vehicle, with its six-light configuration, was built on a Silver Spur ll platform ex-

tended by 24 inches, instead of the 36 or 42 inches applied to the previous Silver Spur Limousines produced by Robert Jankel, making for an overall length of 19 feet 7 inches. The roof, a new one-piece pressing, was raised by 2.2 inches to give increased headroom and incorporated a glass 'moonroof' with an electrically operated blind. Deep rear quarter body panels, together with a small backlight, gave additional privacy for rear compartment passengers and, optionally, silk curtains could be specified for all the rear windows.

The Touring Limousine was de-

signed around the Silver Spur ll body-shell but without that car's rear doors and roof. The usual Silver Spur ll front doors were retained but were fitted with taller stainless steel glass frames, a feature which was carried over to the rear doors. Following the usual anti-corrosion protection, transformation to the longer wheelbase occurred with the engine, gearbox and electrics in place. The build procedure called for the hydraulic piping to be blanked off and the propeller shaft omitted before the platform was cut and the extension panels inserted, along with sill panels

Even a writing table was included in the Mulliner Spur specification. (Courtesy Rolls-Royce Motor Cars Limited & Queste magazine)

and cantrails. The new roof and longer rear doors were then fitted, together with the additional side windows. All new components were appropriately anti-corrosion protected before the whole body was painted in the specified colours to coachbuilding standards.

Virtually all the additional 24 inches were incorporated within the Touring Limousine's rear compartment. In traditional limousine style, the car featured a central division, in this case electrically operated and fitted with a blind to provide further privacy. More akin to a drawing room on wheels, the specification included a burr walnut veneered centre console featuring a complete range of audio visual equipment, comprising a ten inch screen television and a compact disc player with remote stacker unit concealed in the luggage compartment. To one side of the console a magnificent cocktail cabinet contained three silver-topped crystal decanters and four tumblers with space for mixer bottles; on the other side, a fully-trimmed occasional rearward seat folded away into the division when not in use. Maintaining a tradition, exquisitely veneered folding picnic tables were also fitted.

Company press releases declared that the style and choice of the vehicle's interior fittings reaffirmed the long-established expertise of Rolls-Royce personnel, and put aside 'short-lived styling fashions and superfluous gadgetry'. Nevertheless, the all-essential refrigerator was included in the specification, concealed behind the drop-down centre armrest, along with the writing accessories and remote controls for the audio and visual equipment, both of which were contained within the centre cushion. Almost anything was possible: from fitting a fax machine to an infinite variety of features and equipment in accord with customer requirements.

Superlative comfort features included separate fully automatic air conditioning systems for both compartments, with dual-level heating for front and rear seats, the latter being individually adjustable. Amongst the more subtle features were footwell lamps installed at the base of the rear seats which operated when a door was opened, whilst aptly named 'puddle lamps' fitted to the bottoms of the rear doors gave a welcome amount of illumination when alighting from the car at night. Privacy was maintained by an intercom system between the chauffeur and passengers. Naturally, a vehicle such as the Touring Limousine had certain exclusivity and production was strictly limited to approximately 25 cars a year.

The Silver Spur ll's running gear was used to build the Touring Limousine, which, like the 'Mulliner Spur', was constructed partly at Crewe and partly at Willesden. In terms of performance, the new four-speed gearbox fitted to the Series ll Silver Spirits and Silver Spurs for the 1992 model year compensated for the car's increased weight, to provide the somewhat academic official government figures of 17.2mpg at 75mph and 22mpg at 56mph. Rolls-Royce Automatic Ride Control gave similar handling to that

Another variation was the Silver Spur ll Touring Limousine, which was unveiled at the Frankfurt Motor Show in September 1991. The car did not make its British debut until the following year, when it was displayed at the Birmingham British International Motor Show. The Silver Spur platform was extended by 24 inches, and the roof raised by 2.2 inches. (Courtesy Rolls-Royce Motor Cars Limited/SHRMF)

Rear compartment of the Silver Spur ll Touring Limousine. Out of view is the 'moon-roof' with its electrically operated blind. Deep rear quarters afforded passenger privacy and, as an option, silk curtains could be specified. (Courtesy Rolls-Royce Motor Cars Limited/SHRMF)

Silver Spur ll Touring Limousines were built in conjunction with Crewe and Mulliner Park Ward at Hythe Road Willesden, London. Silver Spurs were delivered to Hythe Road almost complete mechanically but without exhaust, propeller shaft, brake and fuel lines. The body was cut in two and the additional section added. (Courtesy Richard Mann)

With the new floor section in place, the Touring Limousines were fitted with new roofs, longer rear doors and new side windows. (Courtesy Richard Mann)

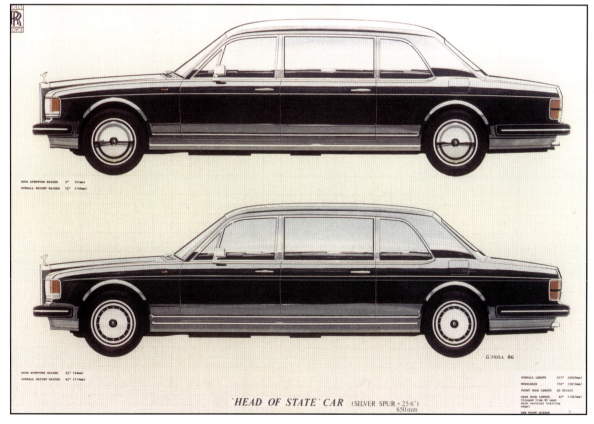

'HEAD OF STATE' CAR (SILVER SPUR + 25·6")
650mm

The Silver Spur also formed the basis of a Head Of State Car as depicted in these drawings penned by Graham Hull in 1986. Rolls-Royce's chief stylist made the point that raising the roof helped counteract the 'stretched toffee' look of some limousines. (Courtesy Rolls-Royce Motor Cars Limited)

of the Silver Spirit ll and Silver Spur ll models.

The third age

For the 1992 model year the Series ll cars received a new four-speed gearbox, which had an electronically operated lock-up clutch on the overdrive 4th speed, depending on road speed and accelerator position. Electronically controlled with the usual electric gear range selector, this was the transmission originally fitted to the Bentley Continental R, which not only ensured the smoothest transmission but improved fuel consumption.

For 1993, specification changes to the model range were less extensive but nevertheless did much to enhance driving pleasure. A new in-car entertainment system featured a combined radio, stereo cassette and compact disc player which could be operated by both front and rear seat occupants. The disc changer unit was, as usual, located in the boot and housed up to six compact discs, a remote controller offering the selection of a particular disc and specific track. Other revisions included an ultrasonic security system which gave three-way vehicle protection: the car could be locked without the alarm being set, but when it was set, bonnet interference or forced entry through the doors or boot was instantly detectable; in the event of a window being broken, for example, the alarm system responded to changes in airflow. An electrochromic interior rear view mirror was fitted which sensed changes in luminance levels; sensors placed fore and aft within the car auto-

matically adjusted the mirror to reduce the effects of dazzle.

In August 1993, Rolls-Royce announced its third generation models, the Silver Spirit lll and Silver Spur lll, which were priced from £104,774 and £119,428 respectively. Introduction of these models arrived at a time of transition for Rolls-Royce, the company, which, not for the first time, had been been severely ravaged by worldwide recession. It was a very much trimmer company in terms of management and personnel that emerged from the boardroom; sweeping changes meant that management levels were restructured and up to 950 jobs, spread over all areas of business, were lost at Crewe. Throughout 1991 and 1992, the company had sought to balance output with depressed sales demand, a policy which resulted in extended periods of reduced output and lay-off. Although retaining the manpower necessary to support an anticipated upturn in the second half of 1992 and throughout 1993, the revival did not happen, and sales in all of the company's major markets remained at very low levels: economic projections for 1993 were equally discouraging. The outcome of a wide-ranging review undertaken by the company's executive board to establish a viable business included reducing capacity to match anticipated

sales. Other measures involved outsourcing certain components or services where these could be produced at a lower total cost, or benefit from increased flexibility, and trimming departmental structures and task teams into a much leaner organisation. In what amounted to one of the most crucial periods in Rolls-Royce's history, adjustments to vehicle production resulted in the profit break-even point being reduced from around 2600 cars annually to 1300, with cars being produced solely to customer demand.

Reading between the lines, the optimistically written press releases revealed the extent of redundancies at Crewe: terms such as 'driving the company to break-even by the end of the year', and '... the company has been radically reshaped and has evolved a business strategy to see it perform profitably into the next century', said much about the extent of the reorganisation.

Developing the third generation Rolls-Royces and Bentleys had cost £30 million, and it was largely accepted that these vehicles represented the final phase in the models' development before introduction of an entirely new range of cars, the design of which was entering its formative stage. The investment in improving an existing model was the greatest ever under-

Along with the Silver Spirit lll, a third generation long wheelbase car - Silver Spur lll - was introduced. Externally there is little to differentiate between these and earlier models except for dedicated badging and distinctive wheel trim. More power was provided as a result of engine modifications which included redesigned cylinder heads combined with larger inlet ports and exhaust valves. American specification cars no longer required the separate rectangular sealed beam headlamp units. (Courtesy Rolls-Royce Motor Cars Limited/SHRMF)

taken by Rolls-Royce and incorporated some seventy modifications. Anyone expecting significant styling changes were to be disappointed, for externally the Series lll cars, apart from those intended for North America, appeared virtually identical to their forebears. One had to look carefully to notice the dedicated badging, and wheel trims with painted rings - a feature the Silver Spirit shared with its long wheelbase sister car. Most significantly, the separate small rectangular sealed beam headlamps were no longer required on North American cars and, accordingly, those Series lll models were fitted with similar headlamp units the same as all other markets.

Substantially, most of the modifi-cations concerned engineering and interior styling. Under the bonnet, revisions to the engine allowed for greater power and even more refined running. Instead of the usual array of equipment - including a plethora of pipes and hoses - what greeted the owner upon opening the bonnet was a neat engine cover with a machined aluminium cooling grille. In essence, the technologically proven 6.75 litre V8 remained: redesigned cylinder heads, combined with larger inlet ports and exhaust valves, improved volumetric and combustion efficiency, whilst a new plenum chamber ram pipe induction system enhanced low speed torque. All this was largely responsible for making these the fastest Spirits and

Spurs to date by pushing maximum speed up to 134 mph with faster acceleration, and increasing mid-range power by 20 per cent. The engine, with its Bosch Motronic 3.3 management system, was designed to meet worldwide emission standards through to the end of the century and, in any case, was within the stringent Californian limits set for 1995 introduction.

Even with a performance boost, fuel economy improved: official figures show that, at 56mph, both the standard and long wheelbase cars could return 24.3mpg, and 19.3mpg at 75mph. As always, the changes to engine specification were introduced only after completion of indiscriminate testing, which included 75,000 miles of

The modified engines fitted to the series lll cars gave a top speed of 134mph and faster acceleration whilst increasing mid-range power by 20 per cent. (Courtesy Rolls-Royce Motor Cars Limited/SHRMF)

steering input meant that handling was in keeping with the new suspension settings and ride characteristics. Even the air conditioning was modified to be CFC-free.

With the emphasis on interior modification and improvement, new seats with additional lumbar and side support, head restraints and seat belt installations provided even greater levels of comfort. A redesigned facia featured an updated information panel with improved illumination. The revisions incorporated airbags; the driver's contained within the steering wheel, and the passenger's concealed behind a veneered panel, which meant that the passenger glovebox was repositioned under the facia. The steering column cowl - because of the driver airbag - was redesigned, the hide finish being colour-keyed to match the rest of the car's interior. Long wheelbase cars were similarly furnished but additionally featured new-style, illuminated picnic tables. The same level of modification was given to the Silver Spur lll Limousine, recognised as the preferred choice for many heads of state and owners of major corporations worldwide. Understandably, the limousine's performance suffered as a result of it's increased size and weight compared to the Silver Spur lll; quoted figures were a top speed of 125mph, 23.3mpg at 56mph and 17.4mpg at 75mph.

For the North American market the Silver Spur lll was fitted with a video cassette player in addition to the in-car entertainment system usually provided. The rear of each of the front

high speed endurance testing in Germany and Italy, and the statutory - for Rolls-Royce - 100,000 mile emissions testing carried out on roads close to the Crewe factory. Additionally, a revised engine underwent a 500 hour full throttle, full load test with complete satisfaction.

Not content at merely providing more power, Rolls-Royce engineers turned their attention once more to the cars' transmission, suspension and handling systems. A transmission shift energy management (SEM) gave even smoother operation, while modified front and rear anti-roll bars added to surefootedness, with roll stiffness being increased to a level halfway between that of previous Rolls-Royces and Bentleys. A reduction in power

A Mulliner Park Ward version of Silver Spur ll was offered, and this picture ably illustrates the company's bespoke design service. Almost anything was possible ... (Courtesy Rolls-Royce Motor Cars Limited / SHRMF)

seat head restraints was fitted with 8cm x 6cm television screens, a system welcomed by both business users and families with young children who could be entertained during long journeys.

In March 1994, Rolls-Royce highly profiled its bespoke design service by marketing the expertise offered by the company's coachbuilding division, Mulliner Park Ward. Since introduction the previous June, the department had received more than 140 enquiries from potential owners around the world, a third of which converted into firm orders. The facilities available to customers were enormous, with craftsmen able to satisfy exactly a customer's requirements, no matter how specific. Along with such features as a refrigerated compartment, laptop computer and facsimile machine, specialised equipment could include a detachable walnut-veneered briefcase, and the limousine's interior could be made to match favourite colours or reflect the design of a customer's home, office, or even a particular piece of architecture. Modifications to the exterior were also possible as long as they did not compromise mechanical integrity or safety legislation.

The Mulliner Park Ward experience evolved eventually to a new limousine, the Rolls-Royce Park Ward. No more than 20 cars a year are to be built

to this design, which can be made to encompass virtually any requirement. Missing from the name is the Mulliner ingredient, which is used in respect of certain Continental models.

Ending an era

Largely unchanged, the Series lll Silver Spirit and Silver Spur remained for the 1995 model year. During 1994, however, Rolls-Royce unveiled the ultimate in the 'Spirit' and 'Spur' ranges, a uniquely named model, the Rolls-Royce Flying Spur. The Flying Spur nomenclature had previously been reserved for the Bentley marque, a four-door version of the Bentley Continental.

The next chapter details the Bentley resurgence and those Winged B emblem cars that were, in many respects, parallel to the Rolls-Royce Silver Spirits and Silver Spurs, and which, with turbocharging, spearheaded the Bentley revival. It is essential to make the point that in the early days of the Bentley turbocharged models, a policy existed to keep the 'sporting' image completely within the Bentley realm, a directive kept intact until the midnineties when the model range had reached full maturity. We see, therefore, what can be possibly described as a hybrid: a Flying Spur with Rolls-Royce appellation, which was quite the

fastest and most powerful model in the Rolls-Royce catalogue.

It could be argued that the £148,545 Flying Spur was, in fact, a Bentley, complete with turbocharging but Rolls-Royce trim specification, badging and radiator. It could be counter-suggested that the car is a Silver Spur in the true sense, but with Bentley turbocharged drive train and a further £25,500 added to the price. Whatever, it really did not appear to matter as customers had decided the car was something very special and orders flooded in upon the model's announcement. Furthermore, the Rolls-Royce Flying Spur was assured of exclusivity from the outset as only 150 were scheduled to be built.

Enjoying similar modifications to those of the Silver Spirit lll, the Flying Spur engine was mated to GM's four-speed gearbox which, in this instance (a first for Rolls-Royce models), included 'sport' and 'economy' modes. The transformation in performance was decidedly noticeable compared to the Silver Spirit and Spur: 0-60mph in under seven seconds and acceleration care of a Garrett AirReseachT4 turbocharger that firmly pushes occupants back in their armchairs is nothing short of phenomenal. The key to unleashing all this performance was engine torque, which was on a par with the Bentley Turbo R engine, and overshadowed that of virtually any other motor car. For such agility there just had to be a penalty: abysmal fuel consumption, a little over 10mpg when the car was pushed to its limit. Economical driving had its rewards, of course;

For the 1996 model year Rolls-Royce introduced what was effectively a series IV Silver Spirit and Silver Spur. Due to marketing decisions, however, the cars didn't get this designation and, instead, were known as the New Silver Spirit and New Silver Spur. The car pictured here is the latter. (Courtesy Rolls-Royce Motor Cars Limited)

by using the lightest possible touch on the accelerator it was possible to almost halve the amount of petrol used to an average of 19-20mpg.

For 1996 the Silver Spirit and Silver Spur cars were again heavily revised, the development programme having called for an investment of £25 million. Unveiled in June 1995, any idea of a Series IV designation was abandoned after the suffix was found to be inappropriate in respect of some Far Eastern countries (it is a symbol of death), and ultimately it was dropped completely. Thereafter, the new models were known as the New Silver Spirit and New Silver Spur.

Mechanically, the engine was modified by revised cylinder heads, a new Zytek electronic fuel injection management system and a liquid intercooler to replace the air-to-air unit on turbocharged cars. A higher final drive ratio - 2.69:1 - which formerly had been specified for turbocharged models, was introduced to all naturally-aspirated cars to provide 40mph per 1000rpm in top gear. All of this gave a 12 per cent benefit in fuel economy whilst increasing performance by 1 per cent.

Changes to external styling amounted to new and distinctively designed 16 inch wheels, with silver painted finish to hub caps (except the Limousine which had a unique centre plaque emphasising the Mulliner Park Ward association) and whitewall tyres, redesigned bumpers, those at the front being integrated with the air dam, and a cleaner line at the rear, achieved by relocating the spare wheel within the well of the boot rather than below it in a drop-down cradle. New window-mounted external mirrors were fitted at the expense of front quarterlights, but the most obvious changes concerned the radiator shell and Spirit of Ecstasy mascot. Due to raising the bumpers, the radiator shell's height was reduced 'from the ground up' to maintain a sense of proportion and, as a consequence, the Flying Lady was reduced in size, by around 20 per cent, to blend in with the grille.

Graham Hull confirms the 1996 styling changes to be the most significant in the vehicle's life. To achieve the raised, cut-through bumpers, several alterations to the sheet metal pressings were necessary. The style of the Continental R's integrated composite bumpers had previously warranted new paint technology and process, and it was this which helped trigger the multi million pound investment in a new paint plant. In turn, the SZ cars reaped the benefit of this plant for their extensive composite bumper mouldings, as well as the application of a polymerised flexible lacquer which was applied to the front of each car to give increased resistance to stone chipping. Rubberised stone chip protection was applied to wheelarches and sills, and was painted in a car's body colour instead of the more usual black. Exterior styling changes, in fact, gave the car a new lease of life as its appearance not only successfully incorporated modern styling trends, but also concealed its age.

Changes to the interiors included a new facia and centre console, with a separate console housing air conditioning controls for rear seat passengers. Minor detail included provision

The 1996 model year cars - unveiled in June 1995 - called for a £25 million investment programme. (Courtesy Rolls-Royce Motor Cars Limited)

of a hinged flap to cover the audio unit head, and concealed ashtray and cigar lighter installation for security purposes; the wash-wipe function on the steering column stalk was modified and the wiper switch repositioned to the upper facia. Moved from a centre console location, the radio telephone speaker was located to the knee roll on the driver's side of the front compartment. On all cars except the Rolls-Royce Limousine, the steering wheel received electrical adjustment to aid entry and exit from the driving seat so that it automatically raised and lowered itself as soon as the doors were opened and closed, or the ignition key removed. Additional adjustment was provided by linking it to 'memory positioning', along with door mirrors and seats. The seats were redesigned with vertical fluting for all Rolls-Royce models except the Limousine, which was given sports-style seats; detailed modifications to the design of the front seats increased headroom by an inch while, on all Rolls-Royce models, seat switches were contained within the centre console layout.

Increased security was a feature and all models, apart from specific

Bentley cars which retained a barrel lock, were fitted with wheel hub caps incorporating a tamper-proof bolt locking system.

The final phase in model development was reached with the introduction of the Silver Dawn, a name which recalled those first postwar Rolls-Royce standard saloons that had almost identical features to the Mk Vl and R-Type Bentleys. As to the choice of name, this was not universally well-received by marque enthusiasts, nor some Rolls-Royce personnel, who considered such an important appellation to be wasted on a car at the very end of its production life. Silver Dawn, some argued, should have been reserved for something very different, and certainly not for a car which, with its sharp corners and flat surfaces, was looking decidedly aged. Those defending the decision contended the choice signalled the very pinnacle of SZ development, and that such an evocative name was fully appropriate.

Talking to Graham Hull about SZ's later styling changes, he admits to SZ, by modern standards, being on the market for an exceptionally long time and acknowledges that most manu-

facturers would have produced three or four models within that car's lifespan. Effectively, the naturally-aspirated Silver Dawn, built on the long wheelbase platform, spearheaded the Rolls-Royce range of cars to complement the Silver Spur. A standard wheelbase version of the Silver Dawn remained available to special order only, when it was known as Silver Spirit.

There were a number of other significant changes for the 1996 model year, which included new in-car entertainment systems. The Silver Dawn was equipped with a combined radio and compact disc unit, whilst the other four-door cars in the model range were fitted with more elaborate and powerful systems that incorporated a radio-cassette with remote mounted CD player. The Limousine's system was even more refined, having a radio-cassette unit in the front compartment and a full suite to the rear which included video player, TV monitor, radio-cassette and 40W per channel music rating amplification.

For the 1997 model year there were fewer - but no less significant - changes to specification. The Silver Dawn and Silver Spur could be option-

Graham Hull explained that the 1996 styling changes were amongst the most significant in SZ's history. Along with new style integrated bumpers and a number of external feature changes, the interiors were also revised. (Courtesy Rolls-Royce Motor Cars Limited)

Interior changes to the New Silver Spirit and Spur included a new facia and central console. Note the cup holders.(Courtesy Rolls-Royce Motor Cars Limited)

wheelbase as well as standard, and both models, SWB and LWB, featured extended front seat cushions to provide greater comfort and support. Rear seat heaters were standard on the Silver Spur but optional on the Silver Dawn, although both cars did feature twin cupholders on the front centre console. Other modifications included seat belt pre-tensioners, improved headlamps and vehicle security and a new range of paint colours. Silver Spurs with a division were available as a Limited Edition model for Middle and Far East markets and featured a 14 inch extended wheelbase, enclosed rear compartment with electric glass division, and rear air conditioning and audio systems. The Park Ward model had an increased body length of 24 inches, a raised roof line of two inches, repositioned passenger doors to aid rear passenger entry and exit, electrically operated division, dual audio systems, rear air conditioning, intercom, a moon-roof, occasional seat and drinks cabinet.

Revisions for the 1998 model year were the final modifications applied to four-door SZ Rolls-Royce models and were mainly cosmetic. External changes amounted to body colour bumper centres and overriders with bright finisher, and blue lettering for the model badge. Interior changes involved a 'commissioning' theme which was designed to let customers choose

ally fitted with Electronic Traction Assistance (ETAS) and, in the case of the latter model, a 25 per cent increase in engine power resulted in an improved maximum speed of 140mph. The Silver Dawn could be ordered with long

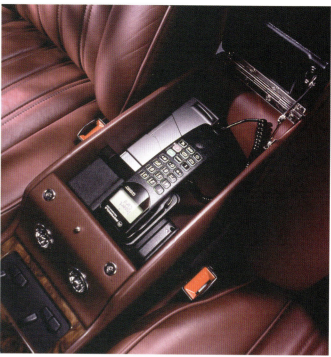

On the fourth generation models the steering wheel was linked to the control memory; it automatically raised and lowered when the ignition was switched on or off. (Courtesy Rolls-Royce Motor Cars Limited)

Detail of the centre console layout which included a telephone. (Courtesy Rolls-Royce Motor Cars Limited)

from various trim options: 'cool' and 'warm'. 'Cool' ambience was based on Silverstone and Light Grey hide, with top roll and carpets co-ordinated with recommended dark colour exterior paint. In contrast was the 'Warm' ambience with Sand and Pebble hide with top-roll and carpeting co-ordinated to match the car's exterior colour scheme. Completing the interior furnishing, hide-covered steering wheel rims could be finished in the same colour as the facia top-roll.

With the Bentley marque now responsible for 70 per cent of overall production in the mid-nineties, the ratio of sales compared to Rolls-Royce-badged cars is in stark contrast to the early eighties, when Bentley accounted for around only three per cent of orders. Ironically, within a generation of models, the tables had turned, and it was towards reviving Rolls-Royce sales that the company directed the projected new models.

By the time the Silver Dawn was introduced, it was generally known

For the 1996 model year a name especially respected was revived and, for a number of customers, evoked fond memories. This latest addition to the SZ range was built as a long wheelbase car and, as such, offered a lead-in to other models. It could also be specified with a standard wheelbase, when the nomenclature reverted to Silver Spirit. Silver Dawn also attracted customers to the marque, who, with the right amount of persuasion, often progressed to the Silver Spur. For 1997 further model changes made Electronic Traction Assistance optionally available. 1998 model year cars were announced during 1997 with the Silver Spur being available in a selected range of co-ordinated exterior colour and interior trim arrangements. (Courtesy Rolls-Royce Motor Cars Limited)

In 1996 Rolls-Royce entered a final phase of SZ development. Heralding the model range was the Silver Dawn, a name recalling one of the first models to emerge from Crewe when car manufacturing began at the shadow factory which had been designed to produce aero engines before and during the Second World War. Although the Silver Dawn of 1996 was a vastly different car to the earlier model, the Rolls-Royce tradition of engineering excellence nevertheless remained. Silver Dawn was built with a long wheelbase, similar to that of the Silver Spur, but represented what is usually termed as a 'lead-in' model. It did not have the turbocharged engine of its sister car and could also be ordered as a standard wheelbase version, in which event it was known as Silver Spirit.
(Courtesy Rolls-Royce Motor Cars Limited)

The interior of the Silver Dawn which, naturally, had all that could be expected of a car carrying the R-R monogram. (Courtesy Rolls-Royce Motor Cars Limited)

that Rolls-Royce was about to introduce a wholly new range of cars. For several months rumours and counter-rumours had circulated; some of the motoring journals published what they claimed to be 'scoop' pictures of the new cars, surreptitiously photographed whilst being tested, but it was not until the end of 1997 that the first of the new models, the Rolls-Royce Silver Seraph, was unveiled. The Bentley version, the Arnage, associated with Le Mans, just as Mulsanne had been, followed in the spring of 1998, and it was clear that a divergence between the two marques, which had begun in the opening years of the Silver Spirit reign, was set to continue.

In addition to the modifications and revisions to particular model years, Rolls-Royce, from time to time, built a

The 1998 model year Silver Spurs were the last to enter production. These cars, with specially designed interiors, were the ultimate development as far as SZ is concerned. Technical specification of Silver Spur included a turbocharged engine, first introduced for the Rolls-Royce Flying Spur in 1994, a facet of Rolls-Royce badged cars that at one time was considered most inappropriate. (Courtesy Rolls-Royce Motor Cars Limited)

number of special edition cars, often in response to dealership or individual demand. One such edition, about which little is known, is the Springfield, intended for the American market, which evoked memories of a period in Rolls-Royce history when cars were built at the Springfield factory in Massachusetts.

The ultimate Rolls-Royce SZ is the Silver Spur Park Ward, built by special commission for a small number of specially selected customers who were directly approached by the company. A specific brochure, with renderings by Robin Page under the direction of chief stylist Graham Hull, gives a clue to the refinement of these cars, around 50 of which were constructed. Various options of interior design afforded total comfort, extending from classic shapes to allow passengers to travel in armchair comfort, to exquisite designs which further the armchair theme of the rear seats to create a spacious, almost colonial, arrangement to include a centre storage console, equipped with fold-away veneered tables, a bottle cooler, storage for cocktail glasses or an ice bucket, and a switch control panel for electronic entertainment or communications equipment. Naturally, there was accommodation for a lap-top computer, housed in a purpose-made compartment built into the back of one of the front seats. The fine craftsmanship was apparent, with burr walnut veneers and distinctive fluted seats trimmed in only the finest selected hides.

Announcement of the Silver Seraph and Arnage was to end a most significant era in Rolls-Royce history. The cars, designed to take Rolls-Royce and Bentley into the new millennium,

114

1998 model year Silver Spur with a 'commissioning' theme interior. Some designs were specified as 'warm', others, like this, as 'cool'. (Courtesy Rolls-Royce Motor Cars Limited)

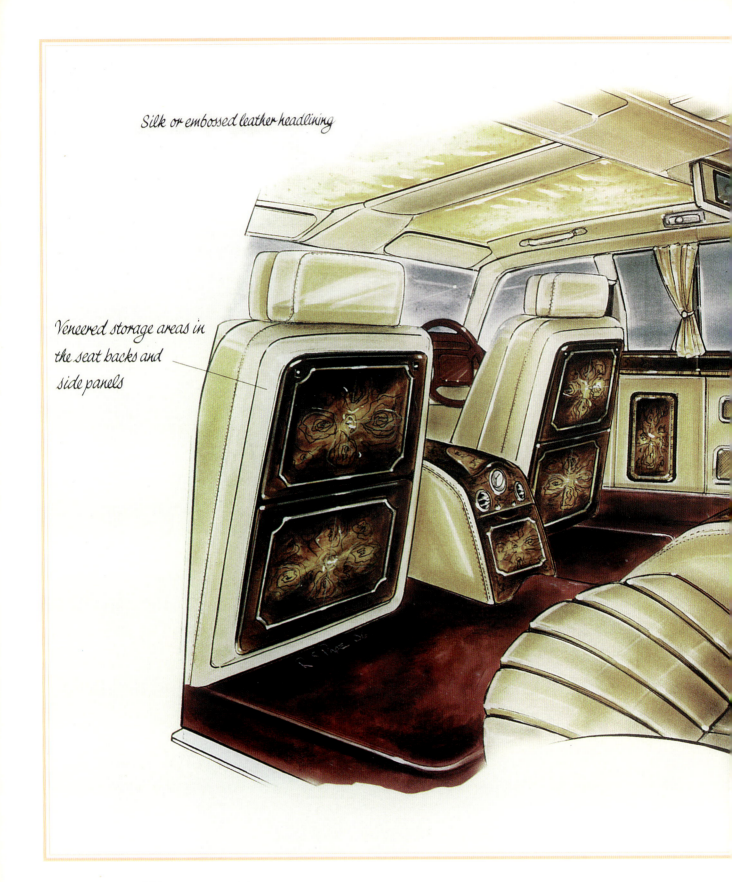

Silk or embossed leather headlining

Veneered storage areas in
the seat backs and
side panels

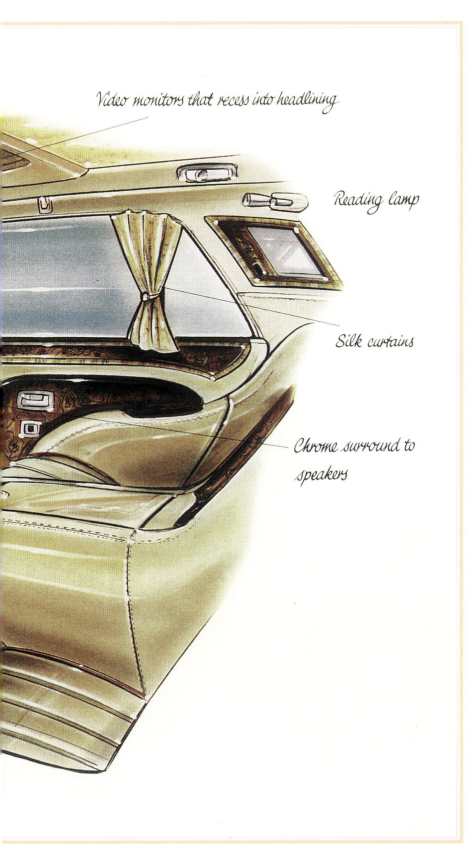

Video monitors that recess into headlining

Reading lamp

Silk curtains

Chrome surround to speakers

The ultimate SZ Rolls-Royce was a special edition Silver Spur Park Ward offered to around 50 specially selected customers. Built on an extended wheelbase, these cars offered the ultimate in luxury. (Courtesy Rolls-Royce Motor Cars Limited)

are also envoys for what will eventually be seen as possibly one of the most contentious periods in the annals of the two marques. Not only did the new models signal the demise of a range of cars which had spanned almost two decades, and which was, effectively, a progression of development with origins in the 1950s, but also heralded new methods by which Rolls-Royce and Bentley built their vehicles. The engines, previously of proven Rolls-Royce design and build with an envious pedigree, were to be the product of BMW, and the car bodies, once built by Pressed Steel, are now constructed in-house at Crewe. Building the Silver Spirit and Silver Spur replacements, along with those cars carrying the Bentley badge, necessitated a massive investment on behalf of Vickers plc, the last such major injection of cash before Rolls-Royce Motor Cars was offered for sale. The familiar V8 so deftly engineered by the late Jack Phillips does live on, however: it is currently fitted to the Bentley Continental models, including the Sedanca Coupé (SC) announced in the autumn of 1998, as well as the Bentley Arnage Red Label introduced for the 2000 model year. The Rolls-Royce V8 engine (with light pressure turbocharging) is also specified for the new Corniche, announced in January 2000 at the Los Angeles Motor Show. Production of the new Corniche is limited to 250 cars a year, which assures the model's exclusivity. For a period the V8 was built by Cosworth Engineering, which was once part of the Vickers empire, but is now produced at the Crewe factory.

In preparing the Silver Spur Park Ward brochure, Robin Page, under Graham Hull's direction, penned a number of interior styling themes, all of which were designed to offer the highest degree of comfort and refinement. Illustrated here is just one of Robin's creations. (Courtesy Rolls-Royce Motor Cars Limited)

The ultimate SZ model proved to be the Silver Spur Park Ward, a very special edition which was offered to around only 50 selected customers. Built on an extended platform, these cars offered the optimum in refinement and, although the cost of producing them is not known, they will surely appreciate in value and remain highly revered and cherished motor cars. (Courtesy Rolls-Royce Motor Cars Limited)

And so the chapter ends as it began: with Vickers' ownership of Rolls-Royce and Bentley consigned to history, other guardians of the marques will carry the two most respected names in motoring history into the new century. At least those owners of the last Silver Spirit-based cars to have left the Crewe factory, whether a Rolls-Royce or Bentley, will have the satisfaction of knowing that they are custodians of cars which represent the end of an era.

Amongst the most lavish of all Rolls-Royce's is the Park Ward Limousine. Built on a 'stretched', platform it had every comfort. (Courtesy Rolls-Royce Motor Cars Limited)

The interior of the Rolls-Royce Park Ward included comprehensive audio and visual equipment and a cocktail cabinet with lead crystal decanters and goblets. When not in use, the occasional seat folded neatly into the division. (Courtesy Rolls-Royce Motor Cars Limited)

Graham Hull styled the Silver Seraph, which was unveiled at the Geneva Motor Show in the spring of 1998. He took several styling cues from what he considers one of the finest cars ever produced by Rolls-Royce, the Silver Cloud, which was created by John Blatchley in the early fifties and introduced in 1955. Amongst the many features of the Silver Seraph is a new engine built in collaboration with BMW, and the body is now built in-house at Crewe. (Courtesy Rolls-Royce Motor Cars Limited)

In 1998 Rolls-Royce unveiled SZ's successor. There were two models, the Rolls-Royce Silver Seraph, illustrated here, and the Bentley Arnage. The cars have different engines: the Silver Seraph is fitted with a BMW V12 and the Arnage with a V8, also of BMW design. For the 2000 model year the Arnage Red Label was introduced and featured the familiar Rolls-Royce V8 6.75 litre engine. (Author's collection)

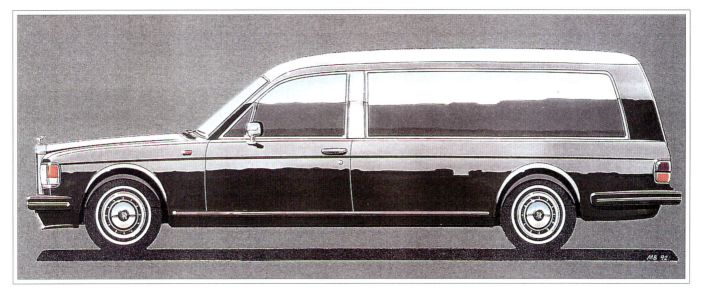

In 1992 a large Midlands firm of undertakers was considering the purchase of six brand-new Rolls-Royce hearses for its fleet. The long wheelbase Touring Limousine underframe was to be used, and the design was worked out and fully drawn quarter-scale by Martin Bourne. The project was eventually cancelled but it was Martin Bourne's final styling assignment before he took early retirement in October that year. Said Martin: "I've always thought what a suitable conclusion it was to my thirty-seven years with the company!" (Courtesy Martin Bourne)

The end of an era: shortly after announcement of the Silver Seraph, Vickers sold Rolls-Royce Motor Cars Limited to Volkswagen; the Rolls-Royce trademark, however, was acquired by BMW. Here, the Silver Seraph is seen alongside its predecessors within the confines of the Crewe factory. From right to left is a Silver Spur, Silver Shadow, Silver Cloud III, Silver Cloud I and Silver Dawn. Significantly, SZ's era coincided with that of Vickers' ownership of Rolls-Royce Motor cars. (Courtesy Rolls-Royce Motor Cars Limited

ROLLS-ROYCE & BENTLEY

4

THE BENTLEY REVIVAL

Mulsanne, as a possible model name, originated in 1977 with the presentation of scale renderings and a small scale model, the Bentley version of which is shown here. There was also a proposal for a Rolls-Royce, which existed as a sketch only. The blunt frontal treatment, 'squared' front wheelarches and lift over the rear axle, along with semi-enclosed rear wheelarches, are all interesting features. The Mulsanne name on the tail, the 'B' emblem on the rear quarters and the Bentley wings on the wheels will be noted. Built as a model depicted as a concept car, the design should be compared with early thoughts for a two-door version of Turbo R, shown elsewhere, which eventually materialised as the Continental R. This scale model styled by Graham Hull was displayed in David Plastow's office at Pym's Lane. (Courtesy Rolls-Royce Motor Cars Limited)

As demand for the Bentley T had all but evaporated, it came as something of a surprise to many motoring commentators that the marque featured at all in the SZ range of cars. That a Bentley version was offered was met with satisfaction, and some relief, by those enthusiasts who had feared the worst: so easily could one of the most celebrated names in motoring history have fallen into obscurity. In retrospect, the fate of Bentley had already been sealed well before introduction of SZ, and the choice of Mulsanne - with its Le Mans connotations - as the model appellation was highly significant.

Mulsanne was initially the choice of name for a Rolls-Royce concept car which came about in 1977 in the form of a scale model and associated wash drawings. The scale model was actually built as a Bentley and for some time was displayed in David Plastow's office at Pym's Lane. The styling of the Mulsanne Concept car was both elegant and futuristic; a two-door car it

sported gracious lines and semi-enclosed rear wheelarches. A wash rendering of a four-door saloon version shows a Rolls-Royce radiator and The Flying Lady, however.

There is little doubt that the name of Bentley and the famous Winged 'B' very nearly went the way of many other illustrious marques, and those members of the Bentley Drivers Club who were present at Pym's Lane when George Fenn give his assurance that Bentley would return, can be forgiven for showing some cynicism. What they did not know, of course, was that plans to revive the name were already well in hand, and that Fenn had a very good idea of the impact a future high-performance Bentley might have on the motoring world.

Introduced at the same time as the Silver Spirit, the Bentley Mulsanne differed in styling from its Rolls-Royce stablemate only slightly. Essentially, the two cars were identical apart from badging and design of radiator shell; the Bentley radiator was a softer shape

The development of SZ is covered in chapter three, but here is illustrated Z-4, the first experimental car which was built to the definitive specification. In this instance Z-4 carries a Bentley radiator shell; the car was completed in the autumn of 1977 and survived well into the 1980s, having amassed in excess of 100,000 miles. Z-4 was used for development of American specification cars and also for emissions testing purposes.
(Courtesy Rolls-Royce Motor Cars Limited)

Z-5, an experimental car built with left-hand steering, makes for an interesting comparison when viewed alongside DY, a full-size model Camargue. Note the American specification headlamps on both cars: Rolls-Royce test driver, John Gaskell, accompanied Z-5 to the USA where he subjected the car to extensive testing throughout the country.
(Courtesy Rolls-Royce Motor Cars Limited)

compared to the more ceremonious Grecian Temple format of the Silver Spirit. Even the bonnet pressings were the same on both cars, which, for the first time, allowed for greater structural integration in the build process of the standard steel saloons. A close look at the front bumper, however, would reveal it to have a curved appearance, which was not evident on the Silver Spirit, and which, as has previously been mentioned, added 1.6 inches to the car's overall length. Neither was there any price difference between the two models: marketing the Bentley a few pounds cheaper than its sister car was considered an anachronism.

There was a very good reason for the curved bumper on Mulsanne. Ron Maddocks was given the task of styling the Bentley's radiator shell which, unlike the S and T Series cars, had to fit a Rolls-Royce bonnet. Ron modelled

Orders for Bentleys had, by the end of the seventies, dwindled to such an extent that it would not have been surprising if the name been allowed to fade into oblivion. With sales amounting to just three per cent of total output, Rolls-Royce directors, encouraged by David Plastow, nevertheless planned a revival of the marque. A Bentley version of the Silver Spirit, the Mulsanne, was included when SZ was introduced in the autumn of 1980; unlike its predecessors, the T and T2, Mulsanne had exactly the same price structure as its Rolls-Royce counterpart, and also shared the same bonnet, with only the radiator shell, front bumper and badging being different. Despite its overall similarity to the Silver Spirit, Mulsanne was, however, sufficiently individual to attract loyal marque enthusiasts, together with those customers who preferred its softer frontal styling to that of the Rolls-Royce. Mulsanne was, of course, only the beginning of the Bentley comeback: under development was a range of models with the potential to encompass all that characterised the marque's magnificent history. (Courtesy Rolls-Royce Motor Cars Limited / SHRMF)

Mulsanne's radiator shell in clay and it quickly became evident that the bumper would have to be curved to protect the shell in the event of an accident.

Driving the Bentley Mulsanne was a truly great motoring experience. The discreet 'B' emblems adorning the facia instruments were reminders of the marque's illustrious pedigree. Sharing Rolls-Royce technology, the Mulsanne's hydraulic levelling system kept the car on an even keel, and the gas springs which supplemented the coil springs at the rear were sensitive to load and

The Bentley Mulsanne, named after the famous Le Mans straight, was introduced at the same time as the Silver Spirit and Silver Spur. Apart from relatively minor design differences and badging, it shared many Rolls-Royce features; the Mulsanne's curved bumper, which added a fraction to the car's overall length when compared to the Silver Spirit, was designed to protect the Bentley radiator shell.
(Courtesy Rolls-Royce Motor Cars Limited/SHRMF)

Despite Bentley's diminishing orders due to customer preference for the arguably more prestigious Rolls-Royce radiator shell and mascot, there were still those enthusiasts for whom nothing but a Bentley would do. In similar fashion to R-R monogrammed cars, Mulsannes were available with a long wheelbase, when it was simply known as the Mulsanne LWB. Marque enthusiasts will deduce this is a 1986 model year car by virtue of its spray jet headlamp washers and alloy wheels which were borrowed from the Continental and were similar to those used on the Turbo R.
(Courtesy Rolls-Royce Motor Cars Limited/SHRMF)

adjusted suspension characteristics, thus maintaining a superlatively supple ride. A pressure priority valve incorporated into each hydraulic system ensured that the braking systems had priority over the levelling, so if pressure in a system fell unduly, the priority valve would close to isolate the suspension system, allowing available pressure to be used for braking purposes.

Comfort was, of course, para-mount and the Mulsanne was fitted with the unique Rolls-Royce Motors designed fully-automatic, two-level air conditioning system. Thermistors mounted behind the front bumper, for external temperature, and on the cantrail, for interior temperature, fed back information to a control centre mounted beneath the facia. The system was sensitive enough to take into account a factor known as solar gain, the warmth of the sun shining through a car's windows. The solar sensor was mounted in the top roll - above the instrumentation - under a central grille.

The Mulsanne's controls were designed with ergonomics in mind, and switches controlling different functions could be recognised by touch alone. The speedometer was electronic; the cruise control employed a built-in memory and, for security, central door locking. Electrically operated remote fuel filler flap release and boot unlock-

During the early 1980s, Rolls-Royce directors were contemplating whether or not to build a smaller car. This in itself was not unique as several such projects were considered throughout the post-war years, and previously. Design parameters resulted in a projected model which, despite being classed as a Rolls-Royce, could easily have become a Bentley. (During the Silver Shadow's and Bentley T's gestation period, similar ideas had been mooted; had the car evolved as initially proposed, that, too, would have been built as a Bentley in preference to a Rolls-Royce.) The full-size model - the project was known as SX - is viewed here alongside a Mercedes, an exercise meant to ensure that the styling had the usual presence associated with the marque when compared to other makes of motor car. This photograph was taken around 1983. (Courtesy Rolls-Royce Motor Cars Limited)

ing were all standard features.

Behind the scenes, discussions at Crewe in the early seventies could easily have resulted in the Bentley name being quietly dropped from the catalogue. The early post-war days when Bentley, as opposed to Rolls-Royce, was preferentially marketed mainly for political reasons, except for the exclusively coachbuilt Silver Wraith, were long past, and the arrival of John Blatchley's Silver Cloud in 1955 had ensured the resurgence of Rolls-Royce. Although the S-Series Bentleys had attracted a loyal and healthy following, this did not prevail with the advent of SY, orders for which were predominantly Silver Shadow. The Bentley marque was allowed to fall further into recession during the seventies, mainly

Built as a full-size model, SX is being prepared for an external viewing. Fritz Feller, standing with the trolley jack, is accompanied by Graham Hull, on his left, and a member of the experimental workshop. In the background are a Mercedes and a BMW, both of which were used for comparison purposes when evaluating SX. (Courtesy Rolls-Royce Motor Cars Limited)

The dimensions of SX are clearly indicated in this photograph which was taken at an external viewing. Proposed as a medium-sized car, SX did not materialise. (Courtesy Rolls-Royce Motor Cars Limited)

because marketing was aimed at promoting Rolls-Royce, especially as far as America was concerned, in the aftermath of the separation of the motor car business from aero engines. Indeed, Bentley never did achieve the same level of reverence in the USA, where Rolls-Royce had historically been deeply respected, although the Winged

It can be safely said that the turning point in the Bentley revival occurred in 1982 with the introduction of the Mulsanne Turbo. At once the car delighted enthusiasts and the media alike with its massive performance - causing at least one motoring journal to herald the car's debut as 'The Return of the Blower Bentley'. Good though the Mulsanne Turbo was, it did suffer from certain handling idiosyncrasies, the cause of which was the suspension, which had been directly borrowed from the unblown 'standard' saloon. This was put right with the unveiling, in March 1985 at the Geneva Motor Show, of the Turbo R, an example of which is pictured here outside the Crewe factory. Peter Ward, then chief executive of Rolls-Royce Motor Cars, standing middle left, is talking to a group of motoring journalists. (Courtesy Rolls-Royce Motor Cars Limited)

B did have its devotees. The fact that the Bentley name survived clearly illustrates what a powerful marketing tool it was, and to have lost such an prestigious name would have been lamentable. Despite Bentley orders having fallen to such a low point in respect of T-Series cars, the opportunity, nevertheless, was seized upon to build on the marque's reputation, thus creating a new and meaningful sales direction for Rolls-Royce Motor Cars. The company had several marketing possibilities to consider, not least of which was producing a smaller car with wider

appeal than might otherwise have been possible.

Not for the first time in its history Rolls-Royce entered into a period of contemplation about whether to produce a medium-sized car. Consideration at Crewe extended as far as building at least one full-size prototype, codenamed SX, the concept of which was paralleled to the mid-range Mercedes, an example of which had been acquired for evaluation purposes. The project did not materialise for a variety of reasons, not least because it was considered uneconomical to pro-

The Bentley revival was confirmed with the introduction of the Mulsanne Turbo in 1982 at the Geneva Motor Show. Externally there was little to differentiate between the turbo model and the standard saloon, other than a body-coloured radiator shell and discreet badging. Under the bonnet it was a different matter, however! (Courtesy Rolls-Royce Motor Cars Limited/SHRMF)

duce, and there was insufficient capacity for large-scale production at Pym's Lane. Ultimately, a smaller car did not fit into Rolls-Royce's corporate directive.

Mulsanne Turbo - the way forward for Bentley

The appearance of the Mulsanne, whilst giving the opportunity for committed Bentley enthusiasts to experience SZ without having to purchase a Silver Spirit, despite the obvious similarities between the two cars, gave Rolls-Royce a lead-in to an entirely new model. The company's marketing department targetted those motorists who demanded high performance potential combined with traditional Bentley (and Rolls-Royce) qualities. From the outset such a car was never going to be anything other than very exclusive, for Rolls-Royce anticipated production would not exceed more than around 100 cars a year.

Thus, the Bentley Mulsanne Turbo was introduced in the spring of 1982 at the Geneva Motor Show. Even if the 'standard' Mulsanne had not, by this time, achieved some measure of recognition, arrival of the turbocharged model afforded the marque a new emphasis: a car so sensational that it took the motoring world by storm and immediately put Bentley sales on track to a spectacular recovery. With the spotlight on this powerful addition to the Rolls-Royce and Bentley catalogue, the Bentley revival began with massive momentum, dramatically affecting Bentley sales as a whole.

The decision to develop the Mulsanne Turbo was taken during the early 1970s, and preliminary investigations into the project's viability (codenamed BZT) began in 1974. It was three years before much of the detail work began, which coincided with the introduction, in 1977, of the Silver Shadow ll and Bentley T2 models. The reason for this hiatus was that work on emissions and US safety requirements, along with development of the second series SY cars and the

After its introduction, the Mulsanne Turbo quickly acquired an enthusiastic following. Even if the car's styling did little to belie its massive performance, the acceleration left no doubt about it's awesome ability. (Courtesy Rolls-Royce Motor Cars Limited/SHRMF)

Camargue, sorely stretched resources at Crewe.

The architects of the Mulsanne Turbo were David Plastow and John Hollings. David Plastow was adamant that the Bentley marque should be revived, and while Hollings was in agreement about developing a Bentley 'supercar', he was mildly apprehensive about the sheer enormity of the project, and was reluctant to allow it to interfere with current priorities. Plastow recognised that the most effective route to revitalising Bentley's share of the business, and thus attracting a clientele that might not otherwise have considered either Bentley or Rolls-Royce ownership, was to offer a car which recalled the sporting image that was once the hallmark of the marque. Whatever David Plastow had in mind, *The Autocar*, when headlining the car's virtues, summed it up quite succinctly; 'The Return of the Blower Bentley'.

There were other, more demanding, reasons for David Plastow's enthusiasm for revitalising the Bentley marque, however. Not for the first time a down-turn in business had seriously affected sales of Rolls-Royce motor cars,

which led Plastow to believe that marketing Bentley - considered an altogether less ostentatious motor car - would actually increase Rolls-Royce sales. He reckoned that during times of recession, a company chairman buying a new Rolls-Royce would not be a popular move, but buying a new Bentley might attract fewer criticisms. Then there was the matter of the Camargue: early predictions had indicated the car to be under-powered, and ways to improve performance were sought. This included turbocharging which, in the event, did not materialise, partly because it was not considered correct policy for a Rolls-Royce to have out-and-out sporting characteristics. Combining turbocharging with promoting the Bentley marque, and concentrating on that car's sporting image seemed to have greater marketing potential. It was further accepted that the Camargue, flagship of the Rolls-Royce range, actually lacked a certain glamour and was something of a white elephant. The development of a car with a different concept was considered a far better business proposition.

As to the Mulsanne Turbo's adopted style of coachwork, there had been little choice about this as developing an entirely new car would have been out of the question on grounds of costs, resources and perceived demand. At a fundamental stage in the car's design, therefore, it was agreed to use the four-door saloon as the Mulsanne Turbo's base, but with sufficient engineering modifications to ensure a substantial increase in performance.

David Plastow's enthusiasm to promote the turbocharging theme was not universally appreciated at Crewe, and some engineers considered the project best left alone. John Hollings, aware that his department was already stretched to capacity, was more than happy to delegate the task of development to a small and select team of six engineers under the auspices of a senior project engineer. That team was headed by Jack Read and included Les Maddock (design), John Humphries, Cliff Williams (now at Cosworth), Guy Morris (development and test), Ken Thornton and Derek Jackson. Jack Read admits the project was very much a 'fun exercise': his

Development of the Mulsanne Turbo was undertaken by project manager Jack Read and a select team of engineers. David Plastow was the architect who delegated a lot of the responsibility to John Hollings who, in turn, was more than happy for Jack Read to get on with the job with as little interruption as possible. Following trials at Crewe, using an experimental Camargue, Broadspeed of Southam conducted some initial turbocharging research on behalf of Rolls-Royce, using a Silver Shadow for the purpose. The results were sensational and showed that torque could be increased by 50 per cent! (Courtesy Rolls-Royce Motor Cars Limited/SHRMF)

team was allowed a relatively free rein to develop the car and, because of its autonomy, it was often possible to cut through red tape. Help was also enlisted from other departments, and two engineers much associated with Jack Read's team were John Astbury and Derek Coulson.

John Astbury was involved with engine development, and for good reason, as he had done much to enable Jack Phillips' V8 to fit into the Burma bodyshell before that project was incorporated into the SY programme. Derek Coulson looked after the handling aspect, suspension and transmission technology, with which he was well versed. The original testbeds for

turbocharging were a variety of cars obtained from the experimental garage at Crewe and included the first prototype Camargue, D1, together with a late model blue Series 1 Silver Shadow which had at one time been allocated to John Hollings for his personal use.

During the gestatory period of the Mulsanne Turbo it was acknowledged that Rolls-Royce had an aversion to turbocharging motor cars, favouring instead large, high torque engines, the type typical of that usually associated with the marque. The company, however, had much experience in this respect, concerning commercial vehicles and diesel engines, and, in fact, the first experiments were undertaken

using a turbo from a diesel engine. As an aside, the question is often asked why Rolls-Royce do not offer diesel - or turbodiesel - versions of its cars. Jack Read explained that the company did at one time consider the idea, but then diesel was not so readily available and refuelling alongside lorries, away from the more friendly confines of the garage forecourt, was a messy business: on test, the interior of a diesel-engined Rolls-Royce became so contaminated and smelly after only 1000 miles that any further plans in this direction were immediately abandoned.

Despite Rolls-Royce favouring big, low-revving engines, the company knew much about turbocharging and would

The Camargue, together with the Silver Shadow, was used during the Mulsanne Turbo's early research. The flagship of the Rolls-Royce range had failed to provide the level of performance anticipated of the production cars, and thus the idea of a high performance Bentley was born. When fitted with a turbocharger, the boost in power was exceptional. Possibly some Camargue owners wish their cars were turbocharged! (Author's collection)

have known that several manufacturers were developing turbocharged cars. BMW had introduced its 2002 Turbo model, Europe's first turbocharged car, in 1973, but, whilst a most desirable motor vehicle, it was inappropriately launched at the height of the energy crisis, a factor largely responsible for it being quickly withdrawn. Porsche followed with a turbocharged version of its 3-litre 911 in 1975, although, in 1977, Saab's turbocharged 99 saloon model had possibly the greatest impact. Suddenly, throughout the motor industry the emphasis was on turbocharging, and Saab was again capitulated to the forefront of technology in 1978 when the Swedish manufacturer successfully fitted its turbocharged engine to the 900 model.

Motor sport, too, had witnessed some important developments: in this respect, Broadspeed was chosen by Rolls-Royce to assist in the Mulsanne Turbo's development. John Astbury recalls that the experimental Silver Shadow was despatched to Ralph Broad of Broadspeed at Southam to see what could be done to boost the car's performance. Of course, this was just the sort of work that Broadspeed specialised in, and a job such as this could be done off the cuff ... Before being despatched to Southam, Rolls-Royce had fitted the experimental car with a downdraught carburettor as this was considered to work well with the Halset turbocharger which had been used in some previous research work. It has to be said that Broadspeed excelled itself, even if the technology at the time

seemed rather crude. No-one - either at Broadspeed or Crewe - expected to achieve standards of engineering usu-

ally associated with production Rolls-Royce or Bentley cars; after all, this was no more than a preliminary evalu-

Following extensive development it was the Garrett AiResearch T04 that was chosen for use with Rolls-Royce's V8 engine. The turbocharger is fitted to increase the power and torque of the engine, which it achieves by taking energy from the exhaust and using it to pump extra air into the engine at wide throttle openings.
(Courtesy Jack Read and Rolls-Royce Motor Cars Limited)

ation. Neither did anyone believe that the car would go like lightning; but it did, and to everyone's astonishment, achieved a maximum speed of 140mph.

Not unexpectedly, Broadspeed had tremendous fun turbocharging the Silver Shadow, achieved at a cost of £7000. The car's performance was transformed: power rose by only 10 per cent whilst torque increased by no less than 50 per cent! The experimental car was kept by Broadspeed for around six months while trials were carried out, and, not surprisingly, all sorts of problems were encountered. Despite these, which suggested that the car's damping would have to be revised, and 50 per cent stiffer roll bars fitted, not to mention adoption of larger diameter wheels and different tyres, Broadspeed proved that turbocharging the still embryonic Mulsanne was distinctly achievable. When delivered to Crewe, the turbocharged experimental car caused nothing less than a sensation and, due to its formidable performance, the power of the turbocharger had to be reduced no less than three times before it was considered safe enough to be fitted to a production vehicle. The future had begun to look very bright indeed for Bentley.

At this time George Ray was the co-ordinating engineer between Crewe and Mulliner Park Ward. On one occasion he drove the turbocharged Camargue down to MPW and on the way overtook a Rover 3500S; the Rover driver overtook the Rolls-Royce and, later, George re-overtook the same car. The Rover driver might have thought George was playing 'cat and mouse'

but was quite baffled when the Camargue, having been subjected to massive throttle pressure, not only overtook but vanished into the distance!

Although turbocharging fever swept through the experimental department at Crewe, with everyone eager to develop a viable motor car, the engineering director nevertheless gently applied the brakes to the project. Not that development ceased, but was slowed down to allow other pressing work to take precedence. By this time SZ's introduction was rapidly approaching and all effort was concentrated on getting the car ready; although a turbocharged Mulsanne was by now no longer merely a dream, it was never the intention to combine its launch date with that of the standard saloon. The turbo theme was, therefore a prolonged affair which took as long to materialise as would an entirely new model. Nothing was to be done in a hurry.

Following Broadspeed's preliminary work, it was clear that much refinement was necessary in order to satisfy Rolls-Royce's exacting standards of engineering. Not least was there the need to resolve certain requirements, such as dealing with excessive heat within the engine compartment, and reducing the amount of turbo lag, a symptom often associated with turbocharged engines resulting in poor throttle response at low engine speed. There was also some debate about when exactly the turbocharger should kick in; the turbo, with its massive thrust, was not really felt on the ex-

perimental Silver Shadow until the engine was well wound up, and Rolls-Royce engineers considered that for it to work properly, it needed to operate smoothly from low revs. Jack Read devised what would today be referred to as an 'energy management system' which, as such, was the first to be developed. Most importantly, however, a decision about what type of turbocharger to use was required, and in this respect the Crewe engineers were faced with a dilemma.

When turbocharging a V8 engine, possibly the most practical choice would be to employ two turbo units; one for each bank of cylinders. A system of this nature would allow the exhaust to be suitably routed from each cylinder's exhaust ports to provide the optimum flow of gases needed to drive each turbine. In the case of the Mulsanne, there was insufficient underbonnet space to fit separate turbines, and engineers looked to an alternative installation. This meant driving a single turbine, fed from exhaust gases collected by harnessing the exhaust pulses from both banks of cylinders.

It was a matter of necessity, therefore, that a single turbocharger be adopted, although for the sake of simplicity, two would have been preferred. The particular unit chosen was the Garrett AiResearch T04 which, at that time, was considered the most suitable for a car of the Bentley's specification. Although Garrett AiResearch was generally supportive, it was very much a case of Rolls-Royce buying the equipment 'off the shelf' and making it work.

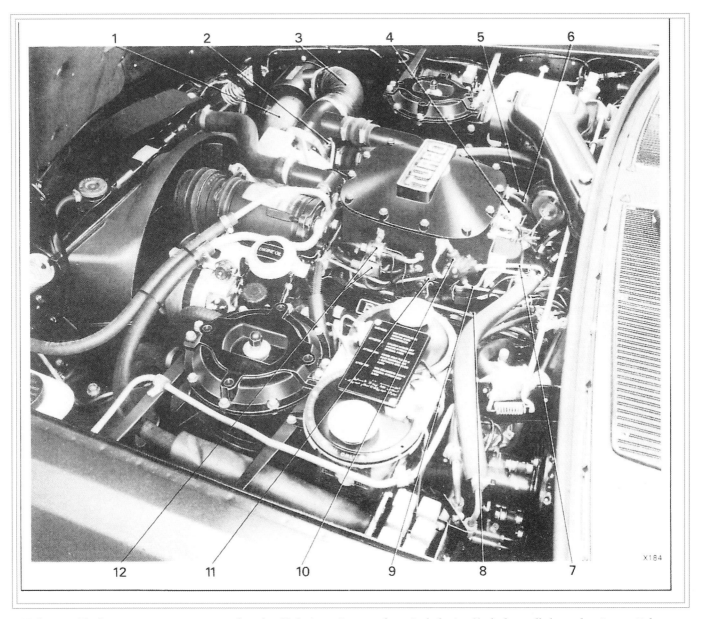

Mulsanne Turbo engine compartment details. 1) Automatic speed control chain; 2) choke pull-down heater switch; 3) air chest; 4) ignition distributor capsule vacuum signal pipe; 5) boost limiter solenoid; 6) turbocharger exhaust turbine housing; 7) turbocharger air compressor housing; 8) exhaust gas wastegate - partially hidden; 9) air dump; 10) ignition system amplifier; 11) air delivery pipe to air chest; 12) crankcase breather pipe. (Courtesy Jack Read and Rolls-Royce Motor Cars Limited)

Although it provided the Mulsanne with markedly increased power and torque, Rolls-Royce engineers certainly did not want any characteristics which meant a rush of power over and above 3000rpm, with little or nothing at the lower end of the performance curve. A more even introduction of power was wanted to provide a useful mid-range boost, as well as giving outstanding performance at upper limits. Rolls-Royce, as usual, was reluctant to disclose the exact amount of power the Mulsanne Turbo had available, and, in this case, 'sufficient plus 50 per cent' certainly did not satisfy those motorists who demanded precise information. The truth was eventually revealed, however, when Rolls-Royce was obliged to register the car's engine details with a German government department in order to qualify for Type Approval in that country. There, the figures were for all to see: 298bhp at 3800rpm; typically, the company had been exact when claiming the Turbo's 50 per cent extra power, the figure for the Silver

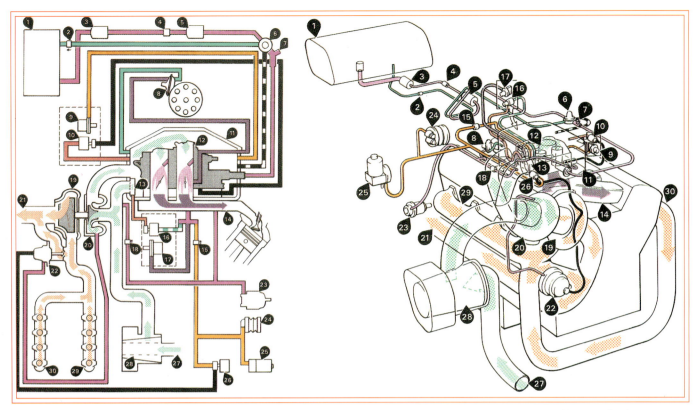

The turbocharging system. 1) fuel tank; 2) non-return valve; 3) fuel pump; 4) check valve; 5) fuel filter; 6) fuel pressure regulator; 7) fuel pressure tapping; 8) ignition distributor vacuum/pressure advance capsule; 9) part throttle enrichment pressure switch; 10) part throttle enrichment cut-in solenoid; 12) Solex 4A1 carburettor; 13) dump valve; 14) engine inlet manifold; 15) one-way valve (speed control); 16) dump valve vacuum signal cut-in solenoid; 17) dump valve vacuum switch; 18) pressure relief valve; 19) turbocharger exhaust turbine; 20) turbocharger intake air compressor; 21) exhaust gas passing to exhaust system; 22) exhaust gas wastegate; 23) transmission vacuum modulator; 24) speed control system bellows; 25) speed limiter vacuum pump; 26) boost limiter cut-in solenoid; 27) ambient air passing to intake system); 28) intake air filter; 29) 'A' bank exhaust manifold; 30) 'B' bank exhaust manifold. (Courtesy Jack Read and Rolls-Royce Motor Cars Limited)

Spirit and Mulsanne was stated as 198.5bhp at 4000rpm.

Fitting the turbocharger under the bonnet was no mean feat, and finding solutions to the many problems encountered became the worry of Jack Read. The housing of the Garret AiResearch T04 was considered the largest available at the time and was sufficient to handle the exhaust mass flow, working a proportionally smaller compressor which, nevertheless, was commensurate with its purpose. Located high up on the engine, ahead of the right hand (A) bank of cylinders as viewed from the driving seat, the installation of the turbocharger meant that some repositioning of ancillary equipment was necessary, including

the power steering pump and belt-driven auxiliaries. Installing all of the associated pipework for the turbocharger also took much effort, which made an already tightly-packed engine compartment even tighter.

Another question which had to be addressed concerned carburation: adequate air throughput was essential and, while the Solex 4A1 met this requirement, the twin SUs as fitted to some cars did not. Even if the Bosch fuel injection system had been contemplated, its use was prevented due to the amount of modification that would have been necessary. Resulting from the decision not to employ fuel injection, sales of Mulsanne Turbo cars were prohibited to America, Canada,

Australia and Japan due to those countries' emission control regulations.

The level of heat generated by the turbocharger was one of the most pressing issues to be addressed; without adequate heatshielding, everything under the bonnet would have been truly cooked. The exhaust manifolds were cast in nickel iron and used in place of the more usual grey cast iron types fitted to non-turbocharged cars. Although more expensive to produce, nickel iron was used as a precaution against the manifolds scaling or flaking internally due to free oxygen in the exhaust, and which could have considerably damaged a hot turbine wheel spinning at around 80,000rpm. The engine ran some 20 degrees centigrade

Despite the Mulsanne's huge increase in power, there were very few modifications to the car's running gear. In hindsight, Rolls-Royce engineers might have wished that suspension and handling had been uprated as the car quickly generated criticism in this respect. (Courtesy Rolls-Royce Motor Cars Limited / SHRMF)

hotter than that of unblown cars, and this temperature increase necessitated fitment of an oil cooler which operated via a thermostat. The electric cooling fan was modified so that it would automatically switch on, even with the ignition off, to cope with engine heat soak. So critical was the issue of adequate cooling that Ford Sierra Cosworth-style catwalk hot air outlets were seriously considered at one stage.

Further engine modifications included fitting Hepolite pistons which, with what were known as steel 'struts' - i.e. two H-shaped pieces of steel strappings per piston - incorporated in their design, reduced any tendency to distortion. Slightly heavier duty cylinder head gaskets were used, and the exhaust manifold gaskets were strengthened to sustain both higher temperatures and greater pressures than otherwise prevailed. In place of the Champion sparking plugs usually fitted, Rolls-Royce opted for the Japanese NGK plug with its wider heat range and copper-cored electrodes.

Apart from the necessary engine modifications, a few major revisions to the Mulsanne's running gear were required. Despite the Turbo's awesome performance, very little was changed

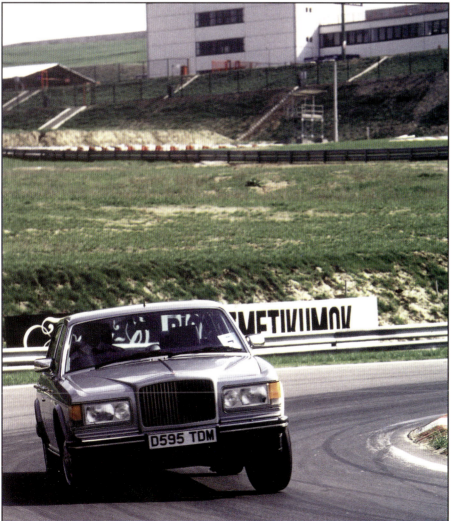

The Mulsanne proved to be very fast. Restricted to 135mph due to current tyre technology, it was certainly capable of higher speeds. Shown being put through its paces, the Mulsanne Turbo delighted journalists when they were invited to the car's media launch. (Courtesy Rolls-Royce Motor Cars Limited)

Media launch for the Mulsanne Turbo. Jack Read recalls taking the car to its limit at Le Mans when it was displayed there; he also remembers with some relish taking Rolls-Royce's chief executive, George Fenn, for a spin around the circuit, an experience neither of them is likely to forget ... (Courtesy Rolls-Royce Motor Cars Limited)

in the way of the standard saloon's handling and suspension characteristics, giving rise to some criticism as the car's ride was considered too soft for the model's performance. For those owners brave enough to lift the bonnet, and who appreciated the sheer complexity contained within the engine compartment, the Bentley and Turbo decals on the engine covers left no doubt about the motor's breathtaking capabilities. The gearbox was subjected to some minor settings adjustment, and the final drive output shafts were enlarged to 34mm diameter, instead of 27mm as applied to the non-turbo cars, along with constant velocity joints which were uprated and positively splined instead of being taper fixed to the hubs. Overall gearing was raised - 3.08:1 as opposed to 2.692:1 - an increase of around 14 per cent. To use Jack Read's words: 'although the car goes faster, there is no noticeable difference in the drive line and engine - up to the final drive pinion at any rate.'

As might be expected, the amount of behind-the-scenes experimental work necessary to prepare the Mulsanne Turbo was enormous. Pri-

orities were given to the engine before anything else, and all other work followed: it was only then that test drivers were able to evaluate exactly how the brakes and gearbox responded to the effects of higher than normal temperatures.

So, exactly how fast was the Mulsanne Turbo? Very fast, is the answer; certainly faster than the governed maximum speed of 135mph. To ensure the car went no faster than the predetermined speed, an ignition cutout actuated the precise moment a wastegate, or air-relief valve, added vacuum to the turbocharger. Rolls-Royce had taken the precaution of limiting maximum speed for reasons of safety, and to keep vehicle performance within the current limitations of tyre technology. Avon was the only manufacturer able to supply a tyre specifically for the Mulsanne Turbo, a special steel-braced affair capable of meeting Rolls-Royce's stringent requirements. As far as technical and performance aspects were concerned, Rolls-Royce proved that a turbocharged Mulsanne, despite its formidable power, could perform as smoothly as a

sophisticated carriage should. Refined and docile in town, the Bentley, once unleashed, showed it was a true sporting motor car in the style of those cars responsible for the Le Mans and Brooklands victories of half a century or so previous.

For Crewe's experimental test drivers, the Mulsanne Turbo was the most exciting car they had driven. The leader of the very select test team was Walter Lea, one of Rolls-Royce's most experienced test drivers, who said of the vehicle: "This car is the most exciting prototype I have driven, its performance capability just has to be seen." Walter's opinion was shared by his team mates, Barry Taylor, Ken Bradshaw and Derek Rowland: Barry was most impressed by the car's massive mid-range torque, whilst Ken appreciated the Turbo's sports car performance with the benefit of a luxury saloon; Derek's comment was that "The car really starts to make an impression when you have got used to the amount of power available."

Mulsanne Turbo on the road
Although the Mulsanne Turbo was

unveiled at Geneva in the spring of 1982, it was several months before any cars actually went on sale. The car had been introduced to the Rolls-Royce and Bentley dealer network, and the media, at the height of the Falklands war, and so it must have been with some relief that the world's press now preoccupied itself, not with fighting, but the arrival of a rather special motor car.

The location for the new Bentley's launch was, appropriately, Le Mans, and Jack Read recalls the occasion most clearly. Rolls-Royce had taken over a chateau and accommodated all its guests very comfortably near to the circuit. Staying at the same chateau at that time was Lord Carrington who, having very recently resigned as Foreign Secretary, was intent on relaxing far from the gaze and glare of the world's news correspondents and photographers. Realising the situation, Jack Read warned Lord Carrington that the chateau was about to be besieged by the paparazzi. The ex-foreign secretary was resigned to the fact that his peace was about to be shattered, however. He entered into the spirit of the occasion and was delighted at being invited to try the Mulsanne Turbo for himself. It was also appropriate that the visiting dealers and journalists were taken to one of the restaurants (the Hotels Moderne and de Paris) which W.O. Bentley and the 'Bentley Boys' had frequented during the famous Le Mans events between 1924 and 1930 in which Bentleys were so successful, winning the Le Mans 24-Hour race no less than five times.

In addition to the usual motoring journalists, one of the first to put the Mulsanne Turbo through its paces was Rivers Fletcher, who was certainly one of the most notable enthusiasts of the marque and who, as a young man, joined W.O. Bentley as an apprentice, having already become an ardent admirer of his cars. Rivers' first love may have been those Cricklewood Bentleys built before Bentley Motors was incorporated into Rolls-Royce, but he also had tremendous affection for the postwar cars, the Mk VI and those that followed, including the Continentals. "Now in 1982", he wrote in his autobiography,"Bentley Motors Limited have announced the 'Mulsanne' Turbo. I have driven it on the road and on the track and sampled its great performance. Its acceleration is like no other production Bentley; it simply goes on and on."

Another person visiting Le Mans was George Fenn, then chief executive of Rolls-Royce Motor Cars. Fenn, of course, had maintained an interest in the Turbo project throughout its gestation and had accepted an invitation from Jack Read to accompany him on a couple of spins round the circuit. Read, by that time, had got fully into his stride having been driving celebrities around Le Mans for several hours. When it came to showing off the car's virtues, he had no anxiety about handling the vehicle at its maximum capability. Jack, of course, enjoyed himself immensely, but the R-R chief executive, clinging on to the seatbelt, his face white with terror, had had enough after only a single lap and gratefully got out of the car.

It was clear from the start that this was a very special Bentley. It wasn't a Silver Spirit in wolf's clothing, and nor, compared to the unblown Mulsanne, was it expensive. Admittedly, it cost an extra £6504, but how little to pay for so much more power and pleasurable motoring! Even the fuel consumption was not that much greater than for the 'standard' car, and anyway, who was going to worry about losing a couple of miles per gallon when, under the bonnet, there existed so much technology? Surging towards 60mph in seven seconds, quicker than a Ferrari, or virtually any other saloon for that matter, the Mulsanne Turbo knocked a clear three seconds off the time it would have taken a naturally-aspirated Bentley or Silver Spirit to reach the same speed. Whereas it would normally have taken a fraction under 31 seconds to 'do the ton', the turbocharged car managed to reach 100mph in almost half that time, taking a mere 17.9 seconds, to be precise. The car, naturally, demonstrated fine roadholding manners with exceptional acceleration and braking which, at all times, was absolutely smooth. In fact, the car was so powerful that some drivers managed to 'lose' their cars by driving too fast into bends, especially in wet weather. At one time there always seemed to be a number of cars undergoing repair at Hythe Road.

In devising some highly emotive publicity material, Rolls-Royce sought to combine the present with the past. 'The Silent Sports Car Returns', it was said of the Bentley Mulsanne Turbo, the advertisement capturing the spirit

The Mulsanne Turbo's interior remained as discreet and refined as that of the standard saloon car. (Courtesy Rolls-Royce Motor Cars Limited)

There were a few clues to the Mulsanne Turbo's performance potential. (Courtesy Rolls-Royce Motor Cars Limited)

of the thirties. And nowhere was there mention of Rolls-Royce, merely Bentley Motors, which signified a concerted effort towards diverging the two marques and letting Bentley exist on its merit once more. For the media, the Mulsanne Turbo performed with alacrity, spinning around Le Mans with the speedometer at the limit - 140mph! And where better for a Mulsanne Turbo to pose for a picture than alongside a road sign at the entrance of the car's French namesake town? Of the Mulsanne Turbo, the *Guardian* noted that it was 'indecently fast'; praise, indeed.

That the Mulsanne Turbo's suspension, which had been directly borrowed from the non-turbocharged cars, was not uprated in keeping with performance potential, attracted much criticism from owners who complained that it was too soft. Tyre design and technology was largely responsible for

some sensitivity to small and high frequency sharp bumps, but, in contrast, the car's suspension coped well with lower frequency undulations. It was over pronounced humps that the springing was really caught out, allowing the car to flop over them; in extreme cases the suspension would reach the limit of travel to the bump stops rather abruptly. Customer feedback suggested that Rolls-Royce and Bentley engineers consider devising a firmer ride, which they did with positive results, and later cars were fitted with revised suspension components.

Inside the car, had a potential owner been expecting to see a restyled facia sporting a comprehensive array

of instruments to include a boost gauge and tachometer, he would have been disappointed. In fact, the instrument board, albeit slightly modified, appeared, at first glance, identical to that of its Mulsanne sister car. Possibly the most subtle difference was the addition of a discreet 'turbo' badge beneath the digital display for outside temperature, stopwatch and clock, which served as a modest reminder of the car's awesome power. Externally there was little to distinguish the turbocharged car from the Mulsanne, other than dedicated badging, which was, of course, unpretentious, adorning the front wings aft of the wheelarches and boot lid. Outwardly

This is the view most motorists had as the Mulsanne roared into the distance.
(Courtesy Rolls-Royce Motor Cars Limited)

it was the radiator shell, painted in the same colour as the body, which was most significant, whilst additional equipment included a headlamp wash/wipe system (on all models) and a pair of Lucas fog lamps fitted beneath the front bumper. For the keen-eyed enthusiast, paired exhaust pipes served to identify this as a particularly capable Bentley.

Neither was there any requirement to furnish the interior of the Mulsanne Turbo any differently to that of the naturally aspirated car; the spacious and well appointed seats were crafted as usual in the finest Connolly hide, although, as an option, a customer could specify Jersey Kapwood cloth upholstery. Of course, only the best veneers, cut by hand and polished to an amber lustre, were used, and for optimum comfort passengers benefited from the unique two-level air-conditioning system which gave a constant and controlled temperature within the interior.

Rolls-Royce influence was clearly evident in the interior appointment of the Mulsanne Turbo, which was virtu-

ally indistinguishable from the standard four-door saloons. This was in no way detrimental, of course, as the comfort, quality and styling was beyond reproach. Rolls-Royce, having identified the market for a dedicated sporting saloon, still had a long way to go before embarking upon an even greater divergence between the two marques.

Mulsanne Turbo sales were generally confined to the home market, not least because its carburation meant it was prohibited from certain countries. There was another factor: Rolls-Royce was anxious to monitor customer opinion as well as initially keeping a watchful eye on the model's overall performance. Notwithstanding overseas marketing constraints, Rolls-Royce was proven very wrong about perceived demand for the car. Anticipating sales of no more than 100 cars a year, far more orders than this poured into Crewe's sales office and Rolls-Royce was obliged to review production, which was doubled. Within weeks of starting delivery there existed a black market for the car, and examples were changing hands at £120,000, about

double the list price. Building 200 cars a year was insufficient to meet demand, and had it been possible to produce engines in greater numbers, more orders might have been satisfied.

Another new Bentley - the Eight

With the Mulsanne Turbo successfully launched, Rolls-Royce looked towards attracting an even wider clientele to the Bentley marque, to include those motorists who might have otherwise considered Rolls-Royce or Bentley ownership beyond reach. The company had by now abandoned all thought of introducing a smaller or 'popular' car and, instead, concentrated on expanding the existing model range. Rather than adding a lower priced 'entry model' car built to lesser standards in order to achieve a lower price, Rolls-Royce went for something even more sophisticated and inspiring. By introducing a derivative of the Mulsanne with special features, the company once again recalled the Bentley's sporting prowess: the Bentley Eight was born.

With media attention focussed on

The Bentley revival had already begun when the Bentley Eight was introduced in July 1984. At the opposite end of the 'Rolls-Royce' market to the Mulsanne Turbo, it succeeded in attracting many new customers as a competitive price and deliberately reduced level of trim offered marque ownership to those motorists for whom this was previously out of reach. (Courtesy Rolls-Royce Motor Cars Limited/SHRMF)

Still a Bentley in the sense of refinement, the Eight had a straight-grained walnut facia and slightly different instrumentation which, Rolls-Royce publicity material claimed, added to the marque's sporting image. (Courtesy Rolls-Royce Motor Cars Limited/SHRMF)

a Bentley resurgence, Rolls-Royce capitalised on the interest in the marque and priced the Eight very competitively at under £50,000. This was a subtle move by chief executive Peter Ward, who wanted the Bentley name to become a separate and powerful identity. On introduction in July 1984 (it was displayed at the Birmingham Motor Show that year), the Eight appealed not only to those customers who might have been attracted to rival cars in the luxury and sporting sectors, such as Mercedes S-Class or Series-4 Porsche, but also to those who previously had aspired to Jaguar or Daimler ownership. In particular, Rolls-Royce wanted to attract the younger executive - young entrepreneurs was the expression used - by whom a Silver Spirit might have been considered too formal or politically incorrect, and, in so doing, no longer underplayed the Bentley image. The prestige of driving a Bentley and experiencing Rolls-Royce standards of

Pictured within the Crewe factory, a Bentley Eight undergoing final preparation.
(Courtesy Rolls-Royce Motor Cars Limited)

motoring had, instead of being no more than a vision, became a possibility.

The Eight similarly had certain appeal for existing Rolls-Royce and Bentley customers; not only those choosing to buy a new car rather than a previously used example, but customers who appreciated the car's sporting characteristics. Priced at £49,497, some £5743 below the Mulsanne, the Eight offered much: beneath the bon-

net lay the familiar Rolls-Royce V8 engine, with its smooth and effortless power combined with the engineering excellence for which the marque was rightly acclaimed.

Although not viewed as an attempt at cost-cutting, there were, however, differences to the car's interior appointment which, whilst not quite as exclusive as that in the Mulsanne, did not in any way compromise quality

or comfort. The companion mirrors built into the rear quarters of the standard saloon were omitted, and the facia was finished in straight-grained walnut. Instrumentation included an analogue clock and outside temperature gauge, both items which, on other models, were digital. The seats could be optionally trimmed in hide or cloth, and the pockets built into the backs of the front seats were of a mesh design in

Right: Photographed in France, this Eight makes a splendid picture. The mesh grille, which suggests the marque's sporting lineage, is part of an image enhanced not only by the car's firmer suspension and improved roadholding, when compared to that of the Mulsanne, but also by interior trim, which was considered more 'purposeful'. (Courtesy Rolls-Royce Motor Cars Limited, Queste magazine, & SHRMF)

As well as the Mulsanne Turbo, a car instrumental in attracting customers to the Bentley marque was the Eight, which was introduced in July 1984. The car, which successfully combined traditional Bentley technical excellence with a slightly reduced level of interior trim, built on the marque's sporting prowess. It was a competitively priced product that made Roll-Royce ownership a distinct possibility for those motorists who had previously believed this to be beyond their reach. A feature of the Eight's styling was the mesh grille, ultimately applied to the entire model range. Here, the Eight is pictured alongside a Bentley Corniche (renamed Bentley Continental in 1985) and a Mulsanne, which is furthest from the camera. (Courtesy Rolls-Royce Motor Cars Limited, Queste magazine & SHRMF)

In terms of performance, the Bentley Eight had better handling than the Mulsanne: stiffer front suspension reduced body roll. A feature of the Eight was its mesh grille which evoked the marque's sporting traditions, an aspect that Rolls-Royce engineers built on with future Bentley models. (Courtesy Rolls-Royce Motor Cars Limited/SHRMF)

For the 1989 model year the Eight, along with the entire Bentley four-door range, was given a new look courtesy of paired round headlamps. (Courtesy Rolls-Royce Motor Cars Limited/SHRMF)

place of leather, known within the factory as 'string vests'; lambswool rugs did not feature and there were fewer options than on the Mulsanne or Silver Spirit. In justifying the slight reduction in specification, Rolls-Royce argued (unnecessarily) that the things omitted were not required by the more sporting owner. Externally the Eight was finished in a limited range of colours, but its distinguishing feature was a mesh grille which evocatively recaptured Bentley's glorious past and those many successes at Le Mans. Also, of course, there were new badges.

Many of the criticisms levelled at the Mulsanne Turbo for its 'soft' suspension and indifferent handling were answered when the Turbo R made its appearance at the 1985 Geneva Motor Show. This picture of a Turbo R prototype car was taken at a test establishment where emissions tests were being conducted.
(Courtesy Rolls-Royce Motor Cars Limited)

The Eight's handling was rather different to that of its contemporaries as it benefited from stiffer front suspension, which helped reduce body roll. Its 120mph capability no doubt pleased the younger and more progressive owner. The change in handling characteristics illustrates clearly that Rolls-Royce was actively reviewing its range of cars, the result of which was the introduction of the much improved Turbo R in 1985.

Rolls-Royce directors must have sighed with relief when it became apparent that the Eight had been well received, and orders were plentiful. Already the Bentley revival was obvious and, with the help of first the Mulsanne Turbo and now the Eight, sales were increasing, reducing the market lead previously enjoyed by Rolls-Royce. From that derisory three per cent in 1980, the sales graphs showed a different profile with the Bentley curve steadily rising upwards beyond twenty per cent.

'R' for roadholding

Those criticisms of the Mulsanne Turbo's handling - too soft suspension - were heeded by Rolls-Royce engineers who implemented dramatic improvements, culminating in an addition to the Bentley model range in March 1985, when the Turbo R was introduced at the Geneva Motor Show.

The R designation could well have had a number of connotations, not least to establish an affinity with that most famous Bentley Continental model, the R-type. In this instance there was no such subtlety, however: R stood for Roadholding! With the Mulsanne Turbo, Rolls-Royce and Bentley had engineered a superlative motor car, and the Turbo R improved upon that success.

Whether or not it was the company's intention to produce both the Mulsanne Turbo and Turbo R simultaneously is debatable. Press releases of the period suggest as much but, in the event, the overlap between the Turbo R's entry into production and withdrawal of the Mulsanne Turbo was minor, the last Mulsanne Turbo car being produced before the end of 1985. A great number of technical modifications were implemented during production of the Mulsanne Turbo. By comparison, there were very few styling changes, the most obvious being the fitting of pressure jet headlamp washers in place of the wash/wipe system.

Mike Dunn's influence in transforming the ride and handling characteristics of Bentley motor cars in particular was very noticeable during the early and mid-eighties, and introduction of the Turbo R, with its 'handling package', was just one of a number of projects with which the chief engineer busied himself. Phil Harding was the engineer responsible for overseeing the suspension modifications and, in this respect, brought together a number of refinements. The suspension itself remained unchanged except that the anti-roll bars were stiffened by 100 per cent at the front and 60 per cent at the rear. The dampers were also slightly stiffened, and the rear subframe received attention and was anchored laterally by its own hard-rate, rubber-bushed Panhard rod. Modifications to the engine mounts eliminated a degree or so of resonance; adjustments were made to the car's self-levelling, and slightly heavier steering was achieved by fitting the power assistance with a firmer torsion bar.

Externally there was little to distinguish between the two Turbo cars. The Turbo R was distinctive, inasmuch as its tyres - big Pirelli 275/55VR15 P7s mounted on low pressure, die-cast aluminium alloy wheels - were fatter and more aggressive-looking than before. The Pirelli tyres were slightly shallower than the Avons fitted to the Mulsanne Turbo they replaced and, as

Turbo Rs were fitted with alloy wheels and special centre caps similar to this American specification car pictured in the experimental workshops at Crewe. (Courtesy Rolls-Royce Motor Cars Limited)

a consequence, the Turbo R had a top speed of 132mph, marginally slower - by 3mph - than its predecessor. The reason for the difference in speeds was the governor, which stopped the engine from exceeding 4500rpm. In reality this mattered little, especially as the Turbo R could fly to 60mph in 6.7 seconds and go on to reach 100mph in less than 19 seconds. Helping to enhance performance was a modified air dam which improved high speed stability and reduced front lift by 15 per cent and drag by seven per cent.

A restyled facia was introduced for the Turbo R, with instrumentation comprising separate gauges, including a tachometer in the style of the earlier Bentley Continentals. These modifications were intended to provide more of a driver bias, and, of course, set the style of the car's interior apart from the other models in the Rolls-Royce and Bentley catalogue. To enhance the car's sporting appeal still further, a leather clad steering wheel was specified soon after introduction, and was a feature which was eventually made standard throughout the Bentley range.

The Turbo R was aimed at differ-entiating the Rolls-Royce and Bentley marques still further, and in this achieved its objective. In a relatively short time, Bentley had once again become the high-performance partner and, for the enthusiast, the application of turbocharging was successful in appealing to that new clientele Rolls-Royce had hoped to attract. For the 1986 model year, distinctive wheel trims were fitted to both the Turbo R and Mulsanne, and were optionally available at extra cost on the Eight.

However, attaining the national one-hour speed record, in September 1986, was what considerably promoted Bentley's sporting image. The title was previously held by a Lamborghini Countach until a Turbo R (SCBZ0409HCH2002) raised the distance attained in exactly one hour to over 140 miles (140 miles, 1690 yards). Achieving the one-hour record had not been without some drama. After the first two-mile lap, taken in 67 seconds from a standing start, subsequent laps were consistently timed at 51 seconds. 57 minutes into the endurance test, and whilst travelling at 141mph round the General Motors Milbrook test circuit in Bedfordshire, the car, driven by

This is the mock-up of Crewe's first alloy wheel, which was fitted to Turbo R. Alloy was as much an engineering choice as it was styling due to problems with steel wheels. (Courtesy Rolls-Royce Motor Cars Limited)

Rolls-Royce test driver Derek Rowland, hit a pheasant, fracturing the windscreen in several places. As well as

Twin headlamps and the body-coloured radiator grille identify this as a Bentley Turbo R. Christopher Leefe's Silver Cloud ll in the background gives this picture real appeal. (Courtesy Rolls-Royce Enthusiasts' Club (R-REC)/SHRMF)

maintaining control, course and speed, Derek also had to contend with fuel starvation caused by the circuit's steep camber. Even with this potentially disastrous accident, the record was achieved without the Bentley being used to maximum potential.

For the 1987 model year there were two significant developments: the Turbo R was fitted with fuel injection, which meant that all models, for all markets, were so equipped, and another model - the Mulsanne S - joined the Bentley range. Significantly, the Mulsanne S, which replaced the Mulsanne, was the first Bentley to be made available in America for more than a decade.

Development of the fuel injection system had been entrusted to Ricardo at Shoreham, Sussex, the respected engineer with whom Rolls-Royce has

enjoyed a long and fruitful association. Ricardo, evaluating Rolls-Royce's requirements, advised the use of the Bosch KE-Jetronic fuel injection system, which was instrumental in pushing the Turbo R's power output up to 328bhp. As previously, the 'secrets' of the engine were published in Germany, although Rolls-Royce remained coy about divulging this detail in the UK. Also for 1987, the Turbo R received anti-lock ABS brakes, and the car's speed was no longer governed to 135mph. When tested by *Autocar*, a maximum speed of 146mph was achieved; motorway cruising suggested fuel consumption to be around 17mpg, although there was a penalty when attempting fast cross-country journeys which reduced the figure to around 14mpg. Had it not been for the efficiency of fuel injection, together with

higher gearing - the final drive having been raised from 2.69 to 2.28-to-1 - the results might well not have been as good.

The Mulsanne S gave the standard saloon a distinctively sporting character courtesy of its style of facia and centre console, inherited from the Turbo R. Unlike the original Mulsanne, the 'S' featured a tachometer but otherwise straight-grained walnut, as on the Bentley Eight, replaced burr walnut veneers, but for those customers insistent on maintaining tradition, burr walnut could be had at extra cost. Sharing technical features, refinement, handling and sparkling performance with the Eight, interior appointment was nevertheless on a par with the model it replaced, and included familiar touches of sophistication such as lambswool rugs and rear companions.

Bentley Turbo R at speed.
(Courtesy R-REC / SHRMF)

The Turbo R - 'R' denoting roadholding - was introduced in response to criticism of the Mulsanne Turbo's handling. The revised model acquired an enviable reputation, the car's modified suspension coping admirably with the 135mph-plus performance potential. It was also the Turbo R which claimed for Rolls-Royce in 1986 the record for covering the most miles in exactly one hour, a feat achieved at the Millbrook circuit in Bedfordshire when the car travelled a little over 140 miles in the time. After 1989 the Turbo R, in accordance with current styling trends, was given a face-lift with the adoption of paired round headlamps, a feature which significantly differentiated Bentley styling from Rolls-Royce. As a matter of interest, it was initially intended that the styling change should include adoption of $5^3/_4$ inch round headlamps, but ultimately, after deliberation, Graham Hull, chief stylist at Crewe, decided in favour of the larger headlamps. (Courtesy Rolls-Royce Motor Cars Limited)

985 FBA 92

Turbo R

A Turbo R outside the showrooms of James Young, the famous coachbuilder, sadly now out of business. The name James Young is steeped in Rolls-Royce history; the coachbuilder from Bromley, Kent, being synonymous with some of the finest cars to carry the Bentley and Rolls-Royce emblems. (Courtesy R-REC/SHRMF)

Left: A new facia was designed for Turbo R. Note the instrument layout and centre console. (Courtesy Rolls-Royce Motor Cars Limited/SHRMF)

Early in the 1980s an exercise was carried out to design a two-door Turbo R. As the styling evolved it became apparent that an all-new body would be required and, in its existing guise, the project was abandoned. It was not forgotten, however, and later re-materialised as Continental R. The two pictures show both sides of a scale model and thus different styling themes. (Courtesy Rolls-Royce Motor Cars Limited)

Another landmark of the Bentley revival was the introduction, in 1987, of the Bentley Mulsanne S. Benefiting from interior styling more representative of the Turbo R, the Mulsanne S had improved handling and roadholding. This is a post-1989 model year car, identified as such by the paired seven inch round headlamps, which gave all Bentleys a purposeful image in keeping with the marque's sporting connections. (Courtesy Rolls-Royce Motor Cars Limited)

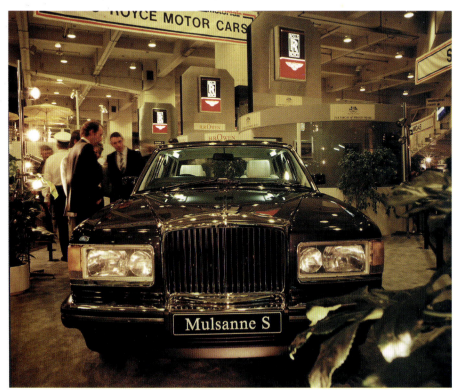

A distinctive image for the Bentley marque

For the 1989 model year, all models in the Bentley range, excluding the Continental, were given a face-lift which effectively distinguished the marque still further from Rolls-Royce. Until the end of the 1988 model year, all SZ-based cars had worn similar headlamp configurations depending upon the market, but for 1989 Bentley models were universally styled with paired seven inch round headlamps. Graham

Introduced in 1987, the Mulsanne S borrowed the Turbo R's facia, console and instrumentation. This, together with a mix of the original Mulsanne's straight-grained walnut, gave the car an appearance that was appreciated by marque enthusiasts. The Mulsanne S, pictured here at London's Motorfair, was also marketed in the USA. (Courtesy Rolls-Royce Motor Cars Limited)

Companion to the Mulsanne S, the Turbo R forged a divergence from the Rolls-Royce marque. Note the headlamp styling on this pre-1989 model year vehicle. (Courtesy Rolls-Royce Motor Cars Limited)

Hull recalls that it had been intended to fit $5^3/_4$ inch diameter lamps in pairs but, ultimately, was glad that the decision to adopt the larger type was taken. In fact, these lamps influenced that styling aspect of the Continental R.

Rolls-Royce and Bentley publicity material referred to the new look as 'purposeful', which it was, and generally it was welcomed by enthusiasts. Substituting existing headlamps for the circular variety successfully enhanced the sporting image and, together with the Bentley type of radiator shell, helped promote the softer styling. The Eight continued to use the mesh type of radiator grille, whilst the Mulsanne S and Turbo R both retained vertical shutters, although the latter continued to feature a colour-keyed arrangement. The Turbo R additionally featured a deeper front air dam, steel sill extensions and a rear skirt, all of which were painted to match body colour. Early styling proposals were for cars to have grey painted lower

Revised frontal styling gave the Bentleys a 'purposeful' look. Here, the first styling mock-up of Turbo R is being prepared at Crewe for evaluation of the revised headlamp arrangement. Masking papers cut to show how 7 inch diameter headlamps would look have been placed over the lenses; originally it had been intended to use $5^3/_4$ inch lamps but, ultimately, the larger diameter units were favoured. Graham Hull admits he is glad he tried the 7 inch lamps as this helped influence Continental R. The mock-up was also considered with a grey lower body section, in case all-body colour was overpowering. (Courtesy Rolls-Royce Motor Cars Limited)

Bentley models did not carry a series ll designation like their Rolls-Royce counterparts. They did, however, receive the same technical changes. Here, a late Mulsanne S is depicted: the model continued in production, together with the Eight, until it was replaced by the Bentley Brooklands in the autumn of 1992. (Courtesy Rolls-Royce Motor Cars Limited/SHRMF)

sections to avoid an all-body colour being overpowering, but the all-body colour on a styling mock-up was considered acceptable. From the rear, as well as by dedicated badging the Turbo R could be identified by a red Winged 'B' badge (on other models this was black) which incorporated the boot lock.

Development of the Turbo R was largely responsible for the Continental R in 1990. Early proposals included a two-door version of Turbo R, which would have meant styling and building an all-new body. The proposal was welcomed and accepted by Rolls-Royce directors who decided the car should, in fact, be marketed as a model in its own right, hence it became the Continental R.

1990 Bentley models did not carry the Series ll designation as applied to Silver Spirit models. They did, however, have the same technical modifications, including facia changes with the exception of the style of woodwork, which remained as before, and without the inlaid style of Rolls-Royce-badged cars. The Eight and Mulsanne S remained in production without any notable modification until the autumn of 1992, when both cars were replaced by a single model, the Bentley Brooklands.

The Brooklands, suitably clad in 'Brooklands Green', made its first appearance at the Birmingham International Motor Show in October 1992, and thus, for the 1993 model year, revived yet another emotive name from the annals of Bentley history. By displacing both the Eight and Mulsanne S, the Brooklands, representing the marque's entry vehicle, came about because of rationalisation. It did, however, enjoy an impressive specification on a par with that of the Mulsanne S, and including ABS anti-locking brakes. External trim incorporated a colour-keyed radiator shell, a new front air dam with discreet integral fog lamps, and new alloy wheels. Unlike those cars it replaced, the Brooklands did not feature chrome moulding along the bonnet centre line. The interior of the Bentley Brooklands was exquisitely appointed with pleated leather door trim and a leather-stitched gear selector located in the centre console in similar style to that of the Continental R introduced in 1990. For those Bentley drivers not overly concerned about having the higher performance of the Turbo R, it was still possible to specify that car's more supportive seats and, optionally, picnic tables that were built into the backs of the front seats. All the usual features were to be available, including automatic split-level air conditioning and an advanced hi-fi sound system complete with CD autochanger. For the 1993 model year only, the badges were enamelled in green.

The Bentley Brooklands made its debut in 1992 for the 1993 model year. This is actually a later car, identified as such by the fact that it doesn't have the moulding along the bonnet. (Courtesy Rolls-Royce Motor Cars Limited/SHRMF)

Power boost

The 1994 Bentley range was announced in early August 1993 and, at that time, comprised the most powerful cars to carry the Winged B emblem. The lead-in model was again the Bentley Brooklands, which was available with either standard (SWB) or long wheelbase (LWB). Top speeds of both cars was 134mph, a substantial increase over previous models, and the 0-60mph acceleration time was reduced from 9.9 to 9.3 seconds. This extra performance was achieved without any increase in fuel consumption; in fact, it slightly improved, the official figures recording 24.3mpg (as against 23mpg) at 56mph and 19.3mpg (18.7mpg) at 75mph.

The specification of the Brooklands models was impressive, with a new black hide-trimmed steering column cowl, a new lockable lower stowage compartment and redesigned front and rear seats. Both SWB and LWB cars were equipped with driver and front passenger airbags and redesigned front seat belt installations, and the LWB models featured new-style illuminated picnic tables. Under the bonnet both cars received the redesigned 6.75 litre naturally aspirated V8 engine and a transmission shift energy management (SEM) to give even smoother gear changing. The mechanical specification also included CFC-free air conditioning, whilst restyled badges with a black background matched the black background wheel trim centres.

As to the interiors, Graham Hull explains that the redesigned seats were essential to comfort. At Rolls-Royce the seat chassis is fine-tuned to get the most out of the leather. The seats fitted to 1994 model cars were, therefore, styled with new longitudinal pleats for greater lateral support, and redesigned squab and cushions were in-line with current orthopaedic research for improved lumbar support. The front seats were electrically adjustable with an electronic memory capable of storing four personal settings.

A new version of the Turbo R was offered for 1994, along with its LWB derivative, the Turbo RL. Mechanically, both cars were identical and, similarly to the Brooklands models, no longer had a chrome moulding along the bonnet centre line. The Turbo models were equipped with new-style, 16 inch alloy wheels with a wider rim section and black background trim centres, and were generally - apart from discreet badging - indistinguishable from the Brooklands. The power of the Turbo cars was exhilarating with 0-60mph taking just 6.3 seconds. Compared to the previous model Turbo R's maximum speed of 140mph, the 1994 model

Pictured at Castle Ashby in Northamptonshire, Turbo R in modified style - note there is no longer a bonnet moulding. New wheels and wheel trims are also evident. (Courtesy Rolls-Royce Motor Cars Limited / SHRMF)

could achieve 147mph without compromising economy. Official figures claimed 26.6mpg (compared to 24.8mpg) at 56mph, whilst at 75mph this reduced to 21.3mpg (20mpg).

Turbo R and RL performance was significantly improved by development of Electronic Transient Boost Control, which was designed to override the normal turbo control system during full throttle manoeuvres, such as overtaking, providing approximately 20 per cent more power before gradually reducing to a normal level. The effect on performance is dramatic as the system produces the maximum power an engine can deliver to provide an incredible power surge.

Turbo models also incorporated another new feature - SEM - Shift Energy Management, which has already been mentioned in connection with the Brooklands models. Coupled with the four-speed automatic transmission, SEM momentarily reduces engine torque before a gear shift takes place, achieving a change that is barely noticeable. Further enhancing performance, Rolls-Royce developed a system called Adaptive Shift Control (ASC), designed to adapt the transmission pattern in accordance with the manner in which a car is being driven. In a situation where a driver repeatedly used progressive acceleration, in the interests of better performance the system would delay gear changes until higher rpm was achieved.

An even more powerful Turbo saloon was introduced in the autumn of 1994, and was designed to be built in very limited numbers to make it one of

Unveiled at the 1992 Birmingham Motor Show, the Bentley Brooklands, successor to the Mulsanne, underwent specification changes for the 1996 model Year. Known as the New Bentley Brooklands, these 'lead-in' models were luxuriously equipped. (Courtesy Rolls-Royce Motor Cars Limited)

the most exclusive Bentley motor cars. Early indications suggested that no more than 100 orders would be accepted and, in the event, as few as 60 cars were built. The Turbo S was built between 1994 and 1996 and enjoyed ultra-high performance with stunning acceleration capable of providing 0-60mph in under 5.8 seconds; maximum speed was governed at 155mph. To allow for such devastating performance, a liquid-cooled inter-cooler was fitted to this and other models, together with an engine management system based on Formula One tech-

nology. A particular feature of the car was its appearance; it had a higher front bumper with integral air dam, and shorter radiator shell from the ground up. Instead of the 16 inch wheels normally fitted to Turbo R models, the Turbo S was equipped with the Continental R's 17 inch wheels and 255/55WR17 tyres.

The Turbo R models, together with the Brooklands, albeit with modifications, remained in production until 1998, when they were discontinued and replaced by the Bentley Arnage. In common with the Rolls-Royce models,

Interior of the 1996 model year New Bentley Brooklands. This left-hand drive car illustrates the change to a console-mounted gear selector (R-R classifies this as a 'floor-mounted' device) in preference to the usual column change so long associated with these cars. (Courtesy Rolls-Royce Motor Cars Limited)

turbocharged cars

* new exterior mirrors on door cheater panels, no quarterlights

* sills and bumpers painted to match coachwork

* new centre console layouts for four-door saloons; tilting steering wheel enabled driving position to be perfectly tailored to individual requirements, whilst preferred steering angle was included in driver's seat memory; steering wheel moved automatically to highest position when ignition key removed or the driver's door opened with the gear range selector in the 'park' or 'neutral' position

* additional ranges of colour arrangements, both exterior and interior

* interior appointments included box-style front armrest with stowage compartment; individually controlled cooling air outlets in rear compartment added to rear passenger comfort; radio head unit protected by hinged flap, and a new smoker's companion installed in centre console with concealed ashtray and cigar lighter

* as a result of detailed developments to the design of the front seat upholstery, an inch more headroom was made possible

Technical modifications included, for naturally aspirated cars:

* a 6 per cent increase in maximum torque

* an improvement in fuel consumption of more than 11 per cent due to detailed engine refinements, adoption of a higher 2.69:1 final drive ratio giving 40mph per 1000rpm in top gear; new lower profile tyres that further improved handling and roadholding

The Bentley Turbo R engine coupled with Electronic Transient Boost Control, propelled the car to 147mph, taking 6.3 seconds to reach 60mph from rest. (Courtesy Rolls-Royce Motor Cars Limited/SHRMF)

Bentleys, in 1995 for the 1996 model year, received important styling and technical changes, which resulted in radiator height being reduced by 2 inches, and adoption of an integrated front bumper and air dam design. Other changes included:

* integrated rear bumper design - made possible by spare wheel stowage in luggage compartment - which was also a feature of the Continental R

* new wheels for all models - 16 inch diameter for naturally aspirated models, and 17 inch diameter for

The Turbo R Sport was a niche model designed to appeal to those customers for whom performance was everything! (Courtesy Rolls-Royce Motor Cars Limited)

Turbo R Sport's impressive facia. (Courtesy Rolls-Royce Motor Cars Limited)

For turbocharged cars revisions included an 8 per cent increase in maximum power and torque, and in excess of 6 per cent increase in fuel economy. All cars had automatic traction control through viscous control differential.

1997 model year Bentleys

Both the Brooklands and Turbo R received a number of technical modifications for the 1997 model year, not least of which was that the Turbo R was specified with a long wheelbase, making it a spacious, turbocharged, water-intercooled model that gave the ultimate four-door Bentley driving experience.

The 300bhp Rolls-Royce Light Pressure Turbo Engine (LPT), known for its silent, smooth drivability and longevity, was installed in the Brooklands models. Power and, in particular, torque, were substantially increased over that of the naturally aspirated engine. Maximum speed of the Brooklands was improved, the car being capable of 140mph, whilst enhanced acceleration resulted in a 0-60mph figure of 7.9 seconds. Electronic Traction Assistance System (ETAS) was optionally available and provided even better traction under difficult driving conditions.

Other improvements to the

Modifications for the 1994 model year included a revised facia and airbag. This is a full-size model showing the first airbag steering wheel; note that at this styling stage the gear selector is still on the steering column and the 'walk-through' console remains. (Courtesy Rolls-Royce Motor Cars Limited)

Turbo R and Brooklands saloons were given even more power for 1995. There were also important stying changes to include a reduced height radiator and integral bumpers with air dams. (Courtesy Rolls-Royce Motor Cars Limited)

1995 models were fitted with 17 inch wheels on turbocharged cars and 16 inch wheels on those naturally aspirated. Styling changes are shown to good effect on this Brooklands model. (Courtesy Rolls-Royce Motor Cars Limited)

Brooklands models included extended front seat cushions, optional rear seat heaters, seat belt pre-tensioners, improved headlamps, greater vehicle security, new paint colours and new, bright finish alloy wheel centres.

The Turbo R was fitted with ETAS as standard which, together with the viscous control differential, allowed power to be fully utilised in all driving conditions. Large diameter micro-alloy front disc brakes (optional on the Brooklands) gave even more responsive braking. The Turbo R was given new, improved head restraints, new-style wheels of improved appearance, together with new, bright finish alloy wheel centres, and a larger range of paint colours.

1998 model year changes

The 1998 model year changes were significant as these were the final revisions made to the SZ Bentleys, the

159

four-door cars being replaced in the spring of 1998 by the Arnage, the first completely new saloon to appear since 1980. For 1998, the Brooklands R was introduced, the addition of the 'R' roadholding package, which included the Turbo R's suspension, complementing the 300bhp engine launched for the 1997 model year. The Brooklands R was fitted with 17 inch wheels and low profile tyres, which increased responsiveness and improved 'turn-in' when cornering. The car's awesome acceleration was matched by its stopping power, made possible by the standardisation of the performance braking system developed for the Continental T. A greater affinity with other Bentley models was achieved by the Brooklands R having a mesh grille, which re-established the lineage with the earliest sporting Bentleys. Additional modifications included new-style bumpers with black lower lip and black mesh inserts to match the mesh grille; headlamp surrounds were in body colour and, internally, the car was fitted with a new ergonomically designed thicker steering wheel rim.

The other four-door car to be introduced for the 1998 model year was the Turbo RT. This car not only incorporated those features which had been specified for the Turbo R for the 1997 model year, but also featured the power train borrowed from the Continental T. The result was staggering performance courtesy of the 400bhp engine which gave immense torque - 590lb ft at 2100rpm, 50 per cent more than the Ferrari F50. An increase in torque at low revs made possible a 0-60mph

The ultimate SZ Bentley is the Turbo RT Mulliner. 50 cars, sold to selected customers, were designed in conjunction with Darren Day, styling engineer at Crewe, working under the direction of Graham Hull. Note the purposeful styling theme which matched the car's very high performance potential courtesy of the Continental T's power train. Customers could specify a push-button starter, drilled metal pedals and a second speedometer fitted in the rear compartment! (Courtesy Rolls-Royce Motor Cars Limited)

time of 5.8 seconds.

Changes in trim included body colour bumpers with chrome finisher and body colour lower lip, together with mesh inserts to match the car's mesh grille. In similar fashion to the Brooklands R, the Turbo RT was de-signed to incorporate marque identity and re-establish the company lineage. Headlamp surrounds were body colour, the new-type steering wheel was fitted and the car received 5 spoke 17 inch aluminium alloy wheels and low-profile tyres.

The final phase of SZ Bentley development included the Brooklands models. 1998 model year changes included adoption of a mesh grille, along with a 'roadholding' (R) version, which is shown here, and the Turbo RT. The Brooklands became a much sought-after motor car. (Courtesy Rolls-Royce Motor Cars Limited)

In launching the new Bentley models Rolls-Royce had very clear customer targets: as well as attracting existing Rolls-Royce and Bentley owners, the company intended that the Brooklands R should appeal to those customers who might otherwise have chosen an S-Class Mercedes or similar. The Turbo RT, standard with LWB, was definitely aimed at motorists who could have been swayed by the Ferrari, and, in particular, those used to Mercedes limousines and BMW L models.

The Turbo RT, therefore, is amongst the most exclusive of Bentley models, and 216 examples were produced. A connoisseur's choice, the Turbo RT had a price premium of a little over £5000 more than that of the Turbo R, but that amount of money really paled into insignificance when comparing the performance of the two cars. At around £71,000 less than the Continental T, the Turbo RT appeared to offer excellent value for money. Top speed was 150mph, and exhilarating acceleration was possible for those customers who appreciated perform-

Viewed from the rear, the Turbo RT Mulliner was just as impressive as from the front. (Courtesy Rolls-Royce Motor Cars Limited)

ance and lavish comfort; apart from the Continental models, this was the ultimate supercar. The Turbo RT was aimed at a particular niche in the market and is unique inasmuch as Rolls-Royce did not produce any publicity material for it.

A strictly limited edition 1998 model was the Brooklands R Mulliner. No more than one hundred of these exquisitely appointed cars were built, and each was specially numbered. Al-

The Brooklands R for the 1998 model year was given a most stylish interior, with black lacquered facia, hide waistrails and chrome inserts on the instrument bezels. (Courtesy Paul Wood & Rolls-Royce Motor Cars Limited)

though these cars were powered by the 300bhp engine, it is possible to increase the output to 400bhp. Mulliner versions - the coachbuilding name was reserved for the Bentley marque, whilst Park Ward was attributed to Rolls-Royce motor cars - were equipped with dark wood veneers and chrome surrounds on the facia instruments, and seats were trimmed in true coachbuilding tradition. These were amongst the last of the SZ generation Bentleys, and, in view of the developments concerning ownership of Rolls-Royce and Bentley, signalled the end of an era. It goes without saying that these vehicles are highly cherished by their enthusiastic owners and can be expected to increase in value. These were the last SZ four-door saloons to use the Rolls-Royce-designed V8 engine which had so successfully powered generations of cars from 1959, including the S-Series Bentleys and their Silver Cloud equivalents, the Bentley T and the Silver Shadow and, of course, the Mulsanne and Silver Spirit, not forgetting the Corniche and Continental models.

The ultimate SZ Bentley is the Turbo RT Mulliner, of which 50 were sold to special customers via renderings by Darren Day, a member of Graham Hull's select styling team at Pym's Lane. The car featured the Continental T's mechanics and wheels, bigger eyebrows over the wheelarches - the front extending over the styling line. New bumpers, aprons and sills were provided and, inside the cabin, features such as a push-button starter and drilled metal pedals recalled that

The Bentley Turbo RT is surely one of the most coveted motor cars in the world. With an impressive specification incorporating the power train borrowed from the Bentley Continental T, the Turbo RT boasted a level of performance higher than that of a Ferrari F50. Capable of 0-60mph in under six seconds, the car's top speed is 150mph. (Courtesy Paul Wood & Rolls-Royce Motor Cars Limited)

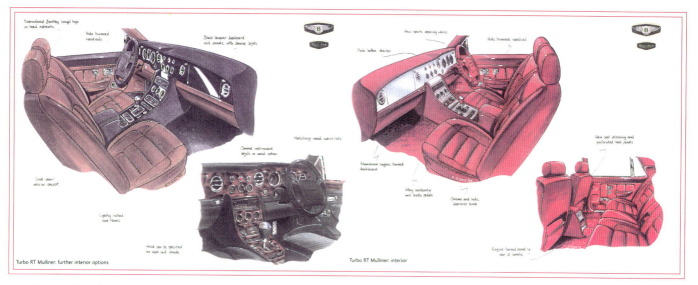

Darren Day's styling arrangements for Turbo RT Mulliner make this the most exclusive four-door Bentley SZ. (Courtesy Rolls-Royce Motor Cars Limited)

The ultimate SZ Bentley, which was offered to 50 specially selected customers, was this Turbo RT Mulliner. Several exterior options were available, including bonnet and wing vents, chrome sports wheels and a matrix grille. (Courtesy Rolls-Royce Motor Cars Limited)

Chrome door mirrors

Bonnet and wing vents

Race number spot

MULLINER

Matrix grille.

Chrome sports wheels

The Turbo RT Mulliner bristled with technical innovation, including Bentley Continental T mechanics and wheels, and the car's styling arrangements included bigger than usual eyebrows, the front extending over the styling line. A push-button starter, drilled metal pedals and the option of a speedometer in the rear compartment were all part of this most impressive package. (Courtesy Rolls-Royce Motor Cars Limited)

great Bentley sporting image. Possibly the ultimate accessory was the optional speedometer in the rear compartment!

The interior trim of the RT Mulliner is nothing less than exquisite: embroidered Bentley 'wings' logo adorn headrests, waistrails are hide-trimmed and the facia and console black lacquered with chrome bezels. Options include a wood or aluminium engine-turned facia and console. Exterior options extend to chrome sports wheels and door mirrors, a matrix grille, bonnet and wing vents and a race number spot on the front doors.

Rolls-Royce, Bentley and the Millennium

The engines that power the Rolls-Royce Silver Seraph and Bentley Arnage Green Label, good as they are, are no longer built by Rolls-Royce. Instead, they are produced by BMW, and are the consequence of several years of collaboration between the two companies. Engine design and manufacture is an expensive business, calling for huge investment, and, as far as Rolls-Royce is concerned, such investment was considered out of proportion for a specialist car producer building exclusive vehicles in limited

numbers. Sharing technology really is not new for it's a long time since Rolls-Royce built and fitted its own gearboxes, and many decades since it produced its own chassis. Similar to other manufacturers, the vast majority of components are bought from a variety of suppliers within the auto industry.

The familiar V8 lives on, however, for the foreseeable future at least. The Continental models - R, T, Azure and SC - use the engine designed by Jack Phillips nearly fifty years ago, even though technology has advanced and improved during the half century.

With the introduction of a new

The Bentley Arnage replaced SZ in 1998. Graham Hull's styling theme, which echoes certain styling cues developed from S-Series Bentleys, is set to become a classic, following the Bentley T and Mulsanne.
(Courtesy Rolls-Royce Motor Cars Limited)

generation of cars, it is Bentley that is the driving force, with something like a 70 per cent share of the company's market. The popularity of Bentley is evident by the fact that there is only one Rolls-Royce model (apart from the very limited Park Ward Limousine and the new Corniche), the Silver Seraph, compared to five Bentley models, the Arnage, Azure, Bentley Continental R, Continental T and the Continental SC (Sedanca Coupé). Significantly, production records show that the Bentley market increased substantially in the SZ era, from around three per cent to forty per cent to reach its present level.

The Continental models are out of the brief of this book and have been very comprehensively covered by Martin Bennett in a companion volume also published by Veloce. The Silver Seraph and Arnage, however, are successors to the SZ standard saloons and, in some respects, have much in common with their predecessors. Both cars were styled by Graham Hull, chief stylist at Rolls-Royce who, under Fritz Feller's direction, was largely responsible for SZ's styling. But it is not the

Silver Spirit or Mulsanne from which Graham derived his inspiration to develop the new cars: instead, he returned to the fifties and the Silver Cloud and S-Series Bentley. Unlike some stylists who have decided on a retro theme, Graham Hull was careful not to create a style that would forever be 1955, and chose a progression of shapes which, taking their cue from a classic form, appear both sequential and modern.

The defining feature of the Silver Seraph ('a celestial being of the highest order' - Oxford English Dictionary) and Bentley Arnage (named after one of the most challenging corners on the Le Mans circuit) is the cars' shouldered waistline which sweeps unbroken from nose to tail, with cabin and boot inset from it. Viewed from the side, the waistline extends just forward of the front door handles before gently falling along the length of the car in a continuous line.

After studying various styling issues, Graham Hull devised what he refers to as a 'yacht element', a form that has a bow and second wave.

Graham describes this as a 'wedge running backwards'.

By Rolls-Royce and Bentley standards, the new generation models enjoyed a relatively short gestation period, initial work having begun in the early to mid-nineties. In fact, Graham Hull and his select styling team commenced work on the project, codenamed P3000, in March 1994 and continued throughout that summer to achieve a definitive outline. All design work was carried out using full-size clay models, the surface of the clay being constantly checked during development, with digital measurement making it possible to allow engineering of the bodyshell to continue in parallel. With exterior styling approved, interior styles were sanctioned in mid-1995 and, in September that year, the definitive model was presented to the 2500 strong Crewe workforce.

In designing the interior of the cars, Graham Hull continued to employ soft styling techniques to produce sculptured waistrails, a crowned facia and console and rounded seat silhouettes. Although both the Silver Seraph

Arnage at Le Mans in 1998. The registration is significant ... (Courtesy Rolls-Royce Motor Cars Limited)

and Bentley Arnage share a common bodyshell, a divergence between the two marques is clearly evident, especially in respect of interior appointment. The Arnage reflects the Bentley marque's sporting association, whilst the Silver Seraph is all that could be expected of a car heralding the R-R monogram.

Under the bonnet the two cars are significantly different: the Silver Seraph has an all-aluminium alloy 5379cc V12 engine, with 24 valves and single overhead camshaft per cylinder bank, producing 322bhp maximum power output at 5000rpm. Coupled to this is a five-speed automatic gearbox with electronic actuation from a steering column-mounted selector.

The Bentley Arnage has an all-aluminium alloy twin turbo 4398cc V8 engine which delivers maximum power of 350bhp at 5500rpm. The engine is the product of combined development between Rolls-Royce and BMW engineers, with expertise from Cosworth, who designed the turbocharger concept. The $4^1/_2$ litre engine enables the Arnage to achieve 0-60mph in 6.2 seconds, plus extremely responsive overtaking acceleration, and is governed to produce a maximum speed of 150mph. The five-speed automatic gearbox has electric actuation, but is controlled via a floor-mounted gear selector. Both the Rolls-Royce and Bentley are fitted with adaptive gear shift management, automatic stability control and transmission torque reduction control.

Sharing a common bodyshell, the

Silver Seraph and Arnage have a wheelbase of 10ft 2.7in, which is approximately mid-way between that of the standard and long wheelbase dimensions of the SZ cars, and the overall length of 17ft 8.2in is around 5 inches more than the Silver Spirit and Mulsanne. The new cars are, however, something like 6 per cent lighter than their predecessors, and the monocoque steel bodyshell has very high torsional rigidity, and is 65 per cent stiffer than those cars it replaces.

Unlike the Bentley Mulsanne, which made its appearance at the same time as the Silver Spirit, the Arnage was launched a few weeks later than its Rolls-Royce sister car. The Silver Seraph was unveiled at the Geneva International Motor Show on 3rd March

1998, but the Bentley's debut was delayed until 26th April when the car was given a spectacular introduction at Le Mans. This proved to be a real Bentley occasion which successfully rekindled those emotive memories of the Bentley Boys and their thrilling 24-Hour race victories which helped seal the marque's reputation for engineering, reliability and sporting ability.

The Arnage's debut was undoubtedly inspired by Bentley's victory in the 1928 24-Hour race of seventy years earlier when, competing for the Rudge-Whitworth Cup, Tim Birkin continued to drive his $4^1/_2$ litre car at speeds exceeding 70mph. This was despite having cut away a punctured tyre and driving on a bare wheel rim until it finally cracked under the pressure on the notoriously difficult Arnage bend. A mid-race wheel change caused him a delay of three hours; nevertheless. Birkin finished the event and managed to qualify for the 1929 final; his team mates, Woolf Barnato and Bernard Rubin, won the 1928 race, securing a Bentley victory for the third time.

Significantly, a Bentley Arnage wore a very special registration plate for the Le Mans introduction. 1 WO had been secured for an undisclosed sum of money, and it was that car which heralded the model's debut to the excited media. Arranging the Arnage's launch was akin to a military exercise for Rolls-Royce had determined that as many as 50 of the vehicles be sent to Le Mans, and this was in addition to around 60 Bentley Drivers Club members who, with their fine Cricklewood, Derby and Crewe cars, had been conscripted to carry out a supporting role. Driving the Arnage cars to Le Mans was entrusted to select members of Rolls-Royce and Bentley personnel, whilst invitations were sent to BDC members to assist in a 'secret project'. Ultimately, 900 guests - which included members of the press and motoring journals - were invited to the launch of the Arnage which proved to be one of the most sensational events in Bentley history.

Now that ownership of Rolls-Royce and Bentley motor cars has been settled, there is some conjecture about what the future holds for both marques. Volkswagen has made a huge investment in the Crewe factory and there is speculation of new models, possibly a medium-sized Bentley, in addition to the existing range, which is intended to attract a wider clientèle.

During 1999 there were two crucial developments at Crewe: resumption at Pym's Lane of production of the Rolls-Royce-designed V8, and the introduction of the Bentley Arnage Red Label model. Bentley owners and enthusiasts will understand the sporting significance of the Red Label appellation given to W. O. Bentleys and, accordingly customers are gratified to see the marque's illustrious heritage promoted.

Long-standing Rolls-Royce and Bentley customers had expressed their disquiet about the use of BMW engines, and enthusiasts lobbied the company and its agents for the return of the much-respected 6.75 litre V8, despite this design being over forty years old. To customers' satisfaction, the Rolls-Royce V8 which powers the Continental models was specified for the Arnage Red Label, an exquisite car that took Crewe's design and engineering team around 18 months to develop. With a huge 835N of torque, the 6.75 litre engine propels the Red Label from 0-60mph in under 6 seconds and from 30-70mph in 5.7 seconds; at 70mph the engine turns over effortlessly at less than 2000rpm. The BMW-engined 4.4 litre Arnage remains in the catalogue and is known as the Arnage Green Label.

As for Rolls-Royce, BMW's plans will eventually be announced. In the meantime, the finely styled new Corniche has made its debut. The engine and chassis have more in common with its forebears of the same name than does the Silver Seraph. To quote from *Queste*, the international magazine for Rolls-Royce and Bentley owners: "The marque is destined in 2003 to part company from the present Rolls-Royce and Bentley Motor Cars owned by the Volkswagen Group AG, and to become part of BMW. The long-term future remains uncertain. Whether or not any such truly exceptional Rolls-Royce motor car as this will ever again be built to such standards is an open question."

Whatever happens, the future promises to be very interesting, and the subject of intense debate amongst marque enthusiasts around the world.

ROLLS-ROYCE BENTLEY

5

LIVING WITH A SILVER SPIRIT OR MULSANNE

An early production car, the Bentley Mulsanne appeared very respectable in its dark blue paint. Having been carefully looked after, there was nothing - apart from styling features - which identified this as being anything other than a much later model. Opening the car's doors, the aroma of well preserved hide was delightful, and second only to the sight and comfort of those broad and supportive seats. Soft carpeting and exquisite burr walnut gave a measure of sophistication seldom found in the modern world, whilst information was discreetly provided by the instruments set within the deftly styled facia.

Turning the ignition key, the engine fired immediately and was no more than a distant growl. The air conditioning started to operate and, with all doors closed, the ambience was one of refined stateliness. The power from the V8 was delivered smoothly and the automatic gearbox changes were imperceptible. Then, when the road was clear, depressing the accelerator of the seemingly docile beast produced massive, tiger-like performance, but always with impeccable road manners. Had the subtle Turbo badges not been noticed there would have been no clue to the car's awesome potential.

Bentleys and Rolls-Royces are like this. They have a charisma rarely found with any other motor car, just one of the many reasons why they attract such a loyal and enthusiastic following. The Silver Spirit and Mulsanne predecessors, the Silver Shadow and Bentley T, have long been regarded as modern classics in Rolls-Royce lineage

and, as such, are revered by marque enthusiasts. Now it is the later generation of cars which has grown to classic status, and early examples especially will appeal to those motorists who might previously have considered this level of car ownership beyond their reach.

Buying advice

Introduced in 1980, the Rolls-Royce Silver Spirit and its long wheelbase sister car, the Silver Spur, together with the Bentley Mulsanne, have enjoyed a production period spanning almost two decades. As well as model designation changes there were, during that time, numerous technical modifications, some of which were more significant than others. Nevertheless, the fundamental image of these cars altered little and, in respect of Rolls-Royce-badged cars, a late nineties model will, at first glance, appear virtually identical to an early one.

Bentleys are easier to identify, if only because of the paired seven inch round headlamps adopted for the 1989 model year in preference to the rectangular sort. Even so, beware, as many owners of early Mulsannes and Eights have replaced the original headlamps for the later type, giving their cars a modern appearance and improved lighting.

For everyday luxury motoring or as a hobby classic, the SZ Rolls-Royce and Bentley can form the basis of a very practical purchase; both cars, particularly early examples, are relatively inexpensive. Later models will command higher prices commensurate with age. Remember, though, that

SZ production spanned almost two decades, during which over 30,400 examples were built. Early cars, those built before the introduction of series ll vehicles for the 1990 model year, can be very affordable. (Courtesy Rolls-Royce Motor Cars Limited)

late series Silver Spirits and Silver Spurs, Silver Dawns, Bentley Brooklands and Turbos will keep their value in the short term at least, and, because these cars represent the end of an era as far as the marques are concerned, may, with time, increase in value.

So, you want to become a Rolls-Royce or Bentley owner. Having established that one of these cars can be surprisingly affordable, depending upon age, condition and mileage, exactly how much will you have to pay? First of all, take a look at the classified advertisements in the major classic car magazines: prices can vary enormously, starting from around £10,000. A car costing £10,000 or less will usually be a very early vehicle and will almost certainly require extensive refurbishment. A similar aged car in top condition will be considerably more expensive, but possibly no more than £15,000. For cars built from 1983, allow from £12,000 to £19,000, and for models dating from 1989 expect to pay

between £20,000 and £28,000, according to condition. More recent cars will obviously command higher values: Silver Spirits and Silver Spurs not more than a couple of years old with relatively low mileages will attract prices of in excess of £50,000-£60,000, and Bentley Turbos will probably be more expensive at £75,000 upwards, depending on the model. Cars under three years old will still be under manufacturer's warranty.

Silver Spirits, Silver Spurs and Mulsannes are complex cars and to work on them proficiently requires considerable knowledge and experience. Without such expertise there is always a risk that an enormous amount of damage can result through ignorance. Such complexity means that routine servicing, maintenance and repairs are likely to be more frequently required compared to many other cars. Some owners, because of the car's build quality, believe it will never need servicing or repair. This, of course, is pure fantasy as every car depends on regular

and full maintenance in accordance with manufacturer's schedules to keep it in top condition. Beware, therefore, of the car without a service history. Remember, too, that running costs, in fuel terms alone, can be high, and that insurance premiums will reflect the likely cost of accident repair.

When considering a purchase it might be advisable to go a respected agent or dealer. Prices will be a shade higher than those of cars offered privately, but a company with a jealously-guarded reputation would not wish for dissatisfied customers. And anyway, once the car has been purchased the pleasures of ownership will outweigh any concerns about price!

A genuine car offered privately may well be a fine proposition, but ascertain its service history and check that regular maintenance has been carried out. If the vehicle has been maintained by an official Rolls-Royce and Bentley agent or respected independent specialist, its true condition should be easy to establish. It's quite

Some early Silver Spirits (such as the car illustrated). Silver Spurs and Bentley Mulsannes with remarkably low mileages can be found. However good a car might seem, though, it's still wise to carry out a full pre-purchase survey. (Author's collection)

The car pictured here at a Rolls-Royce Enthusiasts' Club Rally is an early Silver Spur. Whilst these are attractive vehicles and have an enthusiastic and loyal following, they, and their sister cars, the Silver Spirit and Mulsanne, are technically complex and require specialist knowledge and expertise in order to carry out correct maintenance. (Author's collection)

possible that the vehicle is known within enthusiast club circles, and a check with the local branch of the Rolls-Royce Enthusiasts' Club or Bentley Drivers Club could give peace of mind. Finally, before searching the classified advertisements and disappearing into specialist's showrooms, remember that these are large cars. Modern houses rarely have garages big enough to accommodate vehicles of this size: more than once it's been discovered, too late, that the garage doors won't close with the car inside!

Look before you leap

Buying a car through a reputable specialist will be a vastly different experience to visiting a used-car lot of questionable integrity, where all sorts of problems may lurk beneath gleaming chrome, bright paintwork and unconvincing sales patter. Official agents are less likely to trade in older models unless a vehicle is in truly outstanding condition or is historically important. Anything older than, say, five or six years, will usually be traded to independent specialists or sold at

auction, whilst those cars lacking service history or suffering through neglect may end up in all sorts of emporia.

Unless a vendor can verify a car's pedigree, the buyer should treat the purchase with great caution. It is so easy to be taken in by the character of these cars with their statuesque radiators and charismatic Spirit of Ecstasy or Winged B emblems, not to mention the fine interior appointment; be careful or the heart may rule the wallet!

First of all check the chassis number. This is vitally important as it is not uncommon for registration numbers to change to an owner's personalised plate, often fitted to disguise a car's age. It is essential, therefore, to establish the car's true age and identity, and to do this it is necessary to find the vehicle identification number (VIN). VINs were introduced from October 1980, when the SZ models were launched. On early series models the VIN is situated between the spring pot brackets on the right-hand side of the engine compartment, and also on the nameplate fitted below the upper hinge on the right-hand door pillar. Those cars conforming to a North American specification have the VIN in two additional positions: on the demister panel in the left-hand corner of the windscreen surround to be visible from outside the car (known as the 'visible VIN', as on all new cars), and on the certification plate attached to the left-hand front door hinge pillar. Swedish cars have the VIN within the luggage compartment.

On later cars from 1989, includ-

ing the Silver Spirit ll, Silver Spur ll and relative Bentley versions, the VIN is situated adjacent to the forward spring pot bracket on the right-hand side of the engine compartment. Cars other than those conforming to a Canadian, Middle Eastern and USA specification, have the VIN fitted below the upper hinge on the right-hand door pillar, whilst Australian cars have the VIN on a plate attached to the valance on the left-hand side of the engine compartment adjacent to the coolant expansion bottle. On Middle Eastern cars it is located on the left-hand door hinge pillar, whilst on Canadian and USA vehicles this is on a plate attached to the windscreen surround and can be seen externally. Additionally, USA cars have the VIN in the form of a 'machine readable' bar code label attached to the driver's door closing pillar.

Early cars have the engine serial number stamped on the front face of the crankcase; on later cars this is stamped on the rear face of the crankcase.

Unless buying from an official Rolls-Royce and Bentley agent, or through one of the recognised specialists, it would be wise to have a prospective purchase thoroughly examined. There are marque and model specialists willing to undertake surveys, on a chargeable basis, of course; a worthwhile investment, especially if, once a

Reading the VIN

A car's VIN will appear as a series of 17 letters and digits:

S	C	A	Z	N	0	0	0	0	A	C	H	0	1	0	0	6

or

S	C	A	Z	S	0	0	A	7	L	C	H	3	1	0	0	1

key

1	2	3	4	5	6	7	8	9	10	11	12	13	14	15	16	17

Explanation:

The first VIN relates to a Silver Spur and the second to a Silver Spirit ll. Deciphering the VIN is easy using the sample key.

1) manufacturing origin, Europe; 2) country of origin, UK; 3) marque, A=Rolls-Royce, B = Bentley; 4) underframe, Z=all models other than Camargue or Corniche (Y) or Phantom Vl (P); 5) body type, S=saloon, L=long wheelbase and division, N=long wheelbase without division, D=Convertible, J=Camargue, M=Phantom Vl Limousine and T=Phantom Vl Landaulette. 6) this is a US requirement: 0=cars for other markets, 4=cars with type L410 engines and 8=Bentley Eight, see note 1; 7) type of fuel supply, 1=carburation, 2=fuel injection,T=Turbo, 0=other than USA, see also note 1; 8) occupant safety, A=cars fitted with active seat belts, B=cars with passive belts (USA only),C=cars fitted with airbags, D=cars fitted with driver-only airbag, 0=other than USA market; 9) check digit for security purposes; 10) model year - see note 2; 11) factory, C=Crewe (SZ cars will not carry any other reference); 12) steering, H=RHD, X=LHD; 13-17) sequential build number.

Note 1: From the 1987 model year the codes were superseded by the following: 00=naturally aspirated engines with fuel injection, 01=naturally aspirated carburettor engines, 02=naturally aspirated engines, fuel injection and catalyst, 03=turbocharged engines with catalyst, 04=turbocharged.

Note 2: Model years can be identified as follows:
A-1980; B-1981; C-1982; D-1983; E-1984; F-1985; G-1986; H-1987; J-1988; K-1989; L-1990; M-1991; N-1992; P-1993; R-1994; S-1995; T-1996; V-1997; W-1998; X-1999; Y-2000.

Some prospective owners will choose a Rolls-Royce for the prestige of the famous radiator and Spirit of Ecstasy mascot ... (Courtesy Rolls-Royce Motor Cars Limited)

car has been examined, it is found to be in less than ideal condition.

Choosing the right car

Some prospective owners will choose a Rolls-Royce for the prestige of the name and the Spirit of Ecstasy mascot on the radiator. Others may want all that is special about Rolls-Royce, combined with the more sporting image of the Bentley marque. Should it be out-and-out performance that is required, the choice may be a simple one: a Bentley Turbo.

As price may be the ultimate deciding factor, it pays to buy the very best that can be afforded. Some owners will be happy with a Bentley Eight, with its slightly lower trim level but outwardly greater sporting appeal, combined with firmer handling than that of the Silver Spirit and Mulsanne. Mulsanne Turbos should be very carefully investigated as these would have originally been purchased for performance and, most likely, used to their full potential.

Later cars - Silver Spirit IIs and IIIs, along with their Bentley stablemates - will give substantially better roadholding thanks to their improved handling packages.

What to look for

Early examples of Silver Spirits, Spurs and Mulsannes should be corrosion-free if they have been properly maintained. There should be no sign of accident damage, and cars should have a legitimate Vehicle Inspectorate certificate. Interiors should be clean and undamaged and sympathetically

... whilst others may go for the Bentley's more sporting style. This Bentley Eight has the post-1989 model year headlamps: many Bentley owners with earlier cars fitted these headlamps in order to improve lighting as well as give their vehicle a more distinctive look. (Author's collection)

cared for. Sadly, not all cars are like this and those that look down at heel will almost certainly have been neglected mechanically, too. Check for tears in the upholstery and, if repairs are necessary, ensure the car is entrusted to a recognised and experienced coach trimmer. These vehicles, even the cheapest examples, will be very expensive to renovate as this is a task mostly beyond the capabilities of the average enthusiast. Needless to say, a cheaper model may turn out to be more expensive ultimately than a more expensive car

which is in excellent condition.

Cars should stand evenly and be at showroom height without the assistance of self-levelling. Some early cars suffered from contaminated mineral oil systems due to incorrect brake fluid being used. The remedy is to replace the contaminated hydraulic components, which could cost as much as £6000. Again, some early models suffer from corrosion, especially at the rear of the front wings, around the rear wheelarches, along the sills and around the engine bulkhead. The thick carpeting on these cars can hide all sorts of

Series ll vehicles, this is a Silver Spirit ll, have revised interiors. They also have adaptive ride, and many enthusiasts prefer to pay the extra required to enjoy the advanced technology these cars offer. (Courtesy Colin Hughes, R-REC & SHRMF)

problems which have built up over many years, and it has been known for the floor under the front compartment to virtually rot away. In this respect much of the decay is due to the ingress of water having remained undetected over a long period of time. This is partly due to the air conditioning drains becoming blocked, condensation entering the cabin and being soaked up by carpets and underfelt. Corrosion may also be found where the rear road springs are held in place by plates at the top and bottom: on cars built before 1984, bearing pins on the front suspension were prone to serious wear but, ultimately, design modifications cured the problem. Wear or corrosion affecting the front suspension, often mainly due to a lack of maintenance, will necessitate extensive work, calling - possibly - for a complete suspension overhaul. Spring removal is a difficult and delicate operation requiring specialised equipment, and is best left to a specialist.

Early cars are noted for their indifferent ride and many owners have opted to fit either a Rolls-Royce or Harvey-Bailey handling kit. Noisy shock absorbers were the source of many complaints, and gas springs had a habit of losing pressure, which contributed to poor ride quality. Whilst build quality of SZ cars was very good, there were complaints initially about wind noise, and Rolls-Royce offered a modification kit to deal with this.

Some of the early vehicles had noisy engines which was attributed to the pistons; it was also not uncommon for cars to experience cylinder head gasket failure, which, if not detected through routine servicing and maintenance and remedied, became more acute with use. Overheating of engines was sometimes experienced with early cars, the problem emanating from incorrect radiator maintenance. The air conditioning matrix was sometimes prone to leaks which, if left unchecked, often resulted in corrosion due to the effects of dripping anti-freeze.

Always take a car for a long test drive in various traffic conditions: a mile or two will be insufficient to truly evaluate a vehicle's condition. All of the instruments should operate correctly; the transmission should be smooth, and the brakes capable of bringing the car to a stop evenly and responsively. Should a car have been stored for any considerable length of time, it would be advisable to have the braking system overhauled, as it's possible this could have degenerated from lack of use.

Despite the foregoing problems, SZ cars - even the earliest examples - are generally most reliable and a car in good overall condition can normally be expected to provide long and satisfactory service. It is not uncommon for series l cars (those vehicles built prior to the 1990 model year) to be offered for sale with no more than 40,000 or 50,000 miles recorded, in prime condition and with full service histories, and, as such, represent excellent value for money.

Many of the usually minor problems associated with the early cars were effectively remedied by the time the series ll cars were introduced for the 1990 model year. Their modified handling and active ride made for a much improved motor car and relatively few problems are associated with these, or later, models. They do, of course, have their idiosyncrasies, especially the memory system on the active ride suspension. Occasionally, a fault can be recorded on the facia warning panel and, whilst most owners would be concerned that a malfunction exists, and would be reluctant to drive a car with an apparent defect, the remedy often entails nothing more than having the memory device re-set, a comparatively easy and straightforward task for a specialist.

Prospective owners should be conversant with active ride technology; the system is fed by micro-processors which monitor acceleration and braking whilst another device monitors the speed at which the steering wheel is turned, thus changing the suspension mode from 'normal' to 'sports'. Rolls-Royce cars will usually remain in 'normal' mode, depending upon driving conditions, but Bentleys are set up to switch to sports mode in accordance with performance requirements.

As previously explained, early Mulsanne Turbos should be regarded with caution. Although many of the cars offered for sale might appear attractive, some may have had years of high performance driving combined with negligible maintenance. Such cars will undoubtedly be inexpensive to purchase. Early Turbos were fitted with a Solex carburettor and it can be time-consuming to set up the carburation system for optimum running. It is not unknown for carburettor faces to become distorted, especially with the very high under-bonnet temperatures associated with these cars, and often the only course is to fit an entire replacement. Later cars are fuel injected and can be a more satisfactory investment.

Check on early Turbo cars for

Bentley Mulsanne Turbos are sought-after vehicles, the Turbo R in particular. Sir Elton John once owned this particular car. (Author's collection)

Mulsanne Turbos were often criticised for their 'soft' suspension, a shortcoming remedied with the introduction of the Turbo R. However attractive a proposition a Mulsanne Turbo may seem, take care to have the car thoroughly surveyed as these vehicles were mostly used to their full potential! In this picture, dealers' representatives are enjoying the 'Turbo Experience' for themselves at Donington Park in the spring of 1982, with Ernie Bates and Graham Gibson on the right. (Courtesy Rolls-Royce Motor Cars Limited)

early models. By the middle to late nineties, development of the SZ range had reached its zenith; cars such as the New Silver Spirit and Silver Spur, together with the Silver Dawn, enjoy outstanding levels of performance combined with highly sophisticated technology matched by exquisite comfort. The same applies to Bentley which, having diverged from the Rolls-Royce marque, offered scintillating performance. The Brooklands, Brooklands R and Turbo RT exemplify the SZ series of cars at their best, and are destined to be much sought-after.

As a brief guide the following checklist may be helpful to potential owners when viewing a car, and the author is grateful to Richard Mann for this contribution.

Engine: compartment should be clean with all original equipment in place; check hoses for any signs of leaks, and worn drive belts that indicate wear. Engine oil should be clean. Ensure all fluid levels are correct. The engine should start readily but do listen for tappet and hydraulic pump noise, and look for exhaust smoke with gentle use of the accelerator. Ensure the exhaust system is sound. Make sure air conditioning and all instruments are working properly.

Chassis: tyres should be to original specification and check they are not worn or mixed or that wheels have damaged rims. Steering rack gaiters should not leak. Look for corrosion, especially at the rear under the boot floor; give the underbody a thorough

When buying a Silver Spirit, Silver Spur or Bentley, a relatively brief appraisal of the car's condition can be made quite simply by checking fluid levels, tyre wear, general cleanliness and signs of sympathetic ownership. A specialist will provide a full survey (for a fee) which will confirm whether or not the vehicle is a viable proposition. (Author's collection)

gearbox problems. The input shaft has a habit of failing, which could mean a replacement torque converter and full transmission rebuild. Later, fuel injected cars can, occasionally, suffer from a whine from the differential which might require further investigation.

All Bentley Turbos are capable of exhilarating performance, which will result in high running costs, especially when a car may return only 10-12 miles per gallon. Later cars have much improved handling and firmer suspension, both of which were lacking on the

repainting to be investigated; coach-work, door shuts, boot and bonnet gutters should all be clean; check all brightwork - mouldings and wheeltrim are stainless, badges are chromium-plated over enamelled brass. Radiator shells should be in good condition (Rolls-Royce radiator shells are stainless steel and Bentleys have chromium-plated steel).

Practical ownership and enthusiasts' clubs

There exists a worldwide industry which caters for Rolls-Royce and Bentley owners, through which it's possible to acquire even the most obscure component. Also, as far as specialist services are concerned, help is always at hand. As well as companies and individuals offering sales, servicing and restoration facilities, the recognised enthusiasts' club has much to offer.

Many owners feel a need to meet up with fellow enthusiasts, and in the United Kingdom both the Rolls-Royce Enthusiasts' Club (R-REC) and the Bentley Drivers Club (BDC) serve in this respect. Both organisations attract enthusiasts from around the world, and visiting overseas members are welcomed at their headquarters and club events. As well as publishing informative journals, both organisations arrange events on an international, regional and model basis. Membership can provide all sorts of rewards, not least of which is friendly advice about getting the most enjoyment from your car. The R-REC, which invites membership from both Rolls-

check: it should be undamaged with the underseal intact. The battery should be the correct type and the small tool kit complete, along with wheel changing equipment.

Interior: should be clean, well presented and undamaged; seats, door trim, headlining, carpets and over-rugs should all be in good condition. Woodwork lacquer to be in good order with no lifting or damage to the veneers; windows and seats should operate correctly.

Exterior: damage, repairs or poor

SZ Rolls-Royces and Bentleys are distinctive cars; to get full enjoyment from them many owners decide that membership of one or more of the enthusiasts' clubs is essential. Owning a car such as this is a unique experience. (Author's collection)

Royce and Bentley owners, arranges practical seminars which offer 'hands-on' experience to those members keen to further their practical knowledge. The BDC, which caters exclusively for the Bentley driver, offers members a spares scheme relative to their car, or cars, and, through club specialists, there is always technical advice and information available.

In addition to both clubs having dedicated headquarters which house various marque artifacts, the R-REC has safekeeping of all Rolls-Royce vehicle records and build histories, including post-1931 Bentleys. The BDC retains the records of all pre-1931 Bentleys. Both organisations are able to provide owners with details of their cars. In addition to the R-REC and BDC, other enthusiasts' clubs exist around the world, details of which appear in the appendices.

And finally ...
Ownership of one of these fine cars should be a rewarding experience: exquisite comfort and superlative quality and engineering, not to mention the friendship of fellow enthusiasts. Take as much care over purchasing your car as driving it, treat it to regular and proper maintenance, and it will provide effortless motoring for many thousands of miles.

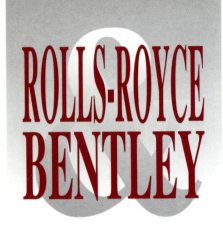

APPENDIX

Original specifications
Silver Spirit, Silver Spur, Bentley Mulsanne & Mulsanne S and Bentley Eight

Brakes
The system comprises two independent power braking hydraulic circuits and a mechanically operated parking brake. Each hydraulic circuit operates a twin piston caliper assembly on each front wheel and a pair of pistons - housed in a four piston caliper assembly - on each rear wheel. 11 inch disc brakes on all four wheels. Warning lamps on facia advise of failure in either of the hydraulic circuits, low level of mineral oil and application of parking brake.

Capacities
Brake and height control hydraulic systems: 4 litres/7pt.Imp/8.4pt.US
Cooling system: 15.9 litres/28pt.Imp/33.6pt.US
Engine oil inc. filter: 9.4 litres/16.5pt.Imp/19.8pt.US
Engine oil exc.filter: 8.4 litres/14.8pt.Imp/17.7pt.US
Final drive unit: 2.6 litres/4.5pt.Imp/5.4pt.US
Fuel tank: 108 litres/23.75gal.Imp/28.5gal.US
Steering system: 0.75 litre/1.33pt.Imp/1.66pt.US
Transmission: 10.6 litres/18.7pt.Imp/22.5pt.US. *(sump):* 2.8 litres/5.0pt.Imp/6.0pt.US
Windscreen & headlamp washer reservoir: 5.0 litres/8.8pt.Imp/10.5pt.US

Dimensions
Length:
    Rolls-Royce: 207.42in (5268mm)
    Bentley: 209.01in (5309mm)
North American spec:
    Rolls-Royce: 207.75in (5277mm)
    Bentley: 209.17in (5313mm)
Width, excluding door mirrors: 74.29in (1887mm), *including door mirrors:* 79.05in (2008mm)
Height: 58.46in (1485mm)
Wheelbase: 120.50in (3061mm)
Track, front & rear: 60.50in (1537mm)
Turning circle - max:
    Rolls-Royce: 38.29ft (11.67m)
    Bentley: 38.42ft (11.71m)
Ground clearance: 6.50in (165.1mm)
Kerb weight: 4950lbs (2245kg)
    Australian spec. cars: 4960lbs (2250kg)
    Japanese spec. cars: 4866lbs (2208kg)
    North American spec.cars: 4980lbs (2259kg)

Silver Spur & Bentley LWB
Length:
    Rolls-Royce: 211.42in (5370mm)
    Bentley: 213.01in (5411mm)
North American spec:
    Rolls-Royce: 211.78in (5379mm)
    Bentley: 213.17in (5414mm)
Turning circle - max:
    Rolls-Royce: 39.50ft (12.05m)
    Bentley: 39.67ft (12.09m)

Kerb weight: 5010lbs (2273kg)
   Australian spec. cars: 5020lbs (2277kg)
   Japanese spec. cars: 4975lbs (2257kg)
   North American spec. cars: 5040lbs (2286kg)

Electrical system
12 volt DC, 68A/h or 71 A/h battery with master switch located in luggage compartment. Alternator, 75 A at 14V, negative earth.

Engine
90 degree V formation, eight cylinders in two banks of four. Bore 4.10in (104.14mm). Stroke 3.90in (99.06mm). Cubic capacity 6.75 litres. Compression ratio 9.0:1 except for Australian, Japanese and North American markets, 8.0:1.

Engine cooling system
Coolant comprises 50 per cent anti-freeze, 50 per cent water circulated by a centrifugal pump and pressurised at approx. 15lbf/in². Thermostatically controlled; facia indicator to warn of low coolant level.

Fuel system
Two SU HIF 7 carburetters with automatic choke control; Japanese and North American cars fitted with Bosch K-Jetronic fuel injection. Fuel consumption 12mpg (23.6 litres/100km) urban driving; constant speed of 56mph, 18.1mpg (15.6 litres/100km) and constant speed of 75mph, 16.1mpg (17.5 litres/100km).

Ignition system
Sparking plugs, Champion RN14Y

Power-assisted steering
3.25 turns of steering wheel lock-to-lock;

Propeller shaft
Single straight tube with a universal joint at the front and rear.

Suspension
The front suspension is mounted on the front sub frame; independent coil spring arrangement with lower wishbones, compliant controlled upper levers, telescopic dampers, anti-roll bar and anti-dive characteristics. Rear suspension has independent coil springs with semi-trailing arms, suspension struts, gas springs and anti-roll bar; trailing arms pivot on rear suspension crossmember. Gas springs operate in conjunction with the suspension struts which act as integral dampers and height control rams. Damping and automatic height control achieved via struts supplied with pressurised mineral oil from hydraulic accumulators through a sensing valve. Bentley Eight has firmer suspension.

Transmission
Gear ratios: 1st: 7.70:1; 2nd: 4.62:1; 3rd: 3.08:1; reverse: 6.16:1. Final drive ratio: 3.08:1, top gear speed per 1000rev/min: 26.3mph.

Wheels and tyres
Pressed steel wheels with flat ledge rims, 6JK x 15; 5 stud wheel fixing. Avon 235/70 HR15 steel braced radial ply or Michelin XVS 235/70 HR15 steel braced, radial ply tyres. Cars for Kuwait, South Africa and North America fitted with Michelin XVS 235/70 HR15 steel braced and radial ply tyres.

Variations

Bentley Mulsanne Turbo
Engine
90 degree V formation, eight cylinders in two banks of four. Bore 4.10in (104.14mm). Stroke 3.90in (99.06mm), Cubic capacity 6.75 litres. Compression ratio 9.0:1. The engine is fitted with an exhaust driven turbocharger which, at large throttle openings, delivers compressed air to the carburetter inlet. The boost pressure generated is limited by a wastegate in the exhaust system, which allows excess exhaust gases to bypass the turbine at a predetermined level. At small throttle openings the output of the turbocharger compressor section is discharged through an air duct valve, and the carburetter operates at atmospheric pressure. Exhaust system has single downtake pipe leading to a twin pipe system with twin intermediate silencers and a dual rear silencer.

Engine cooling system

Coolant comprises 50 per cent anti-freeze, 50 per cent water circulated by a centrifugal pump and pressurised at approx. 15lbf/in^2. Thermostatically controlled; facia indicator to warn of low coolant level. Additional electrically operated booster fan fitted, mounted behind the radiator; engine overheat warning on facia with warning buzzer should cylinder head metal approach critical temperature.

Fuel system

Solex 4A1 carburetters mounted in air chest with automatic choke control; Japanese and North American cars fitted with Bosch K-Jetronic fuel injection. Fuel consumption 11.4mpg (24.8 litres/100km) urban driving; constant speed of 56mph, 21mpg (13.5 litres/100km) and constant speed of 75mph, 16.3mpg (17.3 litres/100km).

Wheels and tyres

Pressed steel wheels with flat ledge rims, 6JK x 15; 5 stud wheel fixing. Avon 235/70 VR15 steel braced radial ply or Michelin XVS 235/70 VR15 steel braced, radial ply tyres. Cars for Kuwait, South Africa and North America fitted with Michelin XVS 235/70 HR15 steel braced and radial ply tyres.

Bentley Turbo R
Capacities

Engine oil capacity, with filter: 9.9 litres (17.4 pt)
Hydraulic systems: 5 litres (8.8pt)

Fuel system

Solex 4A1 carburetters mounted in air chest with automatic choke control; Japanese and North American cars fitted with Bosch K-Jetronic fuel injection. Fuel consumption 11.4mpg (24.8 litres/100km) urban driving; constant speed of 56mph, 21mpg (13.5 litres/100km) and constant speed of 75mph, 16.3mpg (17.3 litres/100km).

Wheels and tyres

Pressed steel wheels with flat ledge rims, 7J x 15AH2ET41; 5 stud wheel fixing. 275/55VR15 tyres.

Silver Spirit ll and Silver Spur ll
Brakes

The system comprises two independent power braking hydraulic circuits incorporating an anti-lock system (ABS), and a mechanically operated parking brake. One hydraulic circuit operates two twin piston caliper assemblies on each front brake disc. The other circuit operates a four piston caliper assembly on each rear brake disc, and also operates the hydraulic levelling system. A pad wear sensor, linked to a warning panel on the facia, is fitted to each leading front brake caliper assembly. Application of the parking brake applies a pair of brake pads attached to the hydraulic caliper onto each rear brake disc.

Capacities

Brake and height control hydraulic systems: 5 litres/8.8pt.Imp/10.5pt.US
Final drive unit: 2.3 litres/4.0pt.Imp/4.8pt.US
Steering system: 0.87 litre/1.53pt.Imp/1.84pt.US
Windscreen & headlamp washer reservoir: 10 litres/17.6pt.Imp/21pt.US

Dimensions

Kerb weight: 5180lbs (2350kg)
Turning circle (max): 42.5ft (12.95m)

Silver Spur ll

Turning circle - max: 44ft (13.40m)
Kerb weight: 5240lbs (2380kg)

Fuel system

Bosch K-Motronic digital fuel injection. Fuel consumption 24.6mpg (11.6 litres/100km) urban driving; constant speed of 56mph, 21.6mpg (13.1 litres/100km) and constant speed of 75mph, 17.6mpg (16.1 litres/100km). Vehicles with catalytic converters: 11.1mpg (25.4 litres/100km), 20.3mpg (13.9 litres/100km and 17.2mpg (16.4 litres/100km) respectively.

Ignition system

Sparking plugs: NGK BPR 4 EVX

Propeller shaft
Single straight tube with rubber jointed couplings at the front and rear.

Suspension
The front suspension is mounted on the front sub frame; independent coil spring arrangement with lower wishbones, compliant controlled upper levers, telescopic dampers incorporating automatic variable ride control, and anti-roll bar mounted on the front sub-frame. Rear suspension has independent coil springs with semi-trailing arms, suspension struts, gas springs and anti-roll bar. The suspension struts, used in conjunction with the gas springs, act as integral dampers and height control rams and also incorporate automatic variable ride control. Damping and automatic height control achieved via struts supplied with pressurised mineral oil from hydraulic accumulators through a sensing valve.

Transmission
Gear ratios: 1st: 6.73:1; 2nd: 4.04:1; 3rd: 2.69:1; reverse: 5.38:1. Final drive ratio: 2.69:1, top gear speed per 1000rev/min: 30mph.

Wheels and tyres
Pressed steel wheels with flat ledge rims, 6^1/$_2$J x 15; 5 stud wheel fixing. Avon Turbosteel 235/70 R15 101V or Goodyear NCT 235/70 R15 103 101V. North American spec cars: Goodyear NCT 70 235/70 R15 103H

Bentley Eight, Mulsanne S and Turbo R, 1990 model year
Dimensions
Kerb weight: 5120lbs (2320kg), 5050lbs (2290kg) (N. America) Eight & Mulsanne S; 5270lbs (2390kg) Turbo R, all markets. Turning circle (max): 42.8ft (13.1m)

Fuel system
Fuel injection, naturally aspirated engines, K-Jetronic, turbocharged engines, KE3-Jetronic

Wheels and tyres
R15 235/70, 255/65 (Turbo R)

Silver Spirit lll, Silver Spur lll
Brakes
Ventilated discs on front brakes

Capacities
Brake and height control hydraulic systems: 5 litres/8.8pt.Imp /10.5pt.US
Final drive unit: 2.3 litres/4.0pt.Imp/4.8pt.US
Steering system: 0.87 litre/1.53pt.Imp/1.84pt.US
Windscreen & headlamp washer reservoir: 10 litres/17.6pt.Imp/21pt.US

Dimensions
Kerb weight: 5360lbs (2430kg); Silver Spur lll: 5440lbs (2470kg)

Fuel system (engine management system)
Bosch M3.3 Motronic digital fuel injection and ignition control system. Fuel consumption: 24.3mpg (11.6 litres/100km) at 56mph and at 75mph, 19.3mpg (14.7 litres/100km).

Transmission
Automatic 4-speed torque converter (electronically controlled) with electric gear range selector

Bentley Brooklands, Turbo R, Turbo RL(LWB)
Dimensions
Kerb weight: Brooklands 5360lbs (2430kg); Turbo R 5400lbs (2450kg); Turbo RL 5440lbs (2470kg)

Wheels and tyres
Turbo R & RL have 7^1/$_2$J x 16 wheels with 255/60 WR16 tyres

Silver Spirit, Silver Dawn, Silver Spur; Bentley Brooklands, Turbo R, Brooklands LWB & TurboRL (1996 model year)
Radiator shell height reduced by 2in; integrated bumper and air dam design; integrated rear bumper design; new exterior mirrors, no quarterlights.

Production figures

Rolls-Royce models

Model	Years	Production
Silver Spirit	1980-1989	8129
Silver Spur	1980-1989	6238
Silver Spirit ll	1989-1994	1152
Silver Spur ll	1989-1994	1658
Silver Spirit lll	1994-1996	211
Silver Spur lll	1994-1996	430
Silver Dawn (LWB)	1994-1998	237
Flying Spur (LWB)	1993-1995	134
Silver Spur	1996-1998	361

Total Rolls-Royce models — **18550**

Total of all SZ 4-door models — **30460**

Bentley models

Model	Years	Production
Mulsanne	1980-1987	531 (49LWB)
Mulsanne Turbo	1982-1985	519 (24LWB)
Eight	1984-1992	1734
Turbo R	1985-1998	6165 (1508LWB)
Mulsanne S	1987-1992	966 (61LWB)
Brooklands	1992-1998	1619 (190LWB)
Turbo S	1994-1996	60
Brooklands R	1997-1998	100
Turbo RT (LWB)	1997-1998	216

Total Bentley models — **11910**

At-a-glance chronology

1980
Silver Spirit, Silver Spur, Mulsanne introduced

1982
Debut of Mulsanne Turbo

1984
Eight, designed as 'market entry model', introduced

1985
Turbo R announced in March. Minor improvements to other models include high-pressure headlamp washer jets and revised facia. Rolls-Royce build the 1000,000th motor car.

1986
Model year cars incorporate several major modifications, including revised suspension and engine cooling. Turbo R wins for Rolls-Royce the national one-hour endurance record. Fuel injection fitted to Australian market cars.

1987
Fuel injection standard for all markets. Mulsanne S introduced.

1989
Model year Bentleys fitted with paired 7 inch round headlamps. Deeper front air dam on Turbo R. Revised air dam for Silver Spirit and Silver Spur models.

1990
Series ll designation given to Rolls-Royce models; Bentleys receive similar modifications but without appellation

1992
Bentley Brooklands introduced for 1993 model year

1993
Silver Spirit lll and Silver Spur lll introduced for 1994 model year. More powerful Bentley models.

1994
Rolls-Royce Flying Spur announced. Bentley Turbo S introduced for 1995 model year. Silver Dawn introduced.

1996
Extensive changes announced in 1995 for 1996 model year. Radiator shell height reduced; integrated front bumper and air dam design, integrated rear bumper.

1997
Model year cars have Light Pressure Turbo engines fitted to Silver Spur and Brooklands; 1998 model year cars announced, Bentley Brooklands R and Bentley Turbo RT.

1998
Production of all SZ four-door cars ceases.

Dimensions
Turning circle Silver Spirit, Brooklands, Turbo R: 39.5ft (12.05m); Silver Dawn, Silver Spur, Brooklands LWB, Turbo RL: 41ft (12.5m)

Engine
Compression ratio 8.7:1, naturally aspirated engines, 8.0:1 turbocharged. Liquid cooled intercooler replaces air-to-air unit on turbocharged engines. New Zytek electronic engine management system for North American cars and all turbocharged models.

Fuel system
Fuel consumption 12mpg (23.6 litres/100km) urban driving; constant speed of 56mph, 18.1mpg (15.6 litres/100km) and constant speed of 75mph, 16.1mpg (17.5 litres/100km).

Transmission
Automatic traction control through viscous control differential available. Adaptive shift control. Gear ratios: 1st: 2.48:1; 2nd:1.48:1; 3rd: 1.00:1; top: 0.75:1; reverse: 2.08:1. Final drive ratio: 2.69:1; top gear speed per 1000 rev/min: 40mph.

Wheels and tyres
Wheel diameter: turbocharged Bentley models 17in; all other models 16in. Rim width: turbocharged Bentley models 7.5in, all other models 7.0in.
Tyres: All Rolls-Royce models Avon Turbosteel 70 235/65 VR15 or Goodyear Eagle GA235/65 VR16; Bentley Brooklands and Brooklands LWB Goodyear Eagle GA235/65 VR16; Bentley Turbo R,RL, Avon RR Turbospeed CR27 255/55 ZR17. Whitewall tyres standard on all Rolls-Royces, optional on Brooklands and Brooklands LWB.

Silver Spirit, Silver Dawn, Silver Spur; Bentley Brooklands, Turbo R, Brooklands LWB & Turbo RL (1997 model year)
Engine
Light Pressure Turbo (LPT) engine fitted to Silver Spur and Bentley Brooklands. Max. power: 300bhp @ 4000rpm; compression ratio: 8.0:1; electronically controlled wastegate for boost pressure control; Zytek electronic management system. Transient boost system.

Transmission
Electronic Traction Assistance System (ETAS) fitted to the 385bhp turbocharged and intercooled Bentley Turbo R; viscous control differential standard. ETAS optional on Brooklands models.

Bentley Brooklands R & Bentley Turbo RT (1998 model year)
Brooklands models fitted with 'R' roadholding package; 17in wheels and low-profile tyres fitted. Bentley Turbo RT fitted with 400bhp engine developed for Continental T

Clubs and specialists

Clubs
Rolls-Royce Enthusiasts' Club
The Hunt House
Paulerspury
Towcester
Northants NN12 7NA
England
Tel 01327 811788, fax 01327 811797
The R-REC caters for members throughout the world. 19 organised sections exist in the UK and 16 in European countries and Canada. Members receive *The Bulletin*, the club newsletter, six times a year together with a monthly *Advertiser*. The club was formed in 1957 and houses at its headquarters the entire Rolls-Royce and Bentley cars histories. Current membership is over 9000.

Rolls-Royce Owners' Club of Australia
Kim Stapleton
PO Box 1578 Crows Nest
NSW 2065

Australia
Tel 02 9398 6949
Formed in 1956, there are six sections throughout Australia. Its magazine, *Praeclarum*, is published six times a year.

Rolls-Royce Club of New Zealand
Tom Williams
78 Kesteven Avenue
Glendowie
Auckland
New Zealand
The New Zealand club has three sections; meetings are arranged on a regional basis. Magazine published six times a year.

Rolls-Royce Owners' Club of America
Headquarters: 191 Hempt Road
Mechanicsburg PA 17055
USA
Tel 001 717 697 4671
The oldest Rolls-Royce Owners' Club in the

world, this club was formed in 1951. There are 33 regions throughout the USA and Canada and members receive the journal *Flying Lady* six times a year.

Bentley Drivers Club
W.O.Bentley Memorial Building
16 Chearsley Road
Long Crendon
Aylesbury
Bucks HP18 9AW
England
Tel 01844 208233
The BDC has eight regions in the United Kingdom and another 30-40 sections around the world. A quarterly magazine, the *Bentley Drivers Club Review*, is supplemented by a bi-monthly *Advertiser* and a monthly newsletter. The club currently has around 4000 members.

Specialists
Rolls-Royce & Bentley Motor Cars Limited
Pym's Lane
Crewe
Cheshire CW1 3PL
England
Tel 01270 255155

Rolls-Royce Motor Cars Limited
London Service Centre
England.
Tel 0181 965 7355

In addition to official Rolls-Royce and Bentley dealers (check local details or contact Rolls-Royce & Bentley Motors Cars Limited), the following companies provide specialist service:

United Kingdom
P & A Wood
Great Easton
Dunmow
Essex CM6 2HD
Tel 01371 870848, fax 01371 870810
Sales, service & restoration

Broughtons
Armstrong Way
Willenhall
West Midlands WV13 2QU

Tel 0121 477 5557, fax 0121 476 8600
Sales, service, parts supply, restoration

R R & B Garages
Shaw Lane
Stoke Prior
Bromsgrove
Worcs. B60 4DT
Tel & fax 01527 876513
Sales, service & restoration

Beare Essentials
16 Sussex Road
New Malden
Surrey KT3 3PY
Tel 01306 631962, mobile 0802 964393
Parts

Bowling Ryan
Unit 5 Fishbrook Industrial Estate
Stoneclough Road
Bolton
Lancs BL4 8EL
Tel 01204 700300
Service, restoration & sales

Frank Dale & Stepsons
125 Harlequin Avenue
Great West Road (A4)
Isleworth
West London TW8 9EW
Tel 020 8847 5447, fax 020 8560 5748
Offices in Germany (tel 49 211 404202, fax 49 211 407764), France (tel 33 553 40 3000, fax 33 553 40 2420), Japan (tel 0081 338 116 170, or via London office, 0171 937 7432, fax 0171 937 4828) Sales, servicing & restoration

S.C. Gordon
10 Cosgrove Way
Luton LU1 1XA
Tel 01582 736633, fax 01582 424202
Restoration, pre-purchase inspections, coachwork

Stantons
61b Pembury Road
Tonbridge
Kent TN9 2JF
Tel 01732 358575
Transmissions

Dennis Pilling &Sons
Old Mason's Yard
419 Manchester Road
Leigh
Lancs WN7 2ND
Tel 01942 607426
Service & repairs, restoration, coachwork

Prescote Motor Carriages
Mill House
Mill Road
Totton
Hants SO40 3ZQ
Tel 01703 666682, fax 01703 666882
Restoration and servicing

Royce Servicing & Engineering
40 The Street
Ashstead
Surrey KT21 2AH
Tel 01372 276546, fax 01372 277704
Sales & service, restoration

Dyer's
Unit 2 Beechwood Clump Farm Industrial Estate,
Tin Pot Lane
Blandford Forum
Dorset DT11 7TD
Tel 01258 455922, fax 01258 480071

D.E.W. Car Services (Oxford)
Unit 5 Fraser Properties
Oakfield Industrial Estate
Eynsham
Oxon OX8 1JN
Tel 01865 882789, fax 01789 883209
Sales, service, repairs

Jack Barclay Limited
18 Berkeley Square
London W1X 6AE
tel 0171 629 7444, fax 0171 629 8258
Sales. Service department situated at 2-4
Ponton Road
Nine Elms
London SW8 5BA
Tel 0171 738 8880, fax 0171 738 8887
Parts hotline: 0171 738 8333, fax 0171 738 8099

Harvey Bailey Engineering (HBE)
Ladycroft Farm
Ashbourne
Derbys DE6 1JH
Tel 01335 346419, fax 01335 346440

Handling systems
Healey Brothers
Irthlingborough
Northants NN9 5RG
Tel 01933 650247, fax 01933 650002
Restoration & parts

Brunt's of Silverdale Ltd
Stonewall Silverdale
Newcastle
Staffordshire ST5 6NR
Tel 01782 625225, fax 01782 717530,
0802 253927 after 9pm
Service, restoration

Servicentre Systems
Somersham Road
St Ives
Cambs PE17 4LY
also in London
24 The Arches
Iverson Road
NW6 2HE
Tel (Cambridge) 01480 463104 (London)
0171 624 5280

Exhaust systems
Ron Stratton & Company Ltd
5 Wolfe Close
Parkgate
Knutsford WA16 8XJ
Greater Manchester
Tel 01565 63222, fax 01565 621144
Sales, service

A & S Engineering
Unit 1 Weyside Park
Newman Lane
Alton
Hants GU34 2PJ
Tel 01420 541257, fax 01420 542122
Mechanical restoration & servicing

Phantom Motor Cars
Pankridge Street

Crondall
Farnham
Surrey GU10 5QT
Tel 01252 850231, fax 01252 850516
Service, restoration, tuning etc

Overton Vehicles
139 The Broadway
Leigh-on-Sea
Essex SS9 1JX
Tel 01702 719489
Sales

Murray Motor Company
Sighthill
Edinburgh
Tel 0131 442 2800
Sales & service

The Chelsea Workshop
Nell Gwynn House
Draycott Avenue
Chelsea
London SW3 3AU
Tel 0171 584 8363/4, fax 0171 581 3033
Sales, service, restoration

Kingsmill Workshop
Unit 7 Maun Valley Industrial Park
Station Road
Sutton-in-Ashfield
Notts NG17 5HS
Tel 01623 651055
Sales, service & restoration

Silver Lady Sales
64-70 Alma Road
Bournemouth
BH9 1AN
Tel 01202 388488
Sales

Douglas Daniels
Church Walk
Bletchingly
Surrey
Tel 01883 743380
Sales, spares

Classic Restorations
Pitnacree Street

Aylth
Perthshire
Tel 01828 633293, fax 01828 632529; 0161
881 6243
Restoration, coachwork

The Real Car Company
Snowdonia Business Park, Coed y Parc
Bethesda
Gwynedd LL57 4YS
Tel 01248 602649, fax 01248 600994
Sales, parts

Flying Spares
Brascote Lane
Cadeby
Warks CV13)BB
Tel 01455 292949, fax 01455 292959
Parts

Hofmann's/Henley
Fairfield Works
Reading Road
Henley-on-Thames Oxon
Tel 01491 573953, fax 01491 573647
Sales, high ratio axle gears

Hanwell Car Centre
Uxbridge Road Hanwell
London W7
Tel 0181 567 6557/9729, fax 0181 579 5386
Sales

Hillier Hill
Unit 14 Stilebrook Road
Yardley Road Industrial Estate
Olney
Bucks MK46 5EA
Tel & fax 01234 713871
Service & restoration

Introcar Limited
1 Manorgate Road
Kingston
Surrey KT2 7AW
Tel 0181 546 2027, fax 0181 546 5058
Parts

Clive Waddingham
199 Wollaston Road
Irchester

Northants NN29 7DG
Tel & fax 01933 350893
Interior restoration

R.W. Cooper
Crewe
Cheshire
Tel 01270 665283
Interior restorations

Rob Jones
Benver Services
Unit 9 Quaker Coppice Crewe Gates
Industrial Estate
Crewe
Cheshire CW1 6FA
Tel 01270 250236
Servicing & restoration

Colbrook
24 High Street
Stilton
Cambs
Tel 01733 243737, fax 01733 243738
Sales, service, restoration, parts

Ristes
Motor Company Limited
Gamble St
Nottingham
Tel 0115 978 5834, fax 0115 942 4351
Parts, engineering

Peter Jarvis
Gildenhill Place
GIldenhill Road
Swanley
Kent BR8 7PD
Tel 01322 669081, fax 01322 662490
Sales, servicing, storage, transmissions

Brian A. Thompson
119 Station Road
Warboys
Huntingdon Cambs
PE17 2TH
Tel & fax 01487 822488
Parts

John Fletcher
Tel 01395 446000, fax 0171 691 9789

Sales

David Haines & Sons
Unit 17 Riverside Business Park
Lyon Road
Merton
London SW19 2RL
Tel 0181 544 1884
Service & restorations

Silver Lady Motor Services Ltd
Hainault Works
Hainault Road
Little Heath
Romford
Essex RM6 5SS
Tel 0181 599 8548/4905, fax 0181 599 8041
Service, restoration, sales

Taylor's
Sidlesham Lane
Birdham
Chichester Sussex PO20 7QL
Tel 01243 513222
Sales, service, restoration

Scotts
59 Staunton Ave
Hayling Island
Tel 01705 466592, fax 01705 461154
Hants PO11 0EW
Service

Michael Hibberd
Unit 31
Middle Green Trading Estate
Langley Slough
Berks SL3 6DF
Tel 01753 531631
Service, restoration & sales

Hooper Alpe Limited
50 Marylebone High St
London W1 3AD
Tel 0171 935 1124, fax 0171 486 1488
Sales & service

Creech Coachtrimming Centre
45 Anerley Road
London SE19 2AS
Tel 0181 659 4135

Coachtrimming

Brian Bilton-Sanderson F.I.M.I.
Maidenhead
Berks
Tel 01628 674674
Vehicle inspections

Derby Plating
148 Abbey Street
Derby
Tel 01332 383408
Plating specialists

David Beswick Coachtrimming
18 Robinsons Lane Industrial Estate
Derby DE23 8NL
Tel 01332 343252
Coachtrimming

Gary Bretherton
Unit J Grove Mill
Eccleston
Chorley
Lancs PR6 9RS
Tel 01257 453 531
Servicing

P J Fischer Classic Automobiles
Northumberland Garage
Dyers Lane
Upper Richmond Road
London SW15
Tel 0181 785 6633, fax 0181 785 6926
Sales

Ivor Bleaney of the New Forest
PO Box 60 Salisbury
Wilts SP5 2DH
Tel 01794 390895, fax 01794 390862
Sales

Alan Dyson Restorations
Honey Farm
Preston Crowmarsh
Wallingford
Oxon OX10 6SL
Tel 0141834818
Restoration

Hightone Restorations Ltd

Unit 5 Enstone Airfield Enstone
Oxon OX7 4NP
Tel 01608 677328
Restoration

Auto Interiors
56 Norfolk Street
Liverpool L1 0BE
Tel 0151 708 8881
Car interiors

G. Whitehouse Autos Ltd
Haden Hill Road
Halesowen
West Midlands B63 3NE
Tel 0121 550 7630, fax 0121 585 6408
Transmission systems

A. J. Hickman
85 Worthington Road
Fradley
Lichfield
Staffs
Tel 01534 252196
Woodwork restoration

Checkmate
Rowney Green
Alvechurch
Worcs
Tel 01527 597555
Vehicle inspections

Woodwork Restoration
Unit 21b Wembley Commercial Centre
East Lane
Wembley HA9 7UR
Tel 0181 908 4438
Concours restoration of woodtrim

Derek E Eames
Vehicle valeting Tel 0800 917 8504

Auto Interiors
Unit 1 Sandow Crescent
Hayes
Middlesex UB3 4QH
Tel 0181 756 1086, fax 0181 561 5311

Leonard Reece & Co Ltd
Clifton Road

Huntingdon
Cambs PE18 7EJ
Tel 01480 451976, fax 01480 453009
Camshafts, valves etc

Shadow Motorcars
The Crest Complex
Courtenay Road
Gillingham
Kent ME8 0RX
Tel 01634 264425 (day) 01795 842932 (eve)
Service, repairs

Europe
Caroline de Jonathan
Rue Libeau 36
B-4682 Houtain Saint Siméon
Belgium
Tel 0032 41 86 48 53/0032 41 86 48 54,
fax 0032 41 86 48 56
Restoration & conversions

Garage De Vaal
Heulweg 78
2295 KH Kwintsheul
The Netherlands
Tel 0031 174 510022/ 297545, fax 0031 174
298175
Sales, service & restoration

Best of British
Hobbemaweg 90
6562 CV Groesbeek
The Netherlands
Tel 0024 3977391, fax 0024 3977244
Sales

Sauzeau Automobiles
Z.I. Quest
6 Rue des Frères Lumière
91160 Longjumeau
France
Tel 0033 1 69348988, fax 0033 1 69348530
New and used parts

Peter Grossegger
A-5020 Salzburg
Elisabethstrasse 36
Austria
Tel 0043 662 453 777, fax 0043 662 451 117
Restoration

USA
Max of Switzerland
6913 East McDowell Rd
Scottsdale
85257 Arizona
Tel 001 602 945 4545
Sales & service

Matthews Motor Co
4901 North Oracle Rd
PO Box 27878 Tuscan
Arizona
Tel 001 602 888 7900
Sales & service

Rolls-Royce of Beverley Hills Ltd
9018 Wilshire Boulevard
Beverley Hills
California
Tel 001 213 659 4050
Sales & service

Peter Satori Co Ltd
285-325 West Colorado Boulevard
Pasadena
91105 California
Tel 001 213 681 8123

British Motor Car Distributors Ltd
901 Van Ness Ave
San Francisco
94109 California
Tel 001 415 776 7700
Sales & service

Imported Cars of Greenwich Inc
217 West Putnam Avenue
Greenwich
06830 Connecticut
Tel 001 203 869 2850
Sales & service

Lauderdale Motor Car Corp
407 North Federal Highway
Fort Lauderdale
33301 Florida
Tel 001 305 764 5881
Sales & service

Val Ward Imports Inc
8700 Tamiiami Trail

Fort Myers
33907 Florida
Tel 001 813 939 4616
Sales & service

Gregg Motor Cars Inc
10231 Atantic Boulevard
Jacksonville
32211 Florida
Tel 001 904 724 1080
Sales & service

Braman Motors Inc
2020 Biscayne Boulevard
Miami
33137 Florida
Tel 001 305 6900
Sales & service

Scarritt Motors Inc
555 34th St S
St Petersburg
33711 Florida
Tel 001 813 327 3700
Sales & service

Royal Motorcar Corp
1314 South Dixie Highway
West Palm Beach
33401 Florida
Tel 001 305 659 1314
Sales & service

Vantage Motorworks Inc
1898 N E 151 St
Miami
33162 Florida
Tel 001 305 940 1161
Sales, service & restoration

R & B Parts
4546 Palm Beach Canal Rd
West Palm Beach
33406 Florida
Tel 001 305 689 7888
Parts

Mitchell Motors Inc
5675 Peachtree Industrial Boulevard
Chamblee
30341 Georgia

Tel 001 404 458 5111
Sales & service

Continental Cars Ltd
1072 Young St
Honolulu
96814 Hawaii
Tel 001 808 526 3258
Sales & service

Worden-Martin Inc
100 Carriage Center
2003 S Neil St
Champaign
61820 Illinois
Tel 001 217 352 7901
Sales & service

Loeber Importers Ltd
5625 North Broadway
Chicago
60660 Illinois
Tel 001 312 728 5000
also at 1111 North Clark St
Chicago 60610
Tel 001 312 944 0500
Sales & service

Continental Motors Inc
420 E Ogden Ave
Honsdale
60521 Illinois
Tel 001 312 655 3535
Sales & service

Dave Lewis Restoration
3825 South St Second St
Springfield
62703 Illinois
Tel 001 217 529 5290
Restoration

Albers Rolls-Royce
360 S Fist St
Zionsville
IN 46077
Tel 001 317 873 2360
Parts

Euro Motor Cars Berthseda Inc
4800 Elms St

Berthseda
0814 Maryland
Tel 001 301 986 8800
Sales & service

Foreign Motors West
253 N Main St
Natick
MA 01760
Tel 001 617 653 4323
Parts

Sears Imported Autos Inc
13500 Wayzata Boulevard
Minnetonka
55343 Minnesota
Tel 001 612 546 5301
Sales & service

Charles Schmitt & Co
3500 South Kingsway Boulevard
St Louis
63139 Missouri
Tel 001 314 352 9100
Sales & service

Cutter Motorcars
2333 South Decatur Boulevard
Las Vegas
89102 Nevada
Tel 001 702 871 1010
Sales & service

Modern Classic Motors
3225 Mill St
Reno
89501 Nevada
Tel 001 702 323 4169
Sales & service

Imported Motor Car Co
34 Valley Rd
Montclair
07042 NJ
Tel 001 201 746 4500
Sales & service

Turner Spares Ltd
Raritan Center Parkway
Box 396
08818 New Jersey

Tel 001 201 225 5800
Parts

Knight-Clarke Services
8 Bodine Ave
Gladstone
New Jersey
Tel 001 210 234 2930
Parts

Perfection Motor Car Co
6012 Acadamy Rd NE
Albuquerque
87109 New Mexico
Tel 001 505 822 8500
Sales & service

Rallye Motor Cars Inc
20 Cedar Swamp Rd
Glen Cove
11542 NY
Tel 001 516 671 4622
Sales & service

George Haug Co Inc
517 East 73rd St
10021 NY
Tel 001 212 288 0173
Service

Park Ward Motors Inc
301 East 57th St
10022 NY
Tel 001 212 688 7112
Sales & service

Premier Resource Group Inc
New York
Tel 001 212 730 5823, fax 001 212 354 1323
Sales

The Belmont Group USA
tel 001 708 945 9603, fax 001 708 945 9636
Sales & purchase worldwide

Bob's Auto Parts
Rt 9W Kingston
12401 NY
Tel 001 914 336 6330
Used parts

Transco Inc
1800 N Main St
High Point
27262 North Carolina
Tel 001 919 885 5171
Sales & service

John McCombie Inc
572 S Nelson Rd
Columbus
43205 Ohio
Tel 001 614 221 2563
Parts

Jackie Cooper Imports Inc
9505 North May Ave
73120 Oklahoma
Tel 001 405 755 3600
Sales & service

Siggi Grimm Inc
2007 East 11th St
Tulsa
74104 Oklahoma
Tel 001 918 582 1151

Mente Shelton Motor Co
1638 West Burnside St
Portland 97228 Oregon
Tel 001 503 224 3232
Sales & service

Keenan Motors Inc
3900 Broad St
Philadelphia
19140 Pennsylvania
Tel 001 215 223 4600
Sales & service

Ascot Imported Cars Inc
418 Walnut St
Sewickly
15143 Pennsylvania
Tel 001 412 761 9310
Sales & service

Dick Dyer Assoc
5717 Two Notch Rd
Columbia
29204 S Carolina
Tel 001 803 786 2010

Sales & service
Autorama Inc
2950 Airways Boulevard
Memphis
38130 Tennessee
Tel 001 901 345 6211
Sales & service

Superior Motors Inc
630 Murfreesboro Rd
Nashville
37210 Tennesse
Tel 001 615 254 5641
Sales & service

Overseas Motors of Dallas
7018 Lemmon Ave
Dallas
75209 Texas
Tel 001 214 358 1446
Sales & service

Overseas Motors Corp of Fort Worth
2824 White Settlement rd
Fort Worth
76107 Texas
Tel 001 817 332 4181
Sales & service

Ken Garff Imports Inc
525 South State St
Salt Lake City
84111 Utah
Tel 001 801 521 6604
Sales & service

Dominion Rolls-Royce Ltd
6517 West Broad St
Richmond
23230 Virginia
Tel 001 804 288 3171
Sales & service

Uptown Motors Inc
2111 North Mayfair Rd
Milwaukee
53226 Wisconsin
Tel 001 414 771 9000
Sales & service

Tony Handler Inc

2028 Cotner Avenue
Los Angeles
90025 California
Tel 001 310 473 7773, fax 001 310 479 1197
Parts

Australia
Fox Rolls-Royce & Bentley
66 O'Riordon St
Alexandria
NSW 2015
Tel 0061 2 9693 9000
Sales, service

Fox Rolls-Royce & Bentley
210 Kings Way
South Melbourne
VIC 3025
Tel 0061 3 9696 0888
Sales & service

McMillan Prestige
25-27 Regatta Road
Five Dock
NSW 2046
Tel 061 02 9744 5111, fax 0061 2 9744 5517
Repairs & restoration

Neil McLean Automotives
14 Beaconsfield Avenue
Midvale
WA 6056
Tel 0061 8 9250 1400, fax 0061 8 9250 1414
Parts

Tom Johnston Motors
13 Stirling Street
Thebarton
SA 5031
Tel 0061 8 8234 5600, fax 0061 8 8234 5607
Service

R.A.M. McDermott & Co
649 Chapel Street
South Yarra
VIC 3141
Tel 0061 3 9804 7977
also at
420 Burnley Street
Richmond
VIC 3121
Tel 0061 3 9428 8844, fax 0061 3 9428
01090
and
8 Hunt Street
Surrey Hills
NSW 2010
Tel 0061 2 212 7200
Restoration, service, parts

ROLLS-ROYCE BENTLEY

INDEX